Black American Refugee

Black American Refugee

Escaping the Narcissism of the American Dream

TIFFANIE DRAYTON

VIKING

VIKING
An imprint of Penguin Random House LLC
penguinrandomhouse.com

Grateful acknowledgment is made for permission to print lyrics from "Billion Dollar Dream"
written by Jiselle Singh and Stephen Singh. Printed with permission.

LIBRARY OF CONGRESS CATALOGING-IN-PUBLICATION DATA
Names: Drayton, Tiffanie, author.
Title: Black American refugee / Tiffanie Drayton.
Description: [New York] : Viking, [2022] | Includes bibliographical references.
Identifiers: LCCN 2021035786 (print) | LCCN 2021035787 (ebook) |
ISBN 9780593298541 (hardcover) | ISBN 9780593298558 (ebook)
Subjects: LCSH: Drayton, Tiffanie. | Trinidadian Americans—New Jersey—Biography. |
Immigrant women—New Jersey—Biography. | African American women—New Jersey—
Biography. | African Americans—Social conditions—21st century—Anecdotes. |
Racism—United States—History—21st century—Anecdotes. | Abused wives—
New Jersey—Biography. | Abused wives—Trinidad—Biography. |
Return migrants—Trinidad—Biography.
Classification: LCC F145.T75 D73 2022 (print) | LCC F145.T75 (ebook) |
DDC 305.896/9729830749—dc23/eng/20211007
LC record available at https://lccn.loc.gov/2021035786
LC ebook record available at https://lccn.loc.gov/2021035787

Printed in the United States of America
1 3 5 7 9 10 8 6 4 2

Book design by Daniel Lagin

For Mom, who taught me how to be a black magic woman.

CONTENTS

PROLOGUE   I

1. Love-Bombing   7

2. Devalued   35

3. Discarded   79

4. Calm   105

5. Moving the Goalposts and Gaslighting   169

6. Healing   199

7. Hoovered   215

8. Lethal Abuse   235

9. The Breakup   279

EPILOGUE: Reconciliation   287

ACKNOWLEDGMENTS   291

NOTES   293

Black American Refugee

Prologue

I write this from exile.

I write to you from Trinidad and Tobago, the home my mother left behind when I was a child, betting on her family's ability to excel in America, in what was pitched—and embraced—as a meritocracy. America's trademark promise of protection for the huddled masses, of freedom for all, and Martin Luther King Jr.'s vision of integration and equality were concepts that I internalized from a young age. I believed that with hard work and impeccable manners I would earn acceptance and recognition. I sought freedom from America's history of dehumanization in the same way Black Americans always have: I worked to set myself apart. I was certain I had access to the mobility to someday lay claim to full citizenship and elite status—trappings traditionally for "whites only." But despite every attempt to pull myself up by my bootstraps, I found myself sinking deeper into despair. Though I sometimes got so close to these designations that I could almost feel them in my grasp, I was never afforded unconditional validation or acceptance.

Instead, over time, I realized I had been unwittingly cast in America's caste system.

In America, I am a Black woman. The position I occupy is diametrically opposed to whiteness, and all that invented designation signifies. Beneath the glittering surface layers of America's promise—a promise whose seduction and lure grew in conjunction with the sway and dominance of capitalism over the global economy—lay layers of bedrock foundation built from the bodies of Black and Native people, bodies whose value to this country was in how they were used, and used up, not in our aptitude for tolerance, assimilation, focus, or commitment. Bodies that could be displaced on a whim; whose inherent humanity could be reduced to stereotypes and tropes. Marginalization and exploitation is the American history I wasn't taught in school but that I learned nevertheless.

In the end, I fled to Trinidad and Tobago as the only means to slip the constraints of the great "American Dream"—a pursuit whose rules seemed to shift under me just when I was sure I was ascending. A project that taught me to revere self-sufficiency but thus kept me isolated, uninformed, and without allies, believing that instead of being alone, I was working toward precious autonomy, a successful striver. Even when I knew I had to leave, I still struggled to help others understand exactly what I felt it was necessary to escape from.

On January 6, 2021, I received a message from a close friend containing a single question: "How did you know?" Washington, DC, was under siege by violent insurrectionists, and my best friend was equal parts shocked and confused as the attack unfolded. The scene itself was of course unbelievable, but what she really couldn't grasp was that I'd warned her about a possible coup attempt over six months earlier.

"I dated a man like Trump," I replied. "I know how far they will go to win."

That's true, but it's also far more complicated than my sharp and pithy reply. My understanding of just how far the former president of the United States would go to avoid the sting of public defeat was gleaned through a set of experiences that I would not wish upon my worst enemy. These personal experiences unlocked an epiphany for me about the trajectory of America by allowing me to finally understand the nature of a narcissist, a term that I once naively believed meant a person obsessed with their own beauty or attractiveness. After years of suffering through (and finally escaping) a romantic relationship with a man who promised me fidelity, bliss, and loyalty and instead dealt me constant abuse and degradation, and ensnared me in a cycle of chaos that oftentimes felt inescapable, I became more informed about what a narcissist really is, and how a narcissistic relationship works. Through my experiences in therapy, I learned that narcissism is an incurable mental-health problem characterized by an excessive preoccupation with self, a lack of empathy, an outrageous sense of entitlement, and a constant need for validation. I learned that it is not easy to escape the wrath of those who suffer with the disorder when you try to end the relationship with them, as America would do by voting Trump out of the White House. As I began to heal and empower myself to take control of my life, I learned more about the cycle of a narcissistic relationship and why they are so hard to leave. That cycle—of being showered with love and offered intimacy, then being devalued and broken down, then being rejected, and finally being pulled back in by promises and grandeur—informs the structure of my story, because I see the power that cycle exerted over my romantic life but also the futility of my quest to find firm footing as a successful and settled American. My deeper understanding of narcissistic abuse illuminated truths that forced me to realize nothing I could do on my own would be powerful enough to save my relationship with my ex or the country I then called home. Toughing it out, working on myself, and even working on the relationship wouldn't be enough to fix it. The liberating realization that gave me permission to move on personally also became a catalyst for me to finally understand my relationship with America as a Black woman who had suffered the repeated blows of systemic racism. It too was an abusive relationship, made glaringly apparent by the election of Donald Trump. I could now accept that I did not have to settle for abuse, not from my ex or even from America.

I left America not only to find freedom but first and foremost as an instinctive act of self-preservation. Leaving was a decision made based on my human drive to survive. In that act, I found rebirth. I discovered a life unburdened by the constant distress of inferiority. In America, my Black life was narrowly defined in a way that colored it gray, dark, and dingy—rife with grit, hardship, and constant disappointment. Upon my return to Trinidad, my Black life became one enveloped in the greens and blues of the ocean; mocha, caramel, and mahogany faces; and the rainbow of pinks, oranges, teals, and yellows of glittering Carnival costumes. A life where I could live out the wildest dreams of my ancestors as a fully liberated African woman in the West. I found freedom by leaving the land of the free, but in that liberation a reckoning was forced: What had I escaped? What did I flee from?

———

Little did I know that I would exit, luckily with my family in tow, just before a powder keg would blow. The combination of four years under the Trump administration—and with it, rhetoric and actions of such blatant racism, sexism, and xenophobia that no claims to color blindness or exceptionalism could blur or blunt the truth—with an unprecedented pandemic revealed what everyone knew but had been able to ignore: America's promise of equality for all wasn't one the country was even trying to live up to. Years of walking back social support systems and civil rights had left America's infrastructure brittle and fragile, and once again abandoned hundreds of thousands of the country's most vulnerable people to have their lives claimed by death, violence, job loss, and psychological instability. I watched in horror as all of this chaos was then interwoven with energetic bursts of mass protest against the killing of unarmed Black Americans by the police. From an ocean away, I had fuller access to my heartbreak and rage in a way I never could when those powerful feelings had to coexist with my drive to survive within the system. I felt haunted by the guilt that I was able to escape while so many I knew and cared for were still trapped in the turmoil. As I watched the only country I had ever called home implode from a distance, I hoped the truth the world was witnessing was one that wouldn't blow over, or be erased.

Finally, America, the abuser, was unmasked.

I was born part of a generation of Black women who inherited the strength, struggles, and insights of our Black ancestors—freedom fighters, artists, intellectuals, and scholars—and I have come into my career and my womanhood in a moment so unique and inspiring. A moment that stands at the confluence of immense data technology and interconnected global reach, one that benefits from decades of research that validates my gut reactions and builds on generations of advocacy that allows Black people access to higher education. The power of arriving at this moment in history, with the tools that I have been afforded through the hard work and dedication of those who came before me, allows me to painstakingly identify and enumerate the various ways that America's vicious racism takes its toll on Black people over the span of their lives. In doing so, I'm able to acknowledge the disturbing impact these systemic forces have had on my own life and the lives of my family, closest friends, and even lovers. What I share with you here is a personal journey, one that gave me permission to be free, to refrain from shouldering the mantle of shame or casting blame upon myself. I share my truth—my triumphs, heartbreaks, mistakes, and even prejudices—to remind us that in our shared humanity there is always room for growth. Mistakes and misconceptions can be catalysts for growth, for individuals, families, countries, and governments alike. The fear of judgment casts a shadow that kept me on the run from the truth. But only by facing the reality of our shortcomings and transgressions could I find a map to realize a greater self.

Only when each individual American is free to achieve self-actualization will we collectively find the strength, and muster the resilience, to heal racial divisions, inequality, and oppression, and finally make the promise of peace, liberty, and justice for all a reality. Which begs the question, America: Are you finally ready to grow and heal with me?

CHAPTER 1

Love-Bombing

It was 1994, and in Trinidad it was the dry season. There was little rain and the colorful poui trees sprouted flowers that blanketed the country's mountains, turning them from green to pink, yellow, and orange. Spring would be different where I was headed to in New Jersey. There, spring meant that the sun had just begun to peek out from behind the winter cloud cover and temperatures were brisk and fresh at last, instead of freezing cold. I was four years old, kneeling on the seat of an airplane, soaring thousands of feet above the shoreline of New York City, and my relationship with America was about to begin.

"Look how dey light up for we!" my brother, Stefan, a brown-skinned, lanky boy only one year my senior, exclaimed in his singsong Trinidadian accent as the city's skyline came into view.

I pressed my face against the plane's tiny window and my eyes lit up at the sight of New York's skyscrapers draped in coruscating lights, which twinkled like tiny stars. Lady Liberty stood proud, her torch bright against the blackness of the sky, beckoning us toward JFK International Airport's landing strip. I accepted my brother's innocent conclusion that the entire skyline was covered in lights just for us and couldn't believe that America would go to such lengths to welcome us to our new home. I beamed in amazement at the spectacle until Granny urged me to sit back so I could put on my seat belt for landing.

The plane bumped onto the tarmac and then crept down the runway toward the terminal. Everyone erupted into cheers and applause—for the pilot who had safely shepherded us thousands of miles, for the new opportunities that surely awaited so many of us here. But I had only one thought as the plane came to a halt: *Mom*. I had not seen her in two years.

My mother had emigrated from our homeland in Trinidad and Tobago with a few dollars, a big dream, and a newfound confidence in her life's purpose. On a quest for a better life for all of us, she left Trinidad with one suitcase and an address in her pocket for a Brooklyn-based agency that placed immigrant women from the West Indies with families who wanted live-in nannies. Mom made two hundred dollars per week yet somehow still managed to send money to my grandmother biweekly for our care, ship down huge barrels filled with goods twice per year—once on Christmas and again right before the summer—and save enough money to buy our tickets when the time came for us to join her. "Forget thy people and thy father's house, so that your children may roam the earth like princes" was one of her few Bible-themed mantras. She became wedded to these words when, looking for a sign from the universe after begging God to help her decide what to do about her failing relationship with our father, she opened the Holy Book exactly to this verse. Its certainty strengthened her resolve to leave for America and helped her cling to the willpower and dedication she needed to survive the heartache of leaving her children in her homeland. That verse helped her focus on the potential she was sure awaited us all in America: stability, maybe even prosperity. The promise of our betterment lulled her to sleep at night and kept her smiling through days that often felt degrading. She toiled for years before she had saved enough money to send for us—her three children and her mother, my grandmother.

When we reunited, after years apart, the moment was quiet. She hugged each and every one of us, then led us to the car, clasping my hand and my brother's hand in hers. I caressed her knit gloves with my fingers, intrigued by the softness of the unfamiliar winter accessory. I peered over my shoulder to make sure no familiar faces had disappeared. Niki, my preteen sister, who was seven years my senior, lagged, dragging her roll-along bag beside our granny, who gave me a small smile and a gentle wave. The ride to our new home was also quiet, with only the hum of the car speeding down the highway and a subtle hint of jazz music playing on the radio in the air between us. Mom kept turning around in the driver's seat to look back at us, as if making sure we were all still actually there and this wasn't just a dream. All of her hard work had finally paid off: we were together again. But the silence in the car was heavy too with the anxieties Mom had lived with for so long while trying to make that dream a reality.

"Dianne, please vacuum the stairs right away," a white woman had demanded the moment my mom arrived at her home, months before the day of our reunion, ostensibly to provide nanny care.

My mother was confused by the request, because the agency that had placed her in the job never said anything about being a maid. Mom's self-esteem was heavily guarded and she felt very protective of her dignity. She wore the status of a graduate of one of Trinidad's most prestigious convent schools like a suit of armor, so she hesitated to accept a position of inferiority she felt was beneath her. The white woman condescendingly pursed her lips and placed one hand on her hip as she held the vacuum's nozzle out to my mother with the other. Mom breathed in deeply and then reached out her hand to accept the machine. She did what was asked of her with only one goal in mind: getting her kids to the United States, where we could have the good life we deserved. Thousands of women like her faced similar indignities—those who ventured from the West Indies in the nineties seeking refuge from the uncertainty of the economy, lured by America's promises of wealth, opportunity, and freedom for themselves and their children. Only years later would I truly understand what it took for her to bring us "home" to her in America—the many nights spent worrying how my grandmother was managing alone with the three young children she had left behind; the days spent exhausting her body and her dignity fulfilling the whims of white families and their children while her own remained back "home," motherless.

Mom's voice finally pierced the silence of our ride.

"It have hot dogs at home," she said.

There was nothing I loved more than food, and there was nothing my brother loved more than hot dogs. The awkwardness of this freighted reunion was broken.

"I doh want any mustard, only ketchup!" my brother piped up.

"It have juice?" I questioned.

"Mummy, we going to our new house?" my sister asked.

There was never very much silence in my household after that first moment—our home was always filled with laughter and storytelling, from then on.

Although she had arrived in America with lofty goals for herself, Mom's early experiences as a live-in nanny led her to believe all Black people in America were servants. Whenever she took her employer's children to the park, she congregated with the other "foreign" nannies. They exchanged jokes and stories about their white employers and their dreams of what they would do with the money they were quietly stashing away, while changing the diapers of blond-haired white babies or dusting the bruised knees of toddlers or older children who took a tumble while playing.

Most of the women, like Mom, were trying to save enough money to bring other family members to the country or return to their native lands, where they would retire or build a home with the fruits of their labor. The only Black faces Mom saw were "the help," so it was hard for her to imagine any other path for women who looked like her. This reality was amended only when a friend recommended she apply for a job at Chase Bank and, to her surprise and delight, she landed a teller position at a branch on Water Street in downtown Manhattan. That's where she worked by the time we arrived.

Mom had managed to secure a one-bedroom apartment for us in North Bergen, New Jersey, a tiny, bustling, hilly immigrant town right on the other side of the Hudson River, directly opposite New York City. The town was run by Italians, and my memories of it are like a canvas painted in watercolor, with vivid splashes of every color representing the diverse faces of my neighbors and friends. There were Hispanic, white, Middle Eastern, and many East Asian first-generation families there, and my tiny Black family blended right in. Mom had followed her sister, my auntie Debbie, to the neighborhood a year earlier from the borough she first called home, Brooklyn—where most Trinidadian immigrants land upon arriving on the shores of America. Debbie was married and had two kids of her own, so Mom imagined the proximity would give her more support, and it did for quite a while. The adults would disappear into their world of work and the older kids would go off to school, and I would spend the first year of my life in America in the care of my grandmother at Debbie's house.

Granny was a very firm caretaker who took pride in the authoritarian parenting style she had adopted to protect her three daughters from the inherent vulnerability of being raised by a single parent who could not read or write. Children left under her care adhered to a strict schedule that dictated the precise time of every meal and the exact length of nap time (when she would watch her "stories": *The Young and the Restless* and *The Bold and the Beautiful*). I loved pressing my fingers into her skin and watching as the imprint changed from white to blush pink. I was intrigued that her skin changed in that way when mine didn't and found it quite peculiar.

"Doh harass me!" she would exclaim when my poke knocked her out of her cooking or cleaning trance, prompting me to run away snickering.

Most of my days were spent watching *Lamb Chop's Play-Along, Barney & Friends, Mister Rogers' Neighborhood*, and *Sesame Street* while my baby cousin Ashley slept or cooed nearby. I longed for adventure and to trudge off into the world with a backpack like my older siblings and cousin did every morning. When Granny announced it was time for me to go to school, about a year into our American life, I was ecstatic. Mom took me school shopping and I picked out a purple backpack, matching pencil case, and lunch box. That day, she also told me that my aunt and cousins would be moving to a town called Edison, New Jersey. But I was too absorbed in my quest to prepare for my first day to get upset. I happily hummed and danced to my favorite songs on my way home. I was excited to get back to show off my new school gear to my siblings and then settle in front of the TV together to watch one of our favorite sitcoms, like *Family Matters* or *Full House*.

In the nineties, American culture had finally made room for Black culture to be assimilated into the media as "all-American." *The Cosby Show* was one of the most-watched television shows, depicting a "successful" upper-middle-class Black family—the Huxtables—who had achieved their American dream. They lived in a two-parent household and resided in a huge townhome. Bill Cosby played the head of the household, the hilarious Cliff Huxtable (a doting father who was also a doctor), but working mom Clair and their five children loomed just as large on-screen. The success of *The Cosby Show* paved the way for other Black sitcoms, like *The Fresh Prince of Bel-Air* and *Family Matters*, to become household names. Posters of the iconic image of Michael Jordan soaring through the air were plastered everywhere, and R&B music topped *Billboard*'s Top 100 charts. Michael Jackson was the world's King of Pop, and various Black female artists were enamoring listeners. My brother, my sister, and I performed daily renditions of the popular songs. Niki was always the lead singer. She had a deep, sultry voice like Anita Baker and Toni Braxton—singers of the era whom we loved. Black women R&B singers of the nineties were powerful, angelic, graceful, and feminine. Most had medium- to light-brown skin, wore their hair permed bone straight, and had long, slender bodies and perfectly straight, pearly-white teeth. They reflected an ideal womanhood I would spend my life aspiring to. One that I now know was carefully curated to be acceptable and wholesome to all Americans.

"*I will always love you,*" we sang along with Whitney Houston, tragically failing to hit her high note at the end.

"*Unbreak my heart,*" Niki belted as Stefan and I played imaginary drums to emphasize Braxton's crescendo before her five-bar finale.

"*What about us?*" we cried along with Michael Jackson as images of dying elephants, a war-torn city, and destroyed Amazon rain forest reversed, springing back to life.

"He officially white," Mom said aloud of Jackson with a chuckle after one of our performances, accompanied by his music video. I thought she was complimenting him and assumed his "whitening" was meant to demonstrate perhaps just how positive his care was for the environment and humanity, so I eagerly nodded along in agreement. She shook her head and continued to laugh before changing the subject to offer a critique of our dance moves. I didn't get the joke, but it was impossible for me to imagine that Mom was actually laughing at the pop star. To me, Michael Jackson was an angel descending to earth, with porcelain skin, white robes, and hair blowing in the wind, like those I saw so frequently in childhood cartoons.

I was totally infatuated with America. I readily assumed that America would love me back.

"With liberty and justice for all!" I proudly pledged allegiance to the flag every morning in class.

I felt it was clear that the liberty in this pledge we all proclaimed in unison extended to me. In between lessons about Christopher Columbus discovering America while sailing aboard the *Niña*, *Pinta*, and *Santa Maria*, stories of the Pilgrims (who sought to escape religious persecution in their homeland) and Native Americans having their first shared Thanksgiving, and learning how to add, subtract, and multiply, I was free to roam the streets of my town for an hour during lunch. With Stefan and the rest of our gang (two brothers named Dylan and Justin) by my side, I fell into a daily routine: grab a dollar slice at the local pizzeria, peruse the bodega for candy or chips, and then walk a few blocks to "the Rocks," a huge rocky formation where all of the kids would meet up to play tag, or shoot hoops at a nearby court. I fiercely believed in the concept of justice and went to great lengths to preserve it at the Rocks. On the playground, I urged kids to share the tire swing instead of fighting over turns and made sure that the collective games we played were always inclusive, even for the younger children or those who were deemed not as fast or strong as the others. I also often led the charge to decide who would be "it" during a game of tag or hide-and-seek.

"Diggy diggy diamond, step right in. Diggy diggy diamond, step right out," I would dutifully recite, tapping on each person's foot until only one was left in the circle.

Cliques of kids in our neighborhood naturally merged with others when it came time for snowball fights during the winter and splintered again when the end of lunchtime neared, sending everyone on a stampede toward the school to avoid the late bell. But a classmate named Anushka, a lanky Indian girl with dark-brown skin and oily, unkempt hair, always stood off to the side of the fun all by herself. She barely ever spoke and often wore clothes that were clearly dirty or old. I sometimes overheard the other kids taunting her with names like "Hindu Bindu" and "Nasty Anushka" and wondered why she never stood up for herself. Eventually, I made it my mission to befriend her and include her in our circle. After all, this was America, where everyone deserves an equal place and fair treatment. When I noticed her shoes were missing laces, I gave her my new ones and laced my sneakers up with an old pair from shoes I had outgrown. I collected all of the T-shirts I had grown out of and left them at her doorstep on my way to school one morning. I felt very proud when she came into class wearing one of the shirts and the new laces. (She waved at me and flashed a big smile before sitting at her desk two rows away.)

None of my interventions worked to stop the other kids from poking fun at her. I decided enough was enough when a group of boys surrounded her one day, threatening to throw an old, dirty diaper at her. Stefan, the crew, and I were making our way up the trail to the Rocks when we saw her trapped between two boys. More were descending like vicious wolves.

"Leave her alone!" I ordered, sprinting in their direction.

Their heads turned toward me in unison.

"You hit her, you're gonna have to hit all of us!" I screamed, putting my hands on my hips, puffing my chest out, and holding my head up high.

Stefan, Dylan, and Justin stood right behind me. Then other kids began to join our lineup, ready for a face-off: Blond-haired twins Anthony and Thomas Ramirez, who both wore huge, wire-framed glasses with thick lenses and a crossbar connected at the bridges of their noses. Jeffrey, a boy whose family was from Belize. The pack of bullies were quickly outnumbered. I could sense their hesitation, and they began to step backward away from the scene. But just when it seemed the confrontation would fizzle without climax, an unexpected voice cracked the tension in the air.

"Don't throw it at me, throw it at him!" Anushka yelled.

She had her finger firmly pointed in a single direction: at Stefan. My eyes darted between her and my brother in shock and disbelief. The boys ignored her instruction and decided to move on to find a more vulnerable target, their leader still toting the dirty diaper pinched between his forefinger and thumb when they departed. I screamed and hurled childish taunts at them as they retreated. Justice had prevailed! But I was haunted by how quickly the young girl I defended had turned on my kin.

"Why would you sell out Stefan?" I asked Anushka. "They were already about to back down!"

She shrugged. I felt both hurt and disgusted and turned to walk away so no one would see the tears that had welled up in my eyes. I avoided her smiles and waves from that day on.

Still, North Bergen summers were idyllic for us as kids. Early mornings were always a dash to get out of the door: Mom rushed to get to work in the city, and Stefan and I rushed to go outside to play. We loved to Rollerblade and traversed the entire town to play with friends, go to the local library, or run around in the sprinklers at a huge public playground at a park ten blocks away.

"Y'all better wear your helmets!" my sister would scream behind us as we skated past her, our pockets jingling with quarters for lunch and a snack. My brother and I would dutifully take our helmets with us, and then ditch them in the bushes near our apartment. We hated how heavy and awkward they felt on our heads. But our sister wasn't the only one looking to enforce a helmet rule: the North Bergen police, who often patrolled the town on bikes, wearing short pants, were quick to quiz us about safety if we ran into them.

"Where are your helmets?" an officer asked us as he rode past one day. We made up an excuse about our mother having them and fibbed that she was waiting for us at the park, and he waved us off.

"Don't let me see you all without a helmet again!" he chided as he and three other officers pedaled past us, continuing on their shared mission to keep us kids safe.

Like many of the neighborhood children, we were home alone during the day in the summer, so we spent all of our time parading the streets of the town. Niki had a best friend, Amanda, an immigrant girl from India whose parents had migrated to the States only a few years before us so her dad could pursue an opportunity in tech, and her apartment became our second home. When we were tired of Rollerblading, we would retreat there, to my sister's dismay.

"What do y'all want?" she would holler from the second-story window when we inevitably showed up.

"Some water!" we would respond in unison, our excuse for simply wanting to spend time with her already concocted.

With an eye roll and a sigh, Niki would let us into their preteen lair, leading us through the foyer and up the stairs to Amanda's apartment. The sound of Britney Spears, the Backstreet Boys, or Missy Elliott typically greeted us upon entry. Back then MTV was completely dedicated to music, and my sister and her bestie were obsessed with memorizing the lyrics to popular songs and choreographing accompanying dance moves. Stefan and I would watch as the pair swapped their different-colored chokers, giggled, laughed, and waved as they sang "Bye Bye Bye" along with NSYNC until we were recharged for another round of Rollerblading. When the sun began its slow descent, we knew we had to head home. We rushed back to the apartment, careful to make it home before Mom did or risk upsetting her over our being out all day. We spent evenings delighting in our favorite shows, like *The Simpsons* or *Goosebumps*, all interspersed with "feed the children" ads featuring impoverished African children, whom I felt grateful not to be.

The Fourth of July—the day that schoolbooks say symbolizes freedom for all Americans—was one of the highlights of summertime. We celebrated the day by making our annual pilgrimage to Donnelly Memorial Park, which sat atop a mountainside and boasted a playground and the most jaw-dropping view of the New York City skyline. At sunset, we trekked up the steep hill from our tiny apartment and traversed several busy intersections before even coming within sight of the park. The streets would be littered with hundreds of other families making their way through the town to marvel at the glistening, brilliant view of hundreds of skyscrapers covered in lights running along the Hudson River. Vendors sold T-shirts, hats, and tiny flags, all emblazoned with the white, red, and blue Stars and Stripes; balloons of superheroes; and fireworks. Mom always pinched off a few dollars from her tiny stash of cash to let us buy a box of sparklers and poppers—tiny, child-friendly fireworks wrapped in white paper that cracked and popped when you threw them to the ground. We lit our sparklers and ran all about the park waving them in the air, pretending to cast magical spells as flames erupted from the far end, while pelting the poppers at each other's feet and giggling when they exploded.

When the sky was completely dark, the real show began: the Macy's fireworks display. At the sound of the first huge explosion, Stefan and I would squeeze through the crowd to lean against the black gate that prevented onlookers from tumbling down the steep precipice and enjoy front-row seats. Bursts of white, green, red, blue, and purple would light up the entire skyline, appearing to stretch from downtown all the way uptown to the Bronx. Onlookers oohed, aahed, and added commentary to the show in all languages. Mothers calmed their babies' angst about the loud noises in English, Spanish, Hindi, or even Arabic. Fathers cautioned kids to stay nearby in hushed voices or with loud orders. As always, Stefan and I sang our songs.

"*And the rocks fury flair,*" I proudly belted, singing the anthem I had only just learned, "*the bombs bursting in air, gave proof through the night that the flag was still there.*"

Every year, we knew the show was finished when four red and green smiley faces appeared in the sky. The experience solidified my belief in America. Those bombs bursting in the air were symbols of my freedom. And the true grand finale of our Fourth of July celebration would arrive just as the fireworks show ended.

Da-duh-duh-da-duh-dum-da-dum, blared the ice cream truck's speakers.

Families lined up and ordered cones, slushies, milkshakes, and superhero ice pops to enjoy on the walk home. I loved the sweet taste of grape slushies and how they turned my mouth purple. I skipped home humming the ice cream truck song, eagerly sucking down my slushy without a care or fear in thought or sight.

For Mom, life in the nineties tristate area was equally liberating. During the week, she boarded the Hoboken-bound bus on JFK Boulevard, a long street that runs through several towns in North Jersey, destined for the PATH station to catch the train to the World Trade Center, near where she worked for Chase Bank on Water Street. She loved the busy city and how it made her feel alive and immersed in endless possibilities. On weekends, she and Granny would drag us kids to window-shop along the town's shopping district: Bergenline. Bergenline was a fortysomethingblock Hispanic oasis. The street gently sloped and ran north to south and in my childhood mind it was bounded by 80th Street Park to the north and Union City to the south.

"Immie" buses were the only rivals to the big New Jersey Transit bus system because they ran more frequently and were cheaper. Driven mostly by undocumented Hispanic men, the small shuttle buses blasted merengue, bachata, or salsa. Selena was the most popular artist then, and her voice would reverberate through the streets from the buses, becoming louder and then growing muffled each time a shuttle swung its doors open and then closed again as the drivers let passengers on and off.

"Don't touch anything, and stay close," Mom would instruct us before we entered one of the local stores to peruse its stock of slippers, socks, and household goods with Granny. Our Bergenline treks typically lasted all day and would sometimes span thirty to forty blocks, but we kids never complained. Mom knew exactly how to keep us in line. While my grandmother preferred utilizing the threat of a verbal or physical lashing, Mom instead cajoled us with the promise of fulfilling our foremost desire: a Burger King kids' meal. With pained feet after a long day, Stefan and I would stuff our faces with fresh, crispy fries and nuggets. The toy in the kids' meal box was like a cherry on top.

When the winter arrived, the right moment to visit my cousins, aunt, and uncle in their new home in Edison finally arose. It was the Christmas season, and the bank closed for a few days, offering Mom a reprieve from her daily commute and long work days. On the day we were to make the sixty-minute drive out to Edison, Mom painstakingly dressed us one by one in layer after layer of pants, undershirts, sweaters, and jackets with matching scarves, hats, and gloves. By the time she was done, I uncomfortably waddled from left to right toward the car, trudging through the snow as it crunched beneath my boots. It was eerily silent when I stepped out into the light of the early morning, with snow flurries gently gliding to the ground like feathers.

"Hey, Tiff!" Stefan screamed from behind me.

Just as I turned around, a cold, icy ball burst on my face. Stefan's laughter echoed into the distance, penetrating the silence.

"Don't start!" Ma pleaded, but it was too late.

I crouched and grabbed a handful of snow, squeezing it in my hand before launching it at my brother. The snow exploded like powdery fireworks across Stefan's chest.

"Get in!" Mom yelled, shooing us toward the car.

But as she flung the car door open, an avalanche of snow came crashing down on her head.

Niki had been dutifully pushing the snow off of the top of the car on the passenger side with a long brush and didn't even notice Mom already opening the driver's side door.

"Sorry, sorry!" Niki sputtered when Mom's surprised scream echoed through the car park.

Stefan and I collapsed onto a pile of snow, giggling uncontrollably as Mom beat the snow off of her jacket.

"Snow Mummy!" I chided.

"We will see who laughs last when I drive fast with the window down and y'all freeze," Mom threatened with a laugh.

We all piled into the car and Mom blasted the heat, then pulled out and carefully descended the steep hill toward Tonnelle Avenue, a long road that connects North Bergen to U.S. Route 1/9, a multilane highway that stretches from New York City to Woodbridge Township.

"*Jingle bells, Batman smells, Robin laid an egg,*" Stef and I sang as we zoomed by the North Bergen police station, a trailer park, and a bunch of used car dealerships.

We turned onto U.S. 1/9 and the car cruised along the highway, which cut through industrial parks, lined with factories billowing dark-gray smoke. Mom couldn't afford the turnpike, the New Jersey toll road that would shave off more than twenty minutes from our travels, so she continued down the local route, stopping at dozens of traffic lights along the way. I suffered with debilitating motion sickness and would moan and groan the entire way. Niki flipped between radio stations, finally settling on the East Coast hip-hop station Hot 97, and we spent the rest of the hour-long ride singing along to Shaggy, the self-declared "lover man" of the nineties, and TLC, who instructed us not to go chasing waterfalls.

Edison was the perfect picture of the American dream. The town had achieved the height of America's ideal—a suburb boasting large homes, perfectly manicured lawns, white picket fences, and families with 2.5 kids on average and a $100,000 median income—and was populated mostly by Asian and white families. We arrived at the front of my aunt's new house and marveled. It was a colonial-style, two-story home with a huge front and backyard. But that wasn't what inspired awe in my brother and me: that day, the huge front yard was covered in untouched snow.

"Two words: snow angels," I whispered to my brother.

He nodded in agreement.

Auntie Debbie appeared at the front door, with my baby cousin Ashley's hand grasped tightly in hers. I hadn't seen her in what felt like years but had only been a couple months. I rushed toward them in excitement, screaming with joy and delight.

"Shhhh, not so loud," my aunt hissed. *The neighbors.*

I stopped dead in my tracks, then slowly resumed inching in their direction before scooping my cousin up into my arms and twirling her around. I was sure she had grown significantly since I had seen her last.

"I have *Mortal Kombat!*" a voice called from in the house.

It belonged to Felicity, my older cousin, who was known back in North Bergen for two things: one, her incredible ability to quickly and effortlessly put together large jigsaw puzzles, and two, swindling all of the other kids out of their video games by making audacious bets about who could climb the highest tree or jump the longest distance.

"Leave your boots here," my aunt instructed, pointing to a mat directly in front of the door. I plopped down and untied the laces of my boots and threw them haphazardly into the ordained boots spot. All of the kids followed behind Felicity, who shepherded us upstairs to her room. Felicity was a lanky, dark-skinned girl and an extreme extrovert with a knack for using puns and telling the most hilarious jokes.

"Who gonna get beat first?" she asked, holding one controller out to me and my siblings.

I knew I was last in line, so I didn't even bother trying to argue for the first turn. My sister grabbed the controller and tossed herself onto a beanbag chair near the television. As the older kids began their Nintendo marathon, I slid out of the room and back down the stairs to look for Ashley. Mom was in the kitchen exchanging hushed words with my aunt and grandmother, so I turned left to venture through the dining room. We kids had been told that the room was off limits, and I wanted to know why. It was impeccably furnished with a black dining room set decorated with a red runner stretching across the table and a glass dish cabinet filled with antiques. I peered into the cabinet, looking at myself in the reflection—my chunky cheeks, hair parted into a few braids, and light-brown skin, which looked a bit ashen from the dry winter air.

"Don't fool around in there!" my aunt's voice erupted.

I scurried into the living room, where I found my cousin quietly playing with a bunch of Barbies on the carpeted floor, right in front of the sliding door, which opened onto the backyard deck.

"Wanna play?" she asked, pushing one of her dolls in my direction.

I scanned Barbie's slender frame—her ponytail of silky, blond, flowing hair and her frilly pink skirt with white blouse—and saw nothing that could possibly be of interest to me. At that point, I was considered a tomboy. I was rowdy, sporty, verbally aggressive, and a bit unrelenting. Mom had long ago given up on trying to adorn my hair with pretty clips or forcing me into pastel-colored dresses. She knew the effort would be in vain. In a single moment, absent supervision, I would find a way to make my neatly combed hair stand on end, and my dress would somehow always become a dingy gray.

"She truly has a talent," Mom always lamented after discovering my state, despite all of her grooming efforts.

It brought me great pleasure that she gave up on trying to safeguard my "girly" status and I was free to tumble around in short pants and T-shirts, free like my brother.

"Nah, let's get Stefan and go play outside in the snow!" I suggested to Ashley.

She lowered her eyes and rejected my offer, returning to her dolls.

I would always be perplexed by my cousin's lack of interest in outdoor activities and equally confused that the town felt quiet and empty every time we went to visit. We never saw kids playing outside. My aunt hushed and hissed for us to settle down at the slightest hint of rowdiness. Unlike loud, boisterous North Bergen, Edison was always still, except for the occasional sound of a passing car.

"Oh my God, it's sooooo boring there," Stefan complained to Mom during one of our hour-long drives to go visit.

One thing we never complained about was our trips with my mother to New York City. My mother worked downtown and sometimes took us along with her to work at the bank, where we would watch movies in a vacant room or color and draw in coloring books on "Bring Your Kids to Work Day."

"Behave and you can pick anything you want for lunch," she would whisper before leaving us to return to her desk.

We were easy to bribe. I always chose the large slice of chocolate cake from a local deli as my reward. Then Stefan and I would sit for the afternoon indulging our appetite for Disney movies. In *Beauty and the Beast*, the animated singing and dancing teacups, wardrobes, brooms, and candlesticks promised that all mean, hideous beasts could be turned into charming princes with the love and acceptance of a kind, gentle, beautiful maiden. I concurred. I held my breath in hopeful anticipation when Pocahontas leaped to the defense of her lover, John Smith, just before her father, the chief, was about to murder him. We sang along to *The Lion King*'s love songs over and over again with incessant fervor. My brother and I bonded over these films, memorizing much of their scripts and all of their soundtracks.

Mom's office was friendly and her coworkers were mostly people of color like her. The bank had many events for families and sometimes gave away coupons and discounts for popular things to do in the city. Even with the discounts, we couldn't afford the city's most alluring attractions. But there was one loophole my mom learned about from her colleagues that she never failed to take advantage of: the Metropolitan Museum's fee was by donation only. She placed a dollar in each of our hands at the entrance to the huge museum, and my siblings and I excitedly traded them in for tiny clips with the letter *M*, indicating that we'd paid for entry. Michael Jackson's "Remember the Time" video, featuring Eddie Murphy, Iman, and Magic Johnson, had inspired my obsession with Egypt, so that exhibit was our first stop in the immense building of historical artifacts. We searched the museum's map for the

African country and found that Egypt had its own exhibit . . . right before Africa's.

"Why would they separate Egypt from Africa?" my mom asked aloud, outraged.

She quietly ranted to us about the European desire to separate Egyptian history from African history so Black people could never lay claim to an ancient culture that inspired wonder and respect, but I was too excited by the idea of finally getting to see a real-life mummy to feel the weight of my mother's words. Could I cast a spell and raise them from the dead? And was it true that their brains were kept in jars? My mind raced with my own questions, but Mom had more to share.

"You know why the nose of the Sphinx and all these other statues are missing?" Mom asked in a whisper.

As I scanned the ancient photos and statues, I did notice that many of them were indeed missing that very prominent, defining feature. Some historians claimed the Sphinx was broken with instruments sometime between the third and tenth centuries CE. Others believed natural weathering caused some of the statues to erode and hypothesized that protruding noses and beards were the most fragile parts of the relics. Mom, however, had her own theory.

"White explorers shot the noses off so Black people wouldn't know their own history," she explained in a hushed voice.

I squinted at the relics, contemplating her explanation. I wondered who these Black people were and why anyone would want to steal their history. I also giggled at the thought that somehow a nose could represent so much complexity and controversy. Whether or not I accepted what my mother said as true, the mystery of the disappeared Egyptian relics' noses sparked a deep curiosity in me.

When I was a child, Blackness was a simple fact of life, one that seemed to require no significant investigation: it was both absent and ubiquitous. Much of the music and media that surrounded me starred Black entertainers, and even though Black families were hard to come by in North Bergen, it wasn't uncommon to see families with brown skin like mine. Many of my classmates shared my hue, and the classroom always felt like a welcoming place. The town's teachers were mostly white, Italians whose families had immigrated there when the area was first established, and they cared deeply about their students and treated my brother, my sister, and me with equal parts curiosity and support.

"This is Nikisia Drayton's little sister," I remember one of the school's front-desk ladies saying as she introduced me to my first-grade teacher. Anytime my sister's or brother's names were uttered in relation to me, teachers or the school's staff would squeal in delight and relay an experience they had had with one of my siblings.

"Niki always stood up like a little soldier when I called her name during attendance," one of her teachers recalled.

"Stefan already knew his ABCs when he came to my class."

"The Draytons are such great kids."

In the eyes of my teachers, my siblings were exceptional, and the same was expected of me. They had never heard of our homeland before, but their impression of it and its people was decided by their interactions with my studious brother and sister, who were used to a school culture where uniforms and strict adherence to authority were the norm. We were from Trinidad and Toe-Bah-Go—an exotic, distant land like Gilligan's island or Neverland. In fourth grade, my teacher recommended I apply to be in the district's "gifted and talented" program. She sent me home with a packet of questions for my mother and a practice test for me to prepare for the entrance exam and assured me I would secure a spot with the "smart kids"—a group of disproportionately East Indian, white, and Asian students. At the time, I didn't understand the delineation, because I enjoyed all of my classmates and marveled when they told me of their homelands. Most were first-generation children of immigrants from the Dominican Republic, Puerto Rico, Cuba, Colombia, or El Salvador. I knew their first and last names and could even point out most of their houses on my walk home from school.

It felt like we were all part of a big, quirky family. *Heart Angie Garcia, Heart Thomas Ramirez, Heart Janita Patel.* I signed cardboard Valentine's Day cards for every one of my classmates, passing them out with lollipops on the day we were taught to celebrate love. The entire school shared the same gym, music, and art teachers and could all tell stories of times that Miss Kaplan, the librarian, slammed a heavy book against a desk to hush the class when things got too rowdy. Our principal, Mr. Sacco—a jovial, round-bellied Italian who wore suits to work and gray wire-framed glasses—also broke the mold. Instead of an absent disciplinarian, he was a warm presence, often seated in his office near the entrance of the school with his door propped open, and was always present for assemblies.

But the inclusivity and success we experienced as a Black family in the Northeast came with a heavy price tag. The cost of living in North Bergen was steadily rising, and rents and bus fares were becoming untenable. Mom knew she had to find a way to make more money, so she embarked on the mission to become a nurse. She applied for a nursing program and prayed she would be gifted with one of the few scholarships on offer. She was delighted to find out that she was selected to receive a completely free ride based on her test scores, but her work had only just begun. To complete the degree, Mom would have to juggle her full-time job in New York City and evening classes in Bayonne and then find time to study at night, all while being a single mother 24-7.

"I think it's chicken pox," Mom said when tiny buttons began to pop up on my skin one day.

She rolled up Stefan's shirtsleeves and discovered similar marks all over his arms. By then, my grandmother had moved to the house in Edison with my aunt, because Debbie had more space and needed help caring for Ashley, who was the youngest of all the cousins. So Mom had a difficult decision to make: leave her children home alone and sick while she braved the world in pursuit of more financial security or stay at home and risk losing her job or flunking the program.

"Students can only miss three classes for the term," the program's head had warned, and she had already missed one.

Chicken pox would require us kids to stay home from school for at least a week, so Mom knew a confrontation was unavoidable. She began to rehearse her position aloud that night.

"My kids are only six and seven, and they are sick," I heard her repeating over and over again, her voice becoming more firm with each rendition. "I cannot leave them home alone."

I felt terrible for Mom as I watched her prepare to battle for time off of work and school. Late that night, I tiptoed over to her bed on the other side of the bedroom and snuggled up next to her.

"It's okay if you have to go to work, Mum," I whispered while I pulled her arm to drape over me. "Stefan and I can take care of ourselves."

"Shhh, go to sleep, baby," Mom sleepily replied.

When I awoke the next morning, I figured Mom had already left for work. I dejectedly sat up in bed, giving myself a few moments to process my feelings. I knew she wanted to stay home with me, but I accepted that she *couldn't*, which eased the sting of the disappointment. Just as I began to find the courage to begin my day of self-care, I caught a whiff of bacon and pancakes. And then the sound of my mom's voice belting out Diana King's "L-L-Lies" burst through the air. I rushed to the kitchen to find her there, cooking and singing with my brother. Stefan's face and arms were speckled with bumps and dots, and he was scratching like a puppy with fleas while he danced and lip-synched to the song, holding a spatula as his fake microphone.

"Go straight to the tub!" Mom ordered when she saw me.

She ushered me to our bathroom, where she was running a warm bath, and instructed me to take my clothes off. Then she poured a cup of oatmeal into the water. As soon as the cotton of my pajamas brushed against my skin as I lifted them over my head, I could feel my brain flooding with the urge to scratch everywhere. I jumped into the warm bath and sank into the water, the urge dissipating as a tingly, calming feeling rushed over me. I felt amazed that somehow Mom had known just what I would need. And I thought she was a superhero for winning the battle to stay home with us that week while our bodies were fighting off foreign, itch-inducing invaders.

With Mom's eighteen-month-long struggle to complete nursing school nearing its end, she dreamed of an easier, more affordable life for us. She dreamed of our having our own rooms and being able to afford more than just basic necessities. She wanted us to have the comforts of a middle-class life. And then her cousin Brian, a loud, short Trinidadian man with curly hair and a tireless ability to talk smack and tell inappropriate, child-unfriendly stories, popped into her life with a bold suggestion.

"Yuh should tink about moving to Houston," he told her one day when she reached out to catch up.

Brian had left Trinidad a few years earlier than she had and had also immigrated to Brooklyn first, but then decided to move to Houston, Texas, at the behest of his wife—with whom he now had a baby. Even after spending years in America, Brian's tongue was still heavy with the sounds and rhythm of his native language.

"Visit, and if yuh like it, move!" he urged.

Mom didn't hesitate to take him up on that offer.

A few weeks later, we arrived at Port Authority Bus Terminal, each of us kids wearing a backpack and carrying a lunch box packed with snacks, ham-and-cheese sandwiches, bags of chips and mini chocolate cookies, and a few boxes of apple juice, bound for Houston, Texas. I didn't know it then, but this trip south was the beginning of a journey into a conception of Blackness that had not been introduced into my consciousness yet and one that my mother certainly couldn't have foreseen—it would be a limited, perilous view of Blackness that I would spend the rest of my life trying to outrun, like an unwarned beachgoer trying to survive an incoming tsunami.

When we boarded the bus, the air was heavy with the smell of pee and Pine-Sol.

"This is gonna be a long two days," Stefan muttered under his breath while holding his nose.

At that time, the journey itself felt like the biggest trial we would have to bear. I tried to convince Stefan that Mom had made sure we were well prepared.

"*SNAAAAAACKS!*" I hissed, pointing at our lunch boxes.

Still ambivalent, he nodded in tepid agreement and continued to follow Mom as she shuffled down the aisle in search of a vacant row of seats. We passed row after row filled with brown and Black faces that belonged to the old and young, men and women. The only empty seats were right beside the bathroom. Mom turned toward us with a completely defeated look on her face, her shoulders slumped forward, waiting for pleas or outrage. I couldn't bear the sight of her tired eyes.

"Can we sit already?" I asked, holding my lunch box up high to ensure she understood my intent. Mom responded with a weary smile and moved aside for us to file into the row. She took the seat right next to the bathroom and endured the smell of urine and feces every time a passenger swung the door open, and cringed through the sound of the watery excrement sloshing side to side when the bus made abrupt turns or decelerated. Finally, we got to Richmond, Virginia, where the bus made its first significant stop and seats were freed up.

It was mandatory for all passengers to leave the bus every now and again so it could be cleaned, but somehow it never smelled any better when it came time to reboard. Most passengers were people of color who could afford no other means of interstate travel, like my mother, and the bus service made sure to reinforce the reality of our poverty with its treatment of us—ordering everyone on and off on a whim.

"Get up, babe." Mom woke me from a deep sleep during one of the routine cleaning stops.

I glanced out of the window. It was pitch-black outside, except for the fluorescent light over the pumps of the gas station. The clock read 3:43 a.m. I had never been awake at that time before and wondered if I would stumble upon a ghost while we inched toward the doors of the bus to exit. We followed a single-file line into a waiting area that featured a small, overpriced store selling snacks and a public bathroom. I collapsed into a blue plastic seat and slouched, falling back to sleep. It felt like I had only been there for a couple minutes when Mom shook me awake to get back on the bus. When I saw the clock again, it was 7:30 a.m.

The two-day trip felt like two weeks, with the bus making stops every few hours during the night and day. By about the fifth time I was awakened out of deep sleep for one of these stops, I was so grumpy and exhausted that I was wired, and I couldn't fall back asleep. I pouted and moaned during the entire hour-long wait to get back on the bus, with my mother gently shushing me. During daytime stops, I busied myself brushing my teeth and splashing water on my face to perform some semblance of normalcy and cleanliness. At every stop, passengers waded on and off the bus like worn explorers crossing a waist-high river. When we finally arrived in Houston, I felt like I had not bathed in weeks instead of in days, and I just wanted to sleep in peace.

"Allyuh reach!" Brian exclaimed when he spotted us in the terminal. "But oh gouuud, ah sure yuh seen better days!"

We all let out chuckles and one by one began to reenact scenes from the treacherous bus ride experience. Stefan crouched down to demonstrate how he almost fell into the bus's excrement-filled latrine when the bus took a sharp turn around a corner, throwing him off balance. I impersonated Mom, hunching my shoulders and pretending to walk like a zombie toward the bathroom-neighboring back-row seats. Mom poked fun at my uncanny ability to fall asleep without a moment's notice and leave puddles of drool on her shoulder. Niki explained that she needed a new toothbrush because hers fell into the sink, which she described as "brown-stained," "stink," and "dutty," while she tried to brush her teeth during a stop. Our storytelling lasted the entire thirty-minute ride to Brian's apartment and was interrupted only by his occasionally screaming obscenities at "shit drivers" and blaring his horn when they acted "too bold-faced."

As we unpacked our things from the car, I overheard Mom telling one last story in a hushed voice.

"Dey searched dee bus for hours with dogs," she whispered to Brian while they both leaned against the car with their arms folded. "And den dey arrest a woman and went through all dee luggage on dee bus until dey found hers."

I thought the dogs must have peed and pooped all over the bus when they let them on. Mom had always explained that pet mess was why she wouldn't let us have a cocker spaniel back in the apartment. *No wonder the bus always smelled so bad!* I thought to myself, outraged.

"Oh. My. God. There's a pool!" Stefan's announcement, from Brian's upstairs apartment, interrupted my snooping.

I made a beeline toward the staircase that led to the apartment, where Stefan was peering into the distance. When I got to him, we rushed to throw on our bathing suits and spent the rest of the evening splashing, paddling, and wading through the cool water. Mom joined us after taking a tour of Brian's three-bedroom condo. The neighborhood was safe, gated, and, most important: affordable. She was sold.

"Yuh-all want to move down here?" she asked as we fell asleep that night in the comfort of Brian's guest bedroom, made extra snug and comfortable by his wife, Avalon.

"We could have a bigger place and a pool," she assured us.

We three kids nodded in agreement, still high-spirited from the enjoyment of the comforts and amenities of the new environment and not yet aware of just how shallow these amenities might feel once we were embedded here. America had love-bombed us—sold us dreams of the perfect union.

The science of psychology calls the early phase of a narcissistic relationship "love-bombing." In these early, idyllic moments, hopeful, fated, and foundational memories are made that keep us coming back to what becomes the cycle of abuse. The abuser sells the victim promises of the perfect life, a life not only rich with comfort but also destined, ordained by a higher power, and thus structured so that the victim won't question the narrative. While the idyllic illusion of this moment isn't sustainable, its power to keep us in the thrall of the narcissist is more durable. Even as the phase psychology refers to as "devaluation" begins.

CHAPTER 2

Devalued

My family and I embarked on our first interstate move between New Jersey and Texas when I was eight years old. We strapped our two full-sized mattresses to Mom's Mercury Sable and began the journey on a warm summer day.

"Are we going to see horses and cows?" I asked her as she herded my brother, my sister, and me to the car.

"Well, it's going to be mostly just highway," she warned.

I couldn't hide my disappointment. As a city kid, I infrequently had the opportunity to see nature, and *Babe*, the nineties film with the talking pig, made me yearn for a farm visit. There was nothing exciting about a highway—I knew that much from driving on them in Jersey.

"We can stop somewhere and visit a farm!" I recommended.

My mom shrugged her shoulders and did not respond for a minute.

"There aren't too many places I'd feel comfortable stopping," she finally said.

Her discomfort made no sense to me, so I figured her ill ease was merely an adult excuse leveraged to avoid giving in to childish requests. I folded my arms in protest and sat in the back seat of the car and stared out the window, avoiding my mother's eyes in the rearview mirror for miles as we sped past the smoky, swampy industrial Newark scene and buildings eventually became grassy, expansive fields.

Our first stop was in West Virginia.

POOL AND COMPLIMENTARY BREAKFAST, a sign at the front of the hotel read.

"There's a pool!" I whispered to my brother. There was only one thing that could get my hopes up after finding out we would not be stopping to visit Babe: splashing around, carefree, in the pool with my brother on a hot summer day. We begged my mother to let us go swim, and after a moment's consideration, she gave in.

"Be careful and don't be too loud," she warned as we ran out of our room, bathing-suit clad. She agreed to meet us there after getting settled in.

The empty pool area greeted us like a brand-new playground. I threw my towel onto a nearby lounge chair and dove in, all in the same action. The cool water gave me goose bumps, and I twirled onto my back and floated to the surface. I breathed a sigh of relief. Then a tornado of splashes from my brother sent water straight up my nose. In between coughs, I chased my brother around the pool, trying to get him back, until we tired ourselves out and just held on to the side, bobbing up and down in the waves created by our play.

"Can we play with y'all?" asked a little boy with dark-brown skin that matched my brother's mahogany complexion. We nodded yes, and he motioned for two of his friends to come over, who appeared from what seemed like the trees near the parking lot. They took off their shirts and jumped into the pool too, splashing us and laughing loudly. Within moments, a middle-aged white woman appeared on the hotel's balcony. She peered down at us, an odd look on her face, as if we were aliens from some distant planet. The boys noticed my gaze fixed on something behind them, so they turned around quickly, trying to figure out what I saw. By that time, a second white woman had appeared and was whispering in the ear of the first woman. The boys quietly got out of the pool, collected their stuff, and left.

My mother materialized from the far corner of the building, wearing her bathing suit and a smile. Only when she caught a glimpse of the looks on our faces, and the group of white guests that had now formed to stare down at us, did she understand what she was walking into. After years of laboring under the white gaze of her former employers and being a fly on the wall during their intimate conversations, she knew what those stares meant. She knew how America viewed Black children.

"Those thugs deserve to be locked up for life," she had overheard the man of the house angrily snarl over dinner once as she cleared the table during one of her live-in nanny jobs years earlier.

In 1989, in what would come to be called the "Central Park Five" case, five Black and Latino teens were found guilty of raping and beating a white woman after the police and the media branded them as "savage" and "thugs" in one of the most heated and racially charged cases of the era. Then businessman Donald Trump spent thousands of dollars advertising the details of the case in newspapers, calling for the teens to be executed, and the national frenzy that ensued was branded "racial hysteria." Black parents across America understood the dangers of committing the grave offense of simply being a Black child playing in America. After spending years in prison, the teens were finally exonerated when the man who committed the crime confessed. By then, many of them bore the scars of being falsely criminalized.[1]

"Lucky we didn't call the cops," one of the women piped up from the hotel's balcony. "Leaving those kids unattended like that."

Mom's smile vanished.

"Get out of the pool and let's go," she hissed angrily.

"Ten mooooore miiiiinu—" my brother and I began in unison, but my mother interrupted us.

"Get out now!"

My mother was not easily angered, and her rage came as a huge surprise to us. We made no further objections and scurried from the pool and fell into line behind her like ducks in a row.

Mom pretended that she didn't hear the woman and ushered us back to the room in silence. Under the guise of concern, the true intent of those white women could be concealed, and so my mom had no room to protest. Their "concern" gave them plausible deniability of any racist intent.

"But we aren't babies and we could all swim," I argued, upset that she wouldn't let us go back to the pool. "And why don't you just come with us?"

Mom breathed deeply and paused for a long while before responding.

"I don't think those ladies cared either way," she said. "And I'm not comfortable going back there."

I sulkily accepted Mom's final verdict, but inside I was seething with anger and disappointment. There was nothing I could do to reclaim my joy. Every Black child remembers the moment they learn that certain white spaces are off limits to them. Through encounters that are technically harmless and legal, but that undermine us anyway, Black children learn from ordinary citizens who take it upon themselves to clandestinely patrol common spaces that we not only are unwelcome but also somehow represent possible danger. At the very least, these encounters leave individual children confused as they are gaslit and sorted apart from the people who are able to patrol and police Black youth without qualification or justification. At worst, this kind of policing threatens to rob us of our physical freedom and dignity. The ensuing trauma of realizing this unspoken agenda threatens to attack and destroy our innocence. Beneath the veneer of the perfect communion America seemed to promise me, tensions were building; something vicious and nasty began to brew. Anything that is combustible and kept under pressure will eventually bubble over.

It took some years and a few more interstate road trips for me to completely understand the subtext of the events of that day and why my mother refused to let us swim not just in that hotel pool but in any more hotel pools at all. It was the same reason we never stopped in certain towns or states, even if we desperately needed to use the bathroom or just wanted to stretch our legs. It wasn't until a middle-school history class, one that spelled out the reason for the Civil War, that I understood what the Confederate flags stuck on cars and trucks throughout the South meant for us and our safety. It was years before I learned white America's terrible history of abusing Black children who dared to try to integrate city swimming pools. And it was only through those years, combined with my personal experience, that I began to be able to explain why all of the white faces in restaurants turned to stare at my family when we ended up stranded with a flat tire nearby. By the time I was a teenager, I knew very well not to venture over to the other side of the tracks—and had learned how to sense where the line between my side and theirs would be. What awaited me there could be ridicule, or even death. A new education began that day at the hotel pool, when my brother and I first experienced what it was like to be unwanted, feared even: what it was like to be Black in the United States of White America. I would never have chosen it and I wouldn't provoke it, but I was given no choice. As a Black child growing up in America, I would be swept up in the push and pull of the country's cycle of abuse.

"The Lord is my light and my salvation; whom shall I fear?" Mom uttered under her breath as she drove along fifty-plus hours of highway with us three rowdy kids in the back seat.

When we arrived in our new Houston neighborhood, it was a depressing sight. The complex's sign was missing letters. The rusted entry gate squeaked as it struggled to swing open after Mom punched the code into a lopsided steel structure. I shot Niki and Stefan glances of disbelief.

"Stifle me," I declared loudly, pressing a pillow against my face.

My siblings giggled, but Mom's body tensed up in discomfort. She shut off the car without saying a word, grabbed the keys, and marched over to the front door. We followed and stood behind her silently as she rattled the keys, trying to match each to its lock.

When the door swung open, though, we could not believe our eyes. *"Wow!"*

Our new place was a three-bedroom townhouse on the back side of the neighborhood, overlooking a bayou. It had huge vaulted ceilings, carpeted floors, and a fireplace. Upstairs had two bedrooms—a master bedroom with an adjoining bathroom and walk-in closet (which my sister and I would share)—and a tiny hallway leading to my brother's room. Downstairs had a spacious living room, a kitchen, and my mom's room.

"And guess what?" Mom said with a satisfied grin. "There's a pool!"

Niki, Stefan, and I darted out of the front door on a quest for the neighborhood pool. We followed a path that led into the center of the complex and bypassed a small playground and tiny field. The pool glistened in the sun, beckoning me.

"Don't do it, Tiff," Niki warned as if reading my mind.

But the allure of the water was unbearable. I ran through the gated entrance and plunged into the pool, bubbles erupting all around me. Stefan joined, and we splashed and played until Mom appeared with towels in hand and a smile on her face, calling for us to come inside because it was dinnertime. We ate our first meal on one of the mattresses that had survived the long journey from Jersey. My mom had contemplated throwing the mattresses in a huge dumpster behind a gas station during one of our pit stops. No one had warned us that the straps we had used to tie them down would cause water to run into the car during every rainfall on our three-day journey, and she was fed up by then with getting drenched. Niki saved the day (and the mattresses) somewhere between Virginia and South Carolina, devising a system of stuffing T-shirts in the cracks of the windows and car doors in order to soak up the rain. We were all glad we had kept the comfy, springy beds as we chomped down our meals amid the otherwise completely bare space. It would take months before Mom could afford to fully furnish the entire townhouse.

Mom had decided on our new neighborhood based on its proximity to a "good" school district. We used a website called greatschools.org to research school demographics and performance ratings. After watching my mom meticulously scrolling through pages of school names and letter grades, we offered to help her out with the search. Anytime we found a "good" school (one ranked with an A or B grade based on student test scores), we took note of its zip code and then tried to find an affordable place to live there. We settled on an elementary school in Mission Bend, a mixed suburb, for Stefan and me, and Niki could attend the local high school.

School in Houston was nothing like what I was accustomed to back in North Bergen. It was far more regimented, organized, and impersonal. But the building was also new, and the curriculum offered more extra activities like band, orchestra, and theater classes. The school bus left every morning from the front of the neighborhood and traveled miles along a desolate road before arriving at the brand-new building with the American flag waving. Students exited the bus in single file and then sat in rows in the cafeteria until the bell rang and we shuffled to our classrooms. Most classes were instructed by white teachers, and I never learned the names of many of my peers. The environment felt cold and unwelcoming, but I always found relief in history class, where I would escape into distant, fantastical worlds of Natives, Pilgrims, explorers, the "New World," kings, queens, and adventure. The great "Land of the Free" sold its history to young, impressionable minds with the same superficial sparkle that Disney wove into stories when it mass-produced fairy-tale classics. The retellings always had happy endings.

"Write a report on your favorite historical character," my fifth-grade history teacher instructed.

Without hesitating, I decided on Pocahontas—the song "Colors of the Wind" from the animated movie hummed in my mind. I drew hearts in my notebook as I imagined the details I would uncover during my research on the Native American princess who unexpectedly fell in love with a white man and united her tribe and the settlers who sought to invade their land. Such was the power of love, I thought.

On the day I presented my findings, though, my voice was very flat.

"Pocahontas was a child like us when she was kidnapped by European colonists," I began.

It didn't take long before my teacher, a plump, middle-aged white woman, hurried me back to my seat.

"You were supposed to use the library resources," the teacher chastised as she explained why I would have to redo the project.

I didn't bother explaining to her that I had used the library resources. I had sat in the library's computer room for hours, teary-eyed as I read the true story of the prepubescent Powhatan girl whose birth name was Amonute and whose life was destroyed by white men who raped and pillaged Native lands and their people. Pocahontas's "love story" was a real-life nightmare, but saying so challenged the order of things, and my teacher quickly asserted her power to put me back in line.

When she said "library resources," I knew deep down that she meant I should rely on sanitized resources, resources that told only an inspiring version of our history, because then, and even now, a painful story couldn't be seen as inspiring or hopeful or galvanizing. My relationship with America entered a new phase. One that Black people have been ensnared by in every era of American history: devaluation.

In an abusive relationship, during the stage of devaluation, an abuser attributes exaggeratedly negative qualities to the victim, thus branding them as fundamentally flawed or worthless. This treatment steals a victim's control over their own narrative and reduces their value in the eyes of not just the abuser but also others in their world and sometimes even the victim themselves. Through the process of devaluation, grotesque, inhumane acts find justification. The abuser no longer feels responsible for their actions around the victim, and the victim is now positioned as if they objectively deserve less than equal consideration. The power of devaluation became apparent to me the more intimately I attuned myself to the style and presentation of my history lessons, though I had no language to communicate what I was seeing at the time.

As I became more immersed in "Black history" lessons, the pain of watching Black bodies shackled, beaten, whipped, and hung from trees like "Strange Fruit" was initially traumatizing and paralyzing. I stared at images of Emmett Till's mutilated face for over fifteen minutes before I was able to turn the page. The visual depiction of violence that I had to digest superseded my desire to find out if the white men who beat Till, shot him in the head, and sank his body to the bottom of the Tallahatchie River ever faced justice for his brutal murder. When I could finally read on and discovered that they were acquitted by an all-white jury but admitted to killing Till in an interview with a magazine a year later, unafraid of prosecution because they were protected by the "double jeopardy" rule, I just stared at the ceiling in bed, unable to fall asleep.

How had white people justified the enslavement and debasement of millions of people who looked like me? As part of my learning, I was presented with images in my schoolbooks of common historical relics from the slavery era, like newspaper clippings that read "For Sale: Two Negro Men" and "Negro Woman and Child," and signs affixed to everything from diner counters to public water fountains from the Jim Crow era that read FOR WHITES ONLY. I flipped through pages with these images over and over again. I found that I would even get out of bed late at night just to reread the schoolbook's captions. The images were doing something to me, and I was paying attention to and digesting a whole buffet of complexity, but on my own, and so young, I could articulate very little about what was taking hold inside of me.

So I anesthetized myself to the horrible outcomes that implications of worthlessness had on marginalized populations in America, like those imposed on Native Americans, many of whom were beaten, raped, tortured, and eradicated by the European colonists, who labeled them "savages." My numbed defense response kept me detached from the fallout and intergenerational damage caused by qualitative terms like "lazy" when they were applied to emancipated Black men by plantation owners who refused to hire them and then criminalized them with Black codes. I was clueless to the fact that colonial stereotypes of Black people as simpleminded Sambos, rapists, overly sexual Jezebels, Jim Crows, servant mammies, and Aunt Jemimahs were rebirthed in the very same culture and music I would consume centuries after these harmful and potent devaluing images were created to justify the abuse and mistreatment of Black people.

I accepted the then-popular stereotyping of poor Black people as "thugs," "crackheads and crack babies," and "welfare queens" as proof of some Black people's inferiority and not expressions of my era's devaluation of Black people, devaluation that justified the continued and systematic ghettoization of people who looked like me. By digging more deeply into my history lessons, I learned that Texas's 1866 Apprentice Act legalized the kidnapping of Black children under the guise of "providing them with guardianship" and providing "good" homes for them. These children were then used as forced, unpaid labor. The very same pretext—the separation of Black children from their families as a means of "bettering" their circumstances—would undergird profitable practices of the twentieth century that disproportionately forced Black children into foster care and child protective services. An education built on the acceptance of the devaluation of Black bodies propels the Black child into adolescence and teenhood. This flawed foundation could offer me only a flawed and destructive form of socialization, one I ultimately couldn't escape even at home, or elsewhere in my community. The tendrils of America's system of devaluation of Black people and other minorities were far too numerous and too nuanced for a young individual to not just flag but rewire all on her own. Looking back, I see that even with all of the love and insight I had, I myself became a "flying monkey" for my own debasement, inadvertently perpetuating a system that continues to position Black people as inferior to, or as having much more to prove than, others.

My paralysis and shock were eased only by the promise of the realization that the dream of full citizenship for Black people was on the horizon in my history books, in lessons of the great civil rights era—a time that eradicated racism and Black oppression. Through my school history textbooks, I was assured that America had righted the wrongs of the past. Once upon a time, I was told, there was a thing called slavery that was a horrible stain on America's otherwise bright history, but Harriet Tubman shepherded slaves to freedom via the Underground Railroad and Abraham Lincoln freed those who remained. Martin Luther King Jr. organized marches, and Rosa Parks refused to give up her front seat aboard a Montgomery, Alabama, bus in protest of segregation. Malcolm X, though perhaps too militant and hostile, united Black Americans in the pursuit of their rights. Voting laws were passed. Schools, ballparks, neighborhoods, and water fountains were integrated. I learned that Ruby Bridges braved crowds of nasty, aggressive whites hurling racial epithets and spitting at her for trying to integrate an all-white Louisiana school in 1960, but it was all worth it in the end and afforded me the opportunity to attend "good" schools. The big, happy American family was now a rainbow coalition of freed people.

"Free at last, free at last, thank God almighty we are free at last." Martin Luther King Jr.'s words reverberated through my soul, putting my anxiety over my skin color to rest. I imagined neither my present circumstances nor my future could be shaped by the evils of racism.

However, some unexplained ill ease still stirred within me. Through those history lessons and by taking cues from my environment, I recognized Black American life to be riddled by a persistent conundrum: America, you learned, was the richest country in the world. Yet Black people were visibly poor, were worn out, and often seemed to get famous only for singing songs of the "ghetto" and life in the "projects" or the "hood." Black people never would have survived nor thrived in America without advocating for themselves, and yet that very advocacy led to the deaths of the country's most prominent Black leaders. My mind was breaking under the cognitive dissonance, and I needed to find a way to settle these discrepancies.

"Just work hard, get good grades, and go to college," my teachers would prescribe when I came to them searching for the remedy.

I thirstily gulped down that magic elixir. My education encouraged buy-in to the American "up by your bootstraps" myth and bound me to ideas that rid my mind of those earlier feelings of cognitive dissonance.

I reconciled the ongoing reality of Black hardship with the idea that Black people were free and equal by internalizing the myth that this conflict was merely meritocracy at work, and that participation in meritocracy could save anyone. If Black people only worked harder, they would not be in such predicaments. America was, after all, the *land of opportunity*. If I got perfect grades, went to college, and then worked my way into a successful career, certainly I would be afforded a good life— and the good grades, college acceptance, and job opportunities were mine to earn. The difficult circumstances of my childhood, I then reasoned, were the fault of my mother for having so many children and leaving my father. It pained me that our hardships were all of my mother's own making, but at least the better decisions I could make would ultimately lead me to a less tumultuous life. I haughtily offered her what I felt were my valuable insights: Things would certainly be better if she paired herself with a mate. Mom was doing both herself and us a disservice by remaining single.

"You should go out with him," I would urge Mom whenever she told us about a coworker or neighbor who hit on her.

"Hush and mine ya business," she would hiss whenever I put forth my case for dating.

My siblings agreed that she was strange but eventually gave up on broaching the subject. Even if Mom pairing with a partner might mean more stability or resources for my family, deep down I wanted her with me and not with some man. Mom was barely home as it was. The thought of her using what little time off she had to entertain anyone else helped me embrace her desire to self-isolate. Plus, our dire financial situation had begun to ease as she settled into her new career as a nurse. A little over a year after our move to Houston, she came home with a surprise she'd been saving for early on Christmas morning: three plastic cases with the titles *The Matrix, Shrek,* and *How the Grinch Stole Christmas* on them. When I cracked them open, I found CDs inside and turned to my mom, eyebrows furrowed and squinting at the disks in confusion.

"We are getting a new CD player?" I unenthusiastically questioned.

"Nope."

Seconds later, a bang on the front door made me jump. Mom opened it and two men wearing shirts emblazoned with the words "Rent-A-Center" and black back braces stumbled in.

"Where do you want it, ma'am?" one asked.

Mom pointed to the empty corner facing the mattress on the floor, where we typically lounged during the day. The men turned to leave and within moments came back rolling a huge sixty-inch-screen Hitachi television. My mouth and eyes were wide open with surprise.

"Those are DVDs," she explained, pointing to the cases I still held in my hand.

We spent the entire morning eating ham and Mom's freshly baked bread and watching Jim Carrey play his best version of the grouchy green Dr. Seuss character. Mom fell asleep within ten minutes of starting the movie, a small smile spread across her face as she rested. Welcoming "Big Mama" (named in tribute to her wide hips and booming audio) to the family was a turning point in my family's financial predicament. When Mom later bought us a computer and we each got our own bed and comforter set, we had officially ascended into middle-class life. There was only one thing left I felt my tiny family was missing: a dog.

"Pleeeeease, Mommmmm," Stefan and I begged anytime we discovered my mother's eyes were open.

Sometimes she would shut them and pretend to be sleeping just to avoid our pleas. After weeks of torment, though, she caved and finally agreed to take us to the local humane society in search of the perfect pup. We found him after two trips: Sam, a nine-week-old Chow Chow fur ball who was rescued along with a litter of about five other puppies. He was the only black one, curled up in a corner all by himself. When the shelter worker lifted him out of the kennel and into my arms, I immediately fell in love. Our family was finally secure and complete. Mom's hard work as a hospice nurse had paid off, just as America promised it would. We were climbing the economic ladder, my mother trudging rung by rung, one patient's comfortable ascent into heaven at a time.

Eventually, my school life also became regular: I boarded the bus in the mornings, sat in long, quiet lines in front of classrooms as teachers shuffled by, listened to history lectures on famous white men, contemplated the scientific method (allegedly first documented by Sir Francis Bacon), and groaned and sighed with heavy reluctance and boredom at Shakespeare's difficult-to-understand-or-relate-to soliloquies. Overwhelmed by the whiteness of my education, I came to view subjects like math, literature, history, and science as a mandate I had to master in order to prove my worth, but I struggled to truly connect with any of it in a meaningful way. There was only one space in the entire school environment that ever called to me: the band room.

At the behest of my mother, I registered to be a part of the orchestra during my first year in intermediate school (for grades five and six). I told her that I could join the band, but she dissuaded me from that option with assurances that playing the violin would be more tasteful and refined. The orchestra class had about seven other students. The instructor was Dr. Miller, a white man with a haughty accent and peculiar penchant for talking down to his students, who were mostly Black. He often ridiculed my posture as I held my violin during class. I couldn't, for the life of me, find the desire to sit upright while listening to his lengthy declamations on the greatness of white male musicians with names I could not pronounce—famous composers, conductors, and violinists. Instead, I spent much of the forty-five minutes in his class daydreaming about lunch and envying the students across the hall.

Across the hall was the band room, and it was always jam-packed with students. The teacher, a short Black woman named Ms. Berry, was equal parts nurturing and disciplinarian.

"All right, y'all need to settle down!" she would command before counting her students down to begin their rendition of a popular song of the era.

I often found myself peering out of Dr. Miller's classroom over at Ms. Berry, deeply drawn to her enthusiasm as she twirled her conductor's baton all about as if casting an incantation. The thumping bass of the percussion, the brazen sound of trumpets, the crashing of the cymbals, and the squeals and laughter of her students all blended together into a spellbinding melody. Every day during the orchestra class period, my soul floated away into the band room, leaving my body hunched over my violin and flaccid as a discarded rag doll. I was bewitched.

"How's orchestra?" Mom asked over dinner one night.

Months earlier, we had driven two hours away to find a music store that would rent us two violins—one for my brother and one for me. Some of the stores would rent instruments only based on the applicant's credit score, which usually meant Mom wouldn't qualify. She spent hours researching and calling stores before one finally gave her its approval. Mom beamed with pride and joy when we walked out with two blue cases in hand, each containing the classical instrument. She wore that same prideful grin as she inquired about our progress that night.

"That white man boring as hell," Stefan responded plainly.

I tried but failed to contain a snicker. Mom's entire demeanor shifted and her head lowered. She had aspirations for us, which she had acquired through her years of education at "convent," a school the richer and whiter children in Trinidad attended. We were to learn how to play tennis, swim, speak French, and play the violin. Those things would make us acceptable in the world she knew could bestow comfort and riches. But we kids were just desperate to feel connected, and Dr. Miller's orchestra was not the environment where that could ever happen.

"You should work on your posture," he criticized me again after my first performance with my violin in front of a crowd of students and their parents.

He offered no kind words.

"I thought it was beautiful," Mom said.

She had managed to make the 10:00 a.m. performance, coming directly from her overnight shift at the hospital. I shrugged. When the next semester ushered in the opportunity to remain in orchestra or decide on a new extracurricular, I chose band. Mom was upset that I gave up on the violin and huffed and puffed when I announced my decision over dinner, but she still supported me.

"Do whatever makes you happy," she acquiesced.

I was near to tears as I toted my alto sax into the music hall and turned left into Ms. Berry's class, overwhelmed by excitement. I anticipated that being in a Black environment, with a Black teacher, would be both comforting and invigorating, and I wasn't disappointed. It didn't take long for me to work my way up to second chair (I took to locking myself in the closet at home and practicing every song from the music book over and over again). When Ms. Berry would call on me to perform a solo, I would proudly sit up and play the most perfectly executed rendition of a beginner band song. I beamed with pride when she applauded my effort. It was like winning the approval of a doting aunt.

On the day I was to compete against a boy from the class for first chair, the music hall was uncharacteristically silent. I crept into the band room, afraid of drawing too much attention to my tardiness. Ms. Berry had rolled a television to the front of the classroom, and all of the students' eyes were fixed on the screen. I settled into my chair and put my sax case onto the floor in front of me. When I finally caught a glimpse of the images on the TV, my heart plunged like a crashing elevator no longer stabilized by cables or brakes.

Dark-gray smoke was billowing from one of the World Trade Center's buildings like blood gushing out of a gaping wound. My eyes shot over to the teacher to gauge her response, but her gaze was on the floor. Moments later, a tiny moving object on the screen crashed into the other tower, which sent exploding glass and debris into the already darkened sky. I couldn't make sense of what was happening, but the tension in the room had my stomach in knots. Then students began to quietly disappear from the class, dissolving from my memory of that day one by one. When Mom arrived, I joined the procession of students marching toward the school's front doors in a zombie-like trance. I got into the back seat of the car and looked in the rearview mirror, trying to gather answers from her usually comforting and steady gaze. Mom's tear-stained face looked exhausted and horrified. I rested my head on my backpack behind the driver's seat and stared into black vinyl as tears blurred my vision and fell onto the car's dark carpet.

It took days for me to understand what happened on 9/11. The *New York Post* and *USA Today* declared the terrorist attacks an "act of war," and the televisions in every home were tuned to the news, which gave constant updates for days after the attack. Images of Americans leaping from the highest floors of the towers haunted my dreams. I wondered what thoughts raced through their minds as they crashed through the depths of the earth's invisible atmospheric ocean. Stefan and Niki argued over dinner about whether or not the terminal velocity and the acceleration of the fall would've created enough pressure to cause the tower's divers to pass out. It brought me great comfort when they both agreed it would, whether or not their analysis was scientifically sound.

"That would've been me," I heard Mummy whisper through sobs when I pressed my ear against her bedroom door one night. "How did you know?"

She never told me until well into adulthood, but right before our move to Houston, one of her longtime Trinidadian friends had called her with an urgent message.

"Dee, you need to leave New York," he told her.

He had had a dream that there was a huge fire in New York City that would kill many people, and he wanted us to leave immediately.

"My friend Pamela, who I used to travel with to work every morning, was in one of the trains that got rerouted back to Newark when the first plane crashed into the towers," Mom later revealed.

The thought haunted me that had she not packed us up and made that cross-country trek, Mom could have been buried in the rubble of the World Trade Center. Though it was unlikely, the possibility alone was unsettling. A total of 2,763 people were killed in the collapses. Four were from North Bergen: Port Authority Police workers Christopher Amoroso, David LeMagne, Lieutenant Robert Cirri, and Sal Edward Tieri. The last photo of Amoroso captured him assisting a woman fleeing from Ground Zero before he returned to the building, where he would die trying to rescue more people. Tieri was only forty years old when he was killed while in a meeting on the ninety-ninth floor of Tower One. He left behind two young sons. One horrific moment changed the lives of so many Americans. One courageous decision drastically reduced the impact of that moment on my family. But the moment the towers fell, my understanding of America did as well. The country was no longer omnipotent if we could be brought to our knees by a few men with box cutters. Americans fired back at whomever they perceived to be Muslim or immigrants by hurling xenophobic, hate-filled language or even threatening violence.

"Take that down," Mom ordered when we rolled into a gas station and strangers peered into our vehicle.

Niki quickly untied a bright red-black-and-white Trinidad and Tobago flag that she had affixed to our rearview mirror to remind us of our homeland. During that time, no one wanted to be perceived as unpatriotic or un-American.

Eventually, in Houston, it felt like my life was hijacked and I couldn't do anything to protect myself. Shortly after the Twin Towers fell, my Black girlhood was also buried by a series of unfortunate attacks. At twelve years old, I was beginning to blossom, and predators in my environment didn't hesitate to take note of that fact. That we were newcomers and northerners in a southern city also made others skeptical of us and even outright hostile at times. Our neighborhood was a huge complex bordered on one side by a highway and on the other by a bayou that teemed with critters like frogs and slugs. Mom worked nights at the local hospital, so I was often left home alone with my older siblings. She didn't have a car to get to work, because ours had broken down shortly after our cross-country road trip, and the public transportation system was so bad that it would take her three buses and two hours to get there, so she typically left home by 8:00 p.m. Stefan, Niki, and I would walk her to the bus stop, cracking jokes and being silly just to try to lighten the mood. Mom would always walk silently, barely responding to our playful banter, which was unlike her. I knew she was holding something back, but her pride and desire to protect us cloaked her deeper feelings. She later admitted to us that she would cry the entire way to the hospital on the bus, saddened by the need for her nightly departures.

After Mom was gone, we'd come home and I'd spend my time loading free AOL dial-up trials onto my computer to go online to play word games. My favorite was Literati, an online version of Scrabble hosted by Yahoo where users could play against one another. I chose a brown-skinned avatar with a short bob haircut and a red hat emblazoned with a yellow *Y*. I took great pleasure in learning the art of scoring points, carefully calculating the value of letter combinations when placed in different positions on the board, where advantageous placement could double or even triple their value. Eventually, I discovered the small chat boxes at the bottom of the screen, and I began to exchange friendly words with my opponents.

"A/S/L?" was the usual icebreaker, an internet greeting and request for "age, sex, and location."

"12/F/TX," I would respond.

Sometimes we would reveal more about ourselves through small talk, but I was usually too deeply invested in the game to participate in more than just game-specific banter. I quickly learned from other players the importance of two- and three-letter words and that using all seven lettered tiles would confer fifty bonus points. It didn't take long before I began to beat my competitors, who were mostly adults from all across America.

"BLACK BITCH," an opponent wrote one day, right after I defeated him 191–72. "YOU FUCKING BLACK WHORE."

I stared at the screen, puzzled. Then I waved at Niki, urging her to come view the spectacle.

"Can you believe this?" I asked her, dumbfounded.

She read the message and turned toward me with a queasy look.

"Yeah, I get a lotta those too," she responded.

Niki confessed that she'd sat through many similar encounters on Literati before she finally decided to change her avatar to a flower, which would not give away her racial identity. She shrugged at me and walked back to bed and continued to thumb through her novel. After that day, it was like the floodgates of online gaming racism had opened. Almost every other win was followed by message after message containing the words "nigger," "black," "bitch," "dumb," or "whore," or some combination of the five. And every time I changed my avatar to a non-race-identifying image (like the flower my sister opted to use or the dog, cat, or alien cartoon drawings) the attacks would cease. At first, I was fueled by the violence and took delight in beating other players with white avatars, anticipating their hateful remarks. But after a while, the reality that those white cartoon faces represented the thoughts of real-life white Americans began to take its toll on me. I realized that I was becoming wary of white people, and the burden of my increasing paranoia began to overwhelm me. So I left Literati and began to venture out into the real world—my neighborhood, where I only saw Black or brown faces. It was the surest way I could avoid encountering or being forced to grapple with white racism. I believed such vitriol and debasement of my personhood existed only online, where cowardly women and men perhaps felt emboldened by anonymity. North Bergen had shown me that basic respect and dignity was the rule in real-world life. But I didn't understand that I no longer lived in that safe little town.

To test the waters, I started making trips to the grocery for snacks, desperate to re-create the freedom I once knew. Here in Houston, Mom always cautioned me against crossing the street after sunset and implored us to stay in the complex. She thought the high fences that surrounded it kept us safe from what was on the outside. But what was inside the neighborhood proved to be a bigger danger. On one particular evening, a group of older men—probably in their thirties and forties—was standing near our townhouse. A screwed and chopped version of the Hot Boys' "I Need a Hot Girl" was blasting from a minivan parked near the curb. As I approached, they waved. I could name every individual in the group.

"Hey, girl, come on over here," one of them, who I knew was named Paul, called out to me over the music.

He was a dark, tall man with huge brown eyes who often waved to me and my family when our car drove past. He sometimes even engaged in light, friendly banter about the weather or some other inconsequential element of daily life with my mom.

I walked over quietly, not wanting to be rude to an adult.

"I always see you going to school," he said.

I nodded but remained quiet.

"You like school a lot, huh?" he asked.

I nodded again.

"I could school you," he said with a smirk. "There's a thing or two I bet you don't know yet."

The crowd of men erupted in chuckles. I gave a weak smile and turned to walk away.

"You know where to find me if you change your mind," he yelled at my back as I sped along.

Tears welled up in my eyes, because I didn't understand the joke, so I couldn't understand why they were all laughing at me. For the rest of my journey to the store, I chastised myself for even going over to them in the first place. I knew better than to talk to strangers—but I hadn't classified him as such. I was torn between feeling victimized and feeling stupid for making a bad decision. On my way back, I ran into my neighbor, a seventeen-year-old brother of one of the men who was in the group.

"Don't pay them any attention. My brother and his friends are just stupid," he assured me.

I didn't say anything but looked up at him with an appreciative smile. He walked me home and showed me a detour that I could use to avoid interacting with those men in the future.

"I got some new, cool movies," he said when we arrived at my front gate. "You should come by tomorrow and we'll watch one."

I accepted his invitation, envisioning the enjoyment we'd share, similar to what I shared with my brother when we watched movies together. By then, Stefan and I had begun to grow apart; puberty and attending different schools created barriers to our ability to relate. I missed our close relationship, and his absence left a hole in my life.

So the next day I showed up to the boy's house, three doors down from mine. The bass from his music was making the front porch rattle.

"It's open," he yelled from inside.

I pushed on the door to find him sitting, completely naked, penis in hand, watching pornography on mute while Juvenile's "Back That Azz Up" pounded out of the speakers. He gestured for me to come closer. But I closed the door and walked back home, both stunned and numb. I sat on the steps outside my house, feeling too dirty and full of shame to enter.

"Hey, you okay?" a voice interrupted my moment of distress.

It belonged to Brittany, a thirteen-year-old white girl who lived next door.

We quickly fell into an easy friendship, spending much of our time comparing and contrasting our northern and southern drawls.

"Tennis shoes aren't just for tennis. They are to exercise with," she told me in between chuckles when I told her I wouldn't need them because I would not be playing tennis.

"Ohhhhh, like sneakers," I responded.

We also enjoyed catching toads in the bayou and singing made-up jingles on our front patios about our excursions.

Skunky went down to the pond one day, ah huh—AH HUH
Skuuuuunky went down to the pond one day, ah huh—AH HUH
Skunky went down to the pond one day, down where the bullfrogs like to play,
ah huh, ah huh, ah huh—AH HUH

Our musical renditions typically ended with our erupting into laughter until tears streamed down our faces. But our musical tastes weren't always so innocent.

Both Brittany and I were obsessed with hip-hop music and culture. We loved the bass and the rhythm of the music, the way it pulsated deep into your soul, making it impossible not to feel like shaking and dancing. By the time we were listening, the music had evolved radically from its humble beginnings, but none of its changes made it any less appealing to young people. In the seventies Clive "Kool Herc" Campbell and Afrika Bambaataa birthed the hip-hop movement, which forged strength and unity in Black urban areas by organizing block parties around the love of Black music and culture. And a decade later, Kris Kross made Black kids all around the world "Jump." But by the nineties, gangsta rap had come to dominate the airwaves, followed by the popularization of southern "dirty" rap, which had raunchy, questionable lyrics.

"Girl, you look good, won't you back that ass up," Brittany and I would rap to one another while shaking our booties around our living rooms like the women we saw in the music video.

African American music was a power inherited from the motherland, but that power, entangled with America's industrialization of music and its history of devaluing Black people, had birthed a stereotype-producing machine. In the late 1800s and early 1900s, American pop music was born in New York City's Tin Pan Alley, a stretch of buildings on West Twenty-eighth Street named for the sound of piano music passersby would hear while traversing the area. Musicians, composers, and sheet music publishers all coalesced on the scene to trade their creativity and artwork for virality, but like everything else at that time in America, even this creative place was plagued by racism. The street housed buildings where some of America's most popular songs were created, but also disturbingly racist tunes including "The Dandy Coon's Parade," "Nigger, Nigger Never Die," and "All Coons Look Alike to Me." Such "coon songs" were a popular trend that sold millions of copies and, in turn, inspired the production of more coon songs. Even a Black man, George W. Johnson, cashed in on the trend when he recorded the first hit by a Black man: "The Whistling Coon." The songs often portrayed Black people as a threat to the white American way of life, which justified Black people's subordination. They also perpetuated the pleasure and amusement the nation got from depicting Black people as racist caricatures—blackface was a national craze. A space that incentivized Black people to perform as racist caricatures meant the American tradition would endure over the years and many Black artists would need to conform in order to cash in, as George W. Johnson did with his coon song.[2]

The exploitative relationship between American music production and Black people had changed very little by the time hip-hop and R&B music took hold in my childhood. Though hip-hop music and culture were conceived as a tool for Black self-expression, they eventually became dominated by "gangsta rap," a subgenre that glorified guns, drugs, gangs, and the exploitation of women. America was enthralled by the style, which depicted Black men as dangerous and a menace to society. Then came rap stars like Lil' Kim, performers whose sexy lyrics and controversial and risqué outfits felt both audacious and alluring, and the rise of "video vixens"—Black female models who sold sex appeal in rap videos.

I watched, transfixed, as Black women's asses bounced on BET in hip-hop music videos or on the network's late-night entertainment show *Uncut* while Black men rapped in videos set in prison or the ghetto. I, too, readily accepted that Black men were likely to be thugs and Black women were unworthy of respect. Black women, I understood, were America's objects of desire, but only insofar as we provided sexy entertainment and performed for consumption. We were born to be commodified, no different from Sarah Baartman, who was paraded by white people through Europe in the eighteenth century because she had a large backside. She died impoverished and undignified, and then white people put her skeleton, brain, and genitals on display in a Paris museum. My exposure to this narrow definition of Blackness and Black femininity became a feedback loop. America's devaluation and abuse of girls and women who shared my hue became glaringly apparent. The dignity of a Black girl or woman was never protected or preserved in popular culture. And the failure to see Black female dignity as sacred was proof of the need for our perpetual oppression and hypersexualization. Black girls and women, I understood unconsciously, had no inherent value.

"I bet you got a fat pussy," a drug dealer from the neighborhood often cooed behind me, following me on his bike when I walked to the bus stop in the morning.

I learned of his vocation via Brittany, whose brother was close friends with most of the neighborhood "dope boys."

"Stay away from him," she urged. "He caught so many charges already, it's a wonder he still out in the streets."

I could barely understand his words through his gold-plated grill when he accosted me in the mornings. But months later, I learned I would no longer have to bear the discomfort of his harassment: police shot and killed him in a drug raid turned sour. Thoughts of his death brought me great pleasure. I smiled while thinking of his body riddled by bullets, even while knowing that he left behind a little boy who would grow up with no father. I thought the kid was better off that way. I feel now that my smile signified the loss of a piece of my humanity. As a Black girl or woman, self-preservation can come with a steep cost: the dilemma of choosing between life and death for another Black person. Living with the burden of knowing a call to the cops could result in the shooting death of a Black man means you have to internally accept Black male death as a possible price for your own survival. At that moment, I sanctioned his death in exchange for peace of mind while I walked to the bus in the mornings. Peace, however, was always short-lived.

Late one night, Brittany's mom, whom I had previously known as a nice woman who perhaps smoked far too many cigarettes, stumbled out of their home, yelling and screaming while staggering from side to side in the middle of the road.

"You wanna leave, motherfucker!?" she yelled.

She stumbled onto our front lawn before collapsing into a crying fit. A middle-aged Black man emerged from her house and ran to a car parked not too far away and hastily drove off. Eventually, Brittany and her brother, a tall, chubby, blond-haired teenager, rushed over to their mom to try to coax her back inside.

"That Black motherfucker," she screamed in between wails.

I stopped seeing Brittany's brother not too long after that incident. The story through the grapevine was that he had been locked up on drug charges.

"I don't know who's gonna pay the rent now," Brittany cried to me when she realized he might not be coming home anytime soon.

Shortly afterward, she begged me to go with her to the house of another boy who lived in the neighborhood. We were all sitting in his living room alone (his mother worked two jobs and was never home) when he pulled down his pants and she got onto her knees in front of me.

"You should try it," she urged me.

It was my first opportunity to assert my preteen perception of feminine power and wield my sexuality, but the moment stood at odds with the stories of "love" and "first times" I saw in the movies. I didn't want to offend her, but I couldn't do it. I slipped away and went home. Our relationship unraveled, and one day weeks later Brittany arrived at my doorstep begging for a fight. A group of fifty or so Black children arrived with her, eager to witness the brawl between us they felt was promised. The group was egging her on and assuring her that she could take me.

"You fixin' ta whoop her ass!" one of the kids cheered.

Unbeknownst to me, my refusal to participate in her close encounter with the local boy's penis had sparked a rage in her that was intensifying. We had not spoken since that day, and I'd avoided contact with her at every turn. No longer having her as a part of my daily life felt strange, but I struggled to process the drama and uncertainty that always seemed to follow her, and I wanted an escape from it all. It was like she had been covered in sticky black tar, and if I got too close, I'd risk being engulfed as well.

"You fucking bitch!" she yelled. "Come out here so I can whoop you!"

It came as a shock to me that the girl I sang childish duets with was now screaming epithets through my window to try to lure me into an altercation. Mom wasn't home yet, working her second shift at the hospital, and Niki hadn't arrived from school. I walked toward the door, then looked back at Stefan as I put my hand on the knob to turn it.

"Don't go out there," he whispered.

I sighed and stepped out into the hot southern sun and squared off with Brittany. Her eyes were filled with tears and rage; her dirty-blond hair was messy, her poorly cut bangs plastered to her face, heavy with perspiration.

"I don't care to fight you," I stated plainly. "What's the point?"

Brittany's eyelids squeezed together in a squint as her body tensed in anger.

"You think you betta than me?" she asked before the tussle began.

The fight lasted maybe three minutes and ended after I tore off her T-shirt in the chaos of it all. When she looked down and noticed her exposed nude-colored bra and left breast, she stared as if the torn shirt were a gunshot wound. She tried to mutter another curse but tripped over her words before turning away and running back into her house next door.

"That white bitch got her ass whooped," a little brown-skinned girl wearing a white shirt, short pants, and dirty Air Force Ones laughed.

Another kid tried to give me a high five. But I turned away and walked back into my house, now with tears in my eyes. It felt like that black, sticky tar had completely engulfed my old friend. Now, in my mind, I was the wicked person who had thrown feathers all over her.

After that day, fights became a regular part of my life. When I tried to neutralize one threat to my safety, others erupted like weeds tormenting a perfectly manicured lawn. A wrong look, an accusation of desiring another girl's "man," refusing to change seats for friends to sit down beside each other on the bus, and even refusing to loan my family's plastic pool to a peer all led to verbal or physical altercations. The worst of the abuse occurred right before or after school. After two girls jumped me while I was walking home from the bus one afternoon, for a reason I remain uncertain of, I skipped school as frequently as possible, hoping to stay off my tormentors' radars. And that's when I had my first run-in with the law.

Mom was working day and night, so she was barely ever home to take note of the fact that I wasn't going to school. At first, I begged her permission to stay home, claiming that I felt ill. She allowed me to miss a few days but sent me back after it was clear that there wasn't anything wrong with me. I never even turned in the handwritten "excuse" notes she tucked into the front pocket of my schoolbag. But during my Mom-sanctioned absenteeism, I noticed a pattern: there was really no reason or way she'd notice if I skipped every day. In her tired stupor, she wasn't tuned in to who was or was not home. In the early hours of the morning, Mom would stagger back from work, drunk with exhaustion, and collapse in bed. It wouldn't be hard to just hide out upstairs until school let out. So instead of adding my being bullied to her exhausting list of stressors, I escaped into the world of American entertainment and music culture while hidden in the walk-in closet that I shared with Niki upstairs. I plugged our little TV into the closet's socket and watched the movie *The Matrix* at least two dozen times, enthralled by the artistry of its storytelling and amazing graphics. I spent hours trying to bend my back, flailing my arms like the movie's main character, Neo, did as he evaded the flurry of bullets shot at him by the agent Mr. Smith. It frightened me to envision the world full of agents who could become life-threatening enemies in the blink of an eye. I also wondered if I would one day be forced to reckon with my own "red pill" moment, if the world that I knew would further crumble and expose a hideous alternate reality.

During that time, I was introduced to southern music artists like Outkast and Erykah Badu. I fell into the trance created by their lyricism. The smooth, sultry sound of their southern drawls paired perfectly with pulsating bass lines. I knew the rhythm; it spoke to my spirit, carrying me away to the swamps of Texas, Louisiana, and Georgia. Their songs intrigued me, as if they held the answers to all of the moment's most pressing issues: Why did the other kids not like me? Why were there fights every day? Was there anything I could do to make it stop? As the artists sang of "the struggle," of "the system," of rising up and finding success in spite of it all, I found solace and hope in their storytelling. They became my southern friends and created a space for me to feel that being different was a strength, not a weakness. Every day I missed school, I sank deeper into the rhythm and the blues. When afternoon came, I would creep downstairs to open and close the front door, as if I had just come home from school, and start my after-school routine. I knew it would be only moments before the phone rang, so I would quickly position myself near it on the living room floor, waiting to intercept the call so the noise wouldn't wake Mom.

"Hello, Dianne?" I always answered on the first ring, and a heavily accented voice would erupt through the receiver.

Before I could even reply, the voice would bark a command: "Dis is Katrin. You have to wok for me today!"

Mom was employed at the city's medical center and also by a Nigerian woman named Catherine who owned a nursing agency and helped to staff hospitals, nursing homes, and home care providers if they were short-staffed. Catherine called almost every day to try to convince my mother to work for her, and Mom, who was usually too nice to say no and couldn't turn down the additional income, barely ever rebuffed the request, even if this was the only time off from her other job. It was my self-appointed job to act as Mom's personal clock, because the buzz or beep of an alarm often failed to be sufficient to shake Mom out of her slumber. So I also took responsibility for relaying Catherine's messages to Mom as she awoke in the afternoon from the coma-like sleep that followed working the night shift. She wanted to be awake to greet us upon our return from school and make dinner. Then she would retire back to bed to get another couple extra hours of rest before she had to get ready to do it all over again.

"Time to get up!" I would announce at about 8:00 p.m. every night.

"All right, all right," she'd sleepily respond, slowly rolling from left to right while pretending to remove the covers from her body as if she intended to rise.

A few times I caught her still in bed after my wake-up call. Ma tried to divert my attention from her bedroom by putting on the light in the bathroom and closing the door to pretend as if she were getting showered or dressed for work.

"GET UP!" I'd scream when I found her still lying in bed while the water cascaded in the shower more than forty-five minutes later. "You are going to be late!"

I refused to burden my already exhausted mother by bringing all of the difficulties I faced in Houston to her attention, because I knew she was struggling to juggle the demands of working and paying the bills. Despite my best effort to manage my situation alone, the cover I'd constructed quickly came crashing down. Not too long after I started hiding out all day at home, a letter came in the mail bearing a bright red stamp and header that read "Office of the District Attorney." Inside was a summons addressed to my mom from the state's family court with a hearing date and an explanation that my continued absence from school could result in criminal charges or her children being taken away by the state. Texas family court was threatening my mom with legal action because I had racked up too many unexcused absences. She immediately got on the phone with the principal of my school.

"How could you do this to a hardworking parent?" she spit through the mouthpiece.

The principal explained that it was Texas law and absences were calculated and reported to the court via an automated system. A student was considered truant once they missed more than three days of school in a four-week period. He also told my mom there was nothing he could do to stop the court from having its hearing, once it deemed it necessary.

"I don't give a damn!" I heard my mom scream. "She is an A student and this is absolutely disgusting."

I had never heard my mother speak so forcefully. It was as if someone had poked a brown mother bear, sending her into a growling, snarling rage. I was terrified that my behavior had evoked such an intense response, and I cowered in my room, unsure if she would turn her anger toward me. Eventually, the school offered to intervene on our behalf and tell the court to back down. I was fortunate that my mom took that strong stance, because only a few years later a study revealed that more than 115,000 cases of failure to attend school—then considered a class C misdemeanor—were filed against students in adult criminal court in Texas in the 2000s.

I returned to school immediately, but the bullying persisted. Even though I had already lived in Houston for two years by that time, as northeasterners and foreigners, my siblings and I were instantly identified as "outsiders," making us prime victims for daily harassment.

"You got a white mama?" I heard a school peer ask my brother one day.

"Um, no," Stefan responded, his forehead furrowed and eyebrows raised in a quizzical look.

"So why you talk like dat, den?"

Inquiries into the origins of our accent were normal.

"Y'all not from here, are y'all?"

Fortunately, I got some reprieve from the constant scrutiny, letdowns, and beatdowns when I befriended Jennifer, a tiny white girl with a bowl-shaped haircut who was my classmate and lived in the neighborhood on the other side of the bayou. She played soccer for a neighboring town's team and wanted me to join her. By then, it felt like Mom was working 24-7, so I knew there was no way she would be able to take me to games.

"It's no problem, we can take you!" Jennifer offered.

All I needed to do was pay the registration fee and buy soccer gear. The request that I demand such an expenditure from my mother was made by my new friend with ease. I nodded my head as if in agreement, even though asking my mom and then bearing witness to the hoops she'd have to jump through to rework our family budget to accommodate my new interest seemed far-fetched at best.

There was no guarantee my mom would have the additional money to fund my desire to participate in extracurricular sports. And I wouldn't want her to feel guilty and take on an extra shift in order to be able to do so. But I still wanted to play. So I carefully crafted my request.

"Ma . . . ," I began, peeping at her through the door with it only slightly open. "You have any extra money?"

She inhaled long and deep and rolled onto her side in my direction, still between the realms of asleep and alert. Her eyes softened and a small smile spread across her face.

"Yeah, what you need, baby?" she asked.

I knew the best moment to ask Mom for money was just before she woke up, because in the event that she didn't have any, it would give me the chance to urge her back to sleep so we could both pretend my request had never happened. Mom hated to disappoint us by admitting she didn't have something we needed. And I hated the way I could feel her entire soul cave under the weight of her guilt. My trick usually saved us both the agony of each other's hurt feelings. In this instance, Mom's contented response let me know I would definitely be playing soccer that season. Early every Saturday morning, Jennifer's mom shuttled me to and from wealthy Houston neighborhoods to play in matches. Typically, I was the only Black girl on the field, but I didn't care. My only interests were goalkeeping and what the halftime snack would be on game day.

Mom also told Brian about all of our hardships, seeking advice on how to find a reprieve. He concluded that we needed to be "saved." And he knew the precise place that could offer us such salvation: his place of worship. One of the largest megachurches in Texas, the Great Light

Baptist Church was a sight to behold. Dressed in our Sunday best, we pulled up to the church for service one weekend and marveled. The almost exclusively Black congregation lined the front of the huge white building, clapping and singing, beckoning members:

Welcome to the light
We're so glad you came
We've all come here today
To gather in Jesus's name!

I cautiously followed behind my mother, counting each step from the parking lot to the front of the church. Then a loud whirring sound interrupted my concentration. The chuff of a copter's blades beat right over my head, prompting me to reflexively duck for cover. I raised my head to see if the copter was about to crash into the building, but it flew past us and then hovered over the nearby parking lot before slowly descending. After the whirring ceased, a Rolls-Royce that had picked up the copter's passengers emerged from the lot and slowly crept toward the church.

When the car arrived at the building, a man opened one of its back doors and the pastor appeared. He was a stocky Black man dressed in a well-fitted black three-piece suit with a black silk tie.

"WELCOME TO THE LIGHT!" the choir screamed.

The pastor smiled and waved to the crowd of congregants that had amassed out front. Mom ushered us through the crowd and through the church's two large white doors. The inside of the church was almost as magnificent as its pastor's arrival. It looked like an elegant castle with a white altar and podium at the front, surrounded by fresh flowers and several huge flat-screens set up on the walls behind it, projecting the images of the church's leaders. The altar was flanked by a choir on one side and a live band on the other. The church had three tiers of seating for its congregants and a concert-style lighting system, as well as various cameras set up and positioned to project the service for anyone who sat too far away and couldn't see very well. The service was also recorded and televised. Mom motioned us toward a row of empty seats near the front of the church, and we all sat down. The choir settled as the pastor took to the stage, and applause erupted as the crowd sprang to their feet to cheer and hoot as if Jesus himself were making a special guest appearance. The Great Light Baptist Church was unlike any church I had been to before.

My mother was raised Catholic and had bribed us with treats to attend Sunday school at the nearby Catholic church back in North Bergen, where we were the only Black family in the congregation. I hated waking up early to rush out of the house only to spend hours horrified by the images of Jesus crucified on a cross, stakes driven through his bleeding hands and feet, with more blood dripping down his head, covered in thorns. The Bible-study kids spent an hour in the basement of the church, reciting the Our Father and the Hail Mary and listening to stories of Eve betraying all of humanity just for an apple (that evil woman!) and Noah filling an ark with animals in the midst of a flood that would wipe out all other life on the planet Earth. Then we would follow the teacher, a young, white Italian woman who always spoke in a soft voice and wore black, flowy dresses, through the church's dark corridors into the main room, where services were held. I usually slept as the priest preached the word of God, sang pitchy psalms, and recited prayer over wafers and wine, turning them into Jesus's body and blood. My favorite parts of Mass were putting money in the baskets when they came around and the moment when the services finally ended, because I knew Granny would be waiting back at home with warm, buttery biscuits and cut-up hot dogs sautéed in ketchup (the aforementioned bribes).

"Allyuh behave in church?" Granny would ask, pausing for our response. We would eagerly nod, prompting her to slap a spoonful of hot dogs onto a plate for each of us.

Sleeping during the Great Light Baptist Church service would have been like attempting to sleep through a Beyoncé concert. I had never been surrounded by so many Black worshippers before, and the energy was both exciting and overwhelming. The bright lights. The music. The energetic and magnetic preacher. His fully engaged congregation hung on every single one of his words.

"It's my wife's birthday!" he boomed one day. "And I want to thank everyone who made her ten-thousand-dollar shopping spree possible in the name of the good Lord!"

My eyes darted toward Niki and Stefan, and we gave each other quizzical looks. As the tithing baskets began to float around the church, members took turns slipping in their tiny white envelopes filled with their monetary contributions to the institution. I crumpled my dollar in my hand.

The church choir and its leader erupted into a call-and-response song:

Choir: Five percent?
Leader: No, that's not good enough.
Choir: Ten percent?
Leader: Yes, giveth to the Lord!
Choir: Twenty percent?
Leader: Yes, and the blessings of the Lord shall rain upon you!

During the early 2000s, a new, more liberal way of interpreting the Bible gave many evangelical American parishioners full license to embrace capitalism. Megachurches were increasingly popular, as were their "faith" teachings that promised God granted wealth to those who obeyed the religious order. The prosperity gospel reigned supreme then, promising congregants infinite material returns on their donations to the church. In truth, Black pastors transferred billions of dollars of Black wealth from their mostly lower- and middle-class followers to white banks, mortgage and insurance companies, landlords, and high-end clothing and shoe designers.[3]

"You giveth to the Lord and you shall receive!" the preacher proclaimed.

But Mom simply didn't have enough to give. So did that mean our returns would never materialize into luxury vehicles or private helicopters? After two Sundays, we stopped attending. Stefan and I begged and pleaded day and night to be absolved of the weekend ritual, so eventually Mom caved. We felt relieved when we overheard her tell Brian we would no longer attend the church. But we continued to sing the songs (which were indeed very catchy).

"Twenty percent!" Stefan's voice would boom as Mom scooped out his favorite meal—curried shrimp, mango, potatoes, and roti.

"No, that's not good enough!" I responded right on cue.

"*Fifty percent!*" we screamed in unison before erupting into chuckles.

Though laughter was never absent from my household, our Houston neighborhood was in steady decline in the years following our move, a fact made glaringly clear by the increase in violence and restrictions imposed by law and the police. Mom was working night shifts almost seven days a week, which meant we kids were even more vulnerable and scared, home alone with my older sister. But Mom did not leave me without escape from the torments of daily life. On my twelfth birthday, I tore cupcake-decorated wrapping paper off a huge, heavy gift to find a clunky book with an illustration on the cover of a disheveled-haired white boy holding a magic wand. I buried myself in that literature, toting it everywhere with me in my backpack, sometimes choosing to carry it to school over a book that I might've needed for class that day. When I got lost in the world of wonder and magic, my daily life of fighting to exist dissolved into the background. I reclaimed the joy of friendship through the tales of Harry, Hermione, and Ron and their journeys through an alternate reality of witches, wizards, ogres, and magical creatures. Through reading, I was able to retreat into a quiet and safe space, even when things felt dizzyingly uncertain and insecure.

Then, one night, screams and begging erupted outside our door.

"Please don't!" a woman's voice echoed into the night. "Aaahhhh!"

The sound of a body crashing into metal followed. My siblings and I rushed to the window and peered into the darkness just in time to catch a glimpse of a Black woman collapsed on the ground in front of a car parked parallel along the road. I knew her face from a few doors down. She was the mother of one of the kids I rode the school bus with.

"You fucking bitch!" a male voice boomed.

He positioned himself near the woman, his foot right in front of her face. Then the man's right leg retracted in slow motion, as if it were a wrecking ball being pulled back by an unseen crane. I cringed and looked away in anticipation of the blow. The impact sounded like a loud thud and a can being crushed simultaneously.

The woman cried out. And the man continued to scream and deliver blows until the sounds of the night became a hellish choir of abuse and croaking frogs. I pressed my eyes tightly shut and started to mumble incoherently to myself. I could feel my heart thumping wildly, as if I held it right in my hands.

"Aye, motherfucker!" A voice pierced through the night, along with the song of screeching tires.

The sound of car doors slamming shook me out of my trance. I plastered my face back against the window, pulling down a single slat of the blinds with one of my fingers. A group of three men was marching toward the scene, one with a shotgun in hand.

"You fixin' to get yo ass beat," one of the men screamed.

The mob unleashed a flurry of violence upon the man.

"You like beating women?" one of them asked between delivering blows.

As violence became more common, the local police implemented a 9:00 p.m. curfew for children under seventeen. We couldn't even go to a Saturday-night movie or hang out with friends at the mall without risking being ticketed. More men stood around idly. The final straw was when Domino's refused to deliver to our neighborhood—the delivery men were being robbed too frequently.

I dropped to my knees and begged Mom to move us back to New Jersey.

"Please, Mom," I whispered. "Please."

Niki and Stefan echoed my sentiment. They were each experiencing their own version of life as ostracized outsiders trapped in a punitive environment, and it was taking a toll on us all.

A police officer had written Niki a truancy ticket when she was caught off campus during lunch hour. That ticket resulted in her first encounter with the ways that the justice system disproportionately punishes Black people, and the experience would cast a shadow for years to come.

"How do you want your trial?" the judge asked when Niki approached her bench during the hearing, passing a terrified-looking Asian boy who was awaiting his turn at judgment. "Judge or jury?"

After the judge saddled Niki with a hearing date, Mom desperately went room to room through the judicial offices asking for someone to intervene on my sister's behalf.

"She is an A student," Mom pressed. "I don't even understand why going out for lunch should lead to a record."

A Black security officer overheard her pleas to a receptionist and urged my mom toward an office where a Black man was seated behind a huge desk decorated with an American flag. Mom explained the story to him, and he scribbled a message onto a sheet of paper and sent my mom and sister back to the judge.

"Tell her *I* said to send you to the counselor," he said authoritatively.

When the judge received the handwritten note, her tone softened.

"I thought I gave you that option," she said before waving Niki off to be escorted by the bailiff.

"Go upstairs," he said, pointing toward a stairwell. "That's where most of the truancy kids go."

When Niki and my mom arrived upstairs, the same Asian boy was sitting in the room, diligently writing on a piece of loose-leaf paper. The counselor motioned for my sister to approach her desk, handed her a piece of paper, and instructed her to write an essay declaring she was sorry for her truancy and would not do it again.

Around the same time, my brother, Stefan, shot up like a beanstalk. By twelve years of age, he stood nearly six feet tall but retained his child-like chubby cheeks and cheeky sensibilities. He had a penchant for collecting little-known snippets of history and science in what we branded his mental "crap scrapbook." However, school staffers, who were mostly white women, did not find him at all amusing. His fifth-grade teacher threatened to call the cops on him when he announced that he would be going to Harvard Law School and was open to taking on clients interested in protesting the absence of chocolate milk from the daily lunch menu. Apparently, he refused to back down when the teacher told him he would never get into the prestigious university, and that standoff led to a verbal altercation that ended with him in the principal's office and threats of suspension.

"He would get into Harvard," the teacher declared during their parent-teacher conference in front of the school's principal, "because of affirmative action that would steal my son's place and give it to him!"

"Your racism cannot stand in his way, because his path has already been decided for him," Mom responded plainly before leaving the room. She proudly told us over dinner that night about her mic-drop moment defending Stefan.

Despite all of this, it wasn't easy for my mom to decide to leave Texas. Mom had to choose between the practical fact of a job that provided the income her family deserved and the more existential problem of the safety and emotional well-being of her children. What was the value of acquired things if you paid for them with your dignity? Ultimately, there was far more to lose than to gain by remaining in Houston, and Mom started the search for a new city for us to call home.

CHAPTER 3

———

Discarded

In 1781, a ship called the *Zong*, bound for Jamaica from the coast of West Africa, faced calamity. Near the end of the twelve-week voyage, fresh water was running low and passengers were trying to contain an outbreak of disease. The ship's captain devised a simple solution: throw enslaved Africans overboard. He knew that his insurance company would pay him for slaves who drowned but not those who died of illness, so he made a "business" decision that would result in the deaths of 132 Black people. Such a brutal story reflects the white tradition of creating systems to control the movement and disposal of Black bodies.[1] Between 1500 and 1866, it is estimated that Europeans transported nearly 12.5 million slaves to the Americas. Of those, 1.8 million died in transit and were thrown overboard into the dark depths of the Atlantic Ocean.[2]

They were simply *discarded*.

The stage in a narcissistic relationship that follows the abuser's devaluing of their victim is the discard stage. Centuries after the official end of slavery, the system of commodifying and profiting from Black bodies and then discarding them when they are deemed no longer profitable still thrives. But it continues to adapt to be more clandestine. By the time I was a teen, American systemic racism had begun to act on my physical being more brazenly. I was hyperaware of the fact that there was an unseen force acting on my life that could drastically alter my world and claim my freedom at any moment. This force, which I sensed but couldn't name, could move and displace my family on a whim.

It is easier to repot a plant that has yet to fully sink its roots into a new environment, and children are no different. Though my family spent four years in Houston, I felt nothing but relief as we prepared for our next move, to Orlando, Florida. Mom stumbled upon an ad for a company that would pay the relocation costs of any nurse willing to move to the state, so she looked to our oracle, the website greatschools.org, and researched the best school district in the Orlando area. She settled on a neighborhood on the outskirts of one of the richest towns in the United States of America, zoned for some of the nation's very best public schools. The prospect of the move fanned the flames of my passion for the country once more, and my hope burned bright. I spent hours on the internet scrolling through photos of the Sunshine State's idyllic, sandy beaches and imagining myself riding all of the attractions at Disney World and Universal Studios with new friends.

Our new neighborhood was right off a four-lane road, where north- and southbound traffic were separated by a grassy median. Drivers sped along as if it were a major highway. Only some portions of the roadway had sidewalks, which we would use to get to the nearby Walmart or a small strip mall with a grocery store that served as both our only shopping and our place of entertainment. The complex had a well-lit entrance sign and a huge green gate that sprang open when you punched a code into a box at its front. When we first arrived, a woman who was the neighborhood's manager gave us a tour. We oohed and aahed as we toured the neighborhood on foot. The complex boasted huge palm trees that swayed in the breeze, apartments freshly painted green and cream, and a clubhouse with a small gym that overlooked a big pool and bubbling hot tub. During my first escapade at the neighborhood pool, I met a girl who would become my best friend.

Karla Garcia was a gorgeous, hazel-eyed Ecuadorian girl with thick, flowing curly hair that fell right above her waistline. Like me, she had recently moved into the neighborhood and she had Jersey roots. Her family had emigrated from Ecuador to New Jersey only a few years earlier than mine and found themselves settling in Florida after her stepfather, like many northerners at the time, found a better-paying job and more affordable housing down south. We were kindred spirits and connected instantly.

"How come you don't have a Spanish accent?" I inquired during one of our very first conversations.

"I unno," she responded with a shrug.

Karla spoke enthusiastically, perfectly enunciating and articulating her thoughts, and was very generous with her laughter, often exploding and beaming while I acted out stories of my family's past moving experiences. She transitioned with ease from conversations with me in plain, standard English to Spanish with her mom, who never learned America's national language.

It was always clear that her two-parent household had more means than my family unit, but that never got in the way of our friendship. Back in Ecuador, when her mom married her dad, he made enough money for her to stay home and be a housewife who got waited on by maids and had her children cared for by live-in nannies. Karla was born on the country's coast in a city called Guayaquil, but her dad moved the family to the mountains in Quito for a job. Her mom hated the "cold" and being away from the family, so she made frequent trips back to the warmth of her newfound city life.

"My dad was Black," she explained one night as we swapped stories about the lives we had left behind in our countries of birth.

She told me that, to her dad, her mom (who had pale white skin and green eyes) was a catch, even though she came from a poor village. He married her and moved her from the village to be with him near his job in the big city and then eventually to Quito. When Karla was born, her family took one look at her bushy, curly hair and brown skin and made an instantaneous declaration: "Negrita." The term was equal parts derogatory and endearing. Karla's family members always pinned her defiant, inquisitive, analytical, and philosophical nature as traits she got from her "Black" father, even though he didn't seem all that Black to me. She was the apple of his eye, and he would rush to defend her whenever her grandmother wanted to hit her for being "altanera" (defiant). Karla and her family lived a life of comfort and luxury, surrounded by maids, family, and friends. Then everything changed one humid day at her aunt's house back in Guayaquil during a family lunch.

"As soon as my aunt turned on the stove to heat up the food, it sparked something in the patio," she told me in a whisper. "The whole patio burst into flames, engulfing all three of them at once. My uncle, who was nearest to the fire, my dad, who was in the middle somewhere, and my grandfather, who was closest to the kitchen door, all got major burns. All three died."

Her mom was overcome with grief and was kept sedated for some time. She couldn't take care of Karla or her little sister for months, and they were forced to move in with their aunt. No one ever said anything to her about her father's death and she was not allowed to attend his funeral. Not too long afterward, her mom picked up and left Ecuador and remarried in America. Karla spent much of her first few years in the U.S. depressed, confused, and confined indoors to avoid the cold weather up north, which she abhorred. But by the time I met her, she was a teen with the perfect hourglass figure and a cheery, bubbly personality.

"Wanna go to Universal Studios Halloween Horror Nights?" I remember her excitedly asking me as we waited for the school bus early one morning. Florida falls were just cool enough for a light sweater, but many of the state's residents often complained that by late October it was "getting cold."

"I don't think my mom would give me that kinda money," I replied, slightly embarrassed.

"When there's a will, there's a way!" she giggled, beaming triumphantly.

She instantaneously devised a plot: she would use her all-year pass to get into the park and then deliver it to me through the gate for me to get in.

"Can I bring Stefan?" I asked, not wanting him to miss out.

"Yeah, sure!"

The invitation list grew from there as we added a couple other neighborhood kids to the plot: Dennis, a Black boy with island roots, and Brielle and Rochelle, two white sisters who had recently moved from upstate New York. That evening, we all excitedly piled into my mom's car for the ten-minute ride to the park. Using Karla's plot, we managed to get everyone in with only two passes (the other belonged to Karla's younger sister), high-fiving one another when the last person pushed through the turnstiles and entered into the majesty of American entertainment. The park was huge, and roller coasters twisted and turned in the sky. We spent the evening screaming through haunted houses and a cornfield maze where workers, made up to look like zombies, carried fake chainsaws and blood-covered hatchets. We spent the entire ride home engaged in a long, drawn-out debate about who screamed the loudest and which attraction was the scariest.

"How did yuh all pay to get in the park?" Mom asked before she opened the front door to our apartment when we arrived home. She had given us only a twenty-dollar bill, and she knew the park cost almost a hundred dollars per person.

"If we tell you, we might have to kill you," Stefan coyly responded.

"Ah, Lordy, I don't wanna know," Mom said with a chuckle.

I was elated to finally feel settled and embraced again, both at home and with friends.

"Thanks for moving here," I whispered to my mom as we stood in my doorway that night.

She responded with a small smile and a nod and gently closed the door.

I was a year older than Karla, so I didn't have the support of her friendship at school. Our age difference meant that we never shared the same class in middle school and I went to high school a year before she did. My heart thumped with anxiety as I walked to the bus stop on my first day of high school without her, flashbacks of Houston racing through my mind and an overwhelming feeling of helplessness consuming me. I stood as far away from the other kids as possible as we waited at the stop. They were all embroiled in conversations about their schedules, huddled together to compare and contrast their homerooms, classes, and teachers, so they barely took note of my presence. One group of kids exploded into loud banter in Portuguese and another sang a reggaeton song. Almost every demographic was represented.

"Hiya!" a girl said, waving in my direction.

Michelle was a tall, adorable Black girl with her hair straightened and cut into a bob. She was also a friendly goofball who was clearly eager to make friends. I waved back and she approached, sauntering toward me with peppy steps.

"What's your schedule?" she asked, wasting no time.

I unfolded the piece of paper with my classes, teachers, times, and rooms printed in tiny letters across the top. They were all AP or honors classes.

"Uhhhhhhh," she said, scanning the schedule and comparing it to her own as we rode the rowdy bus. "Nope, I don't have none of these, but we have the same lunch period!"

Michelle and her little sister, Deanna, lived with their aunt and uncle in the neighborhood. Her mom was incarcerated after a boyfriend she lived with got busted for dealing drugs—officers found them both in the house filled with cocaine hidden in the walls. Michelle maintained that her mother was innocent and I believed her. I knew even then that it wasn't uncommon for innocent Black women to get swept up in the drama between police and Black men committing crimes. In the nineties, a young Black woman named Kemba Smith made national news after a judge sentenced her to twenty-four and a half years in prison for her drug dealer boyfriend's crimes. She met him while attending Hampton University, and the pair started a relationship. Sadly, it didn't take long before he became mentally and physically abusive and allegedly used her as a gopher in his drug ring. After he died, the U.S. government charged her for all of his crimes, resulting in her over-two-decade-long sentence. She gave birth to a baby boy while incarcerated.

I saw Michelle's mom, like Smith, as just another casualty in the nation's "war on drugs." In 1971, President Richard Nixon declared a "war on drugs" and said that drug abuse was America's biggest public enemy. In the 1980s, Ronald Reagan expanded many of Nixon's policies and signed into law severe penalties for drug-related offenses, which fueled the rapid expansion of the country's prison population. By the late twentieth century, the prison industrial complex was a multibillion-dollar business, circulating $182 billion annually through the incarceration of millions of Americans, the vast majority of whom were Black.[3]

Between 1977 and 2007, the population of women in prison grew by 832 percent and Black women were being locked away at nearly two times the rate of white women.[4]

Michelle hadn't seen her mom in four years by the time she started high school and we met. Her mom's brother had agreed to raise her and Deanna, which was a saving grace. Michelle and her sister were fortunate they weren't among the thousands of children raised in foster care or behind bars alongside their incarcerated mothers who, in exchange for "good behavior," were rewarded with the chance to rear their kids in prison.

"She'll get out soon," she declared one evening as we journaled together, her eyes downcast.

Her cheery demeanor vanished as she hunched over her notebook, where she was doodling flowers and hearts next to a paragraph she had written. A single tear ran down her face and splatted onto the paper, blurring the letters written in pen into illegible scribbles.

"She will definitely get out in time for prom and graduation," she said, her face springing back to life.

I nodded and offered a supportive grin, but I knew she was trying to convince herself more than me.

Olympia High was in Windermere, one of Orlando's wealthiest suburbs, and had a huge campus with a parking lot for student drivers. Lines of buses off-loaded kids like Michelle and me from the surrounding neighborhoods, but the local kids arrived in brand-new Hondas, BMWs, and Mercedeses. Olympia High also had a reputation for offering the most advanced placement classes (which could help students earn college credits while in high school) and an expansive list of extracurricular activities like journalism, languages, and music and arts classes, as well as a highly regarded athletic program. At the school's center, there was a huge courtyard enclosed by a two-story building with glass doors that opened into the school's hallways, where the classrooms were located. Thousands of children of every color bustled about the campus, rushing to their first class of the day. That first morning, we unfurled a map of the campus and discovered that Michelle's hall was nearest to the bus drop-off. I agreed to walk her to her class before making my way through the large campus to mine. Most of Michelle's classes were remedial because she had been struggling to maintain good grades. When we arrived at her rowdy hallway, filled with mostly Black and Hispanic kids, I was grateful that I would not be staying. We had been tracked—put on early academic paths that were hard to break from. Our paths had diverged. I waved her off and promised to meet her at lunch where I'd dropped her off.

I was already seated when the first-period bell rang. Most of the students in my class were white. I didn't know it at the time, but in-school segregation had created a great chasm between me and the other Black children like Michelle. School tracking separated the "good" among us from the "bad" apples, and that distinction all too often broke across racial lines. It created distinct and separate paths for students within a single school and in school systems and divided children early, setting them off on trajectories they'd likely have trouble transcending or breaking out of. For many Black students, their schooling began in "special education" or "remedial" classes, and that path often led to underachievement or even imprisonment. But America had once again decided I was exceptional, and I was more than okay with embracing the fast-tracking.

"Play tennis and take French" were my mom's only requests when it came time for me to select my high school schedule.

I obliged on both counts.

Tryouts for the tennis team were at a large local park surrounded by trees and lakes. The varsity girls were all white. The top two among them, Katie and Taylor, were homeschooled so they could pursue their athletic careers more aggressively. They all wore athletic skirts with matching visors, shirts, and sneakers and carried huge multicompartment tennis bags. Though I had spent years haphazardly batting balls back and forth over nets with my brother, I barely had any training and showed up in short pants and a T-shirt with my cheap Walmart racket in hand. I was paired with Taylor for my first match. I gave up on any hope of being a worthy opponent after her first serve. Fortunately, I still made it onto the JV team, where there were other girls of color.

"You need to get you some gear," one of my teammates recommended.

I knew Mom couldn't afford any and breathed a sigh of relief when they handed out the uniforms.

Florida State had a scholarship program that afforded students who graduated with at least a 3.5 GPA and completed one hundred hours of community service the opportunity to attend any local university or college for free. As soon as I learned about the opportunity, I started looking for volunteer work. I made an appointment with my assigned guidance counselor, a middle-aged white woman with messy blond hair and silver-rimmed glasses, to ask if the school could place me.

"I think we have something that may be the *perfect* spot for you," she responded when I made my inquiry.

She scribbled a few details on a sheet of paper and then handed me the paperwork.

"You are going to be tutoring kids at an elementary school!" she exclaimed. "The community needs young people like you."

Her excitement was infectious, and enthusiasm pumped through me. I was thrilled by the idea that I was needed and appreciated. I explained the details to my family over dinner.

"Stefan, you should volunteer there as well. That way you can complete your hours," Mom suggested.

He agreed. Mom would have to sacrifice some of her sleep to pick us up from school and drop us off forty minutes away and then wait to bring us home, but she was willing to be sleep-deprived for a few months so that we could be assured a higher education.

"Niki, you will have to make dinner from now on."

"Please, for the love of God, no curry tuna!" Stefan pleaded.

Mom's go-to inexpensive and quick meal would finally be scrapped because of our volunteer opportunities.

"You see, good things happen when you give," I said to Stefan with a wink.

When we arrived in the neighborhood where we were meant to work as tutors, Florida's usual sunniness seemed to dissipate. A heavy feeling weighed on me as we passed by homes with unkempt front lawns and busted cars parked along the streets and in driveways. Occasionally, a resident came into sight—a little Black girl sitting on her front porch playing with a white Barbie doll or a woman braiding the hair of a young man.

The school where we were to volunteer consisted of a main building surrounded by several trailers. As we walked down the path toward the campus, which was framed by overgrown grass, we made a small game out of trying to hop over the cracks and craters in the cement walkway. When we pushed the front door open, a damp, swampy smell rushed out like air from a deflating balloon. It was already after school hours, so the building was empty except for ten or so kids playing in a small gym next to an office near the entrance. They were all Black. I poked my head into the office.

"Um, excuse me, we're here to volunteer," I announced.

No response.

I tried again a bit more forcefully and then turned to follow Stefan, who was already making his way over to the gym. A tall Black man wearing slacks, a shirt, and shiny black dress shoes was in a crowd of kids, rebounding their shots and cheering them on. He was Mr. Adebayo, the school's principal.

"Are you the volunteers?" His voice echoed through the room as the sound of bouncing basketballs reverberated all about, creating a cacophony.

We both nodded. He rushed over and warmly greeted us.

"I'm so excited that you will be joining us," he began. "We don't get too many volunteers for the after-school program, but so many of the kids need tutoring."

He gave us a short tour of the building (there wasn't much more to see) and then sat us down in the office to assign us mentees. Stefan and I exchanged looks of disbelief over the disgraceful condition of the school. I zoned out while Mr. Adebayo told Stefan about his charge but snapped to attention when the principal began to address me. My student was Da'Quan, a second grader who needed help with reading and writing, according to his report. I accepted the pack of workbooks the principal pushed in my direction, along with a pen and a couple pencils.

"You can go to classroom number two with Da'Quan," the principal said, pointing to a door that exited to the back of the building onto a big field filled with trailers.

He disappeared into the gym and returned with a small boy whose shirt was rumpled from romping about. He was wearing the school's uniform, khaki pants and a blue collared shirt, and carrying a Batman backpack on his right shoulder.

"This is your tutor, Tiffanie," the principal told him.

I gave him a weak smile and a small wave. The boy's eyes quickly lowered.

"Have fun!"

I led him out the back door and toward the classroom, desperately trying to kill the tension between us with small talk.

"You like Batman?" I asked.

He shrugged.

"How old are you?" I asked.

He remained silent.

We climbed up a small wheelchair-accessible ramp that ran along the front of the trailer to its entrance. A few desks and chairs were littered about the room, facing a white dry-erase board that was bordered by cutouts of the letters of the alphabet. I pulled two desks right beside one another, sat down in one, and indicated that he should take a seat in the other. He reluctantly obliged.

"So what subjects do you like in school?" I said, trying again to get him to open up. "I really hate math, but I'm pretty good at reading and writing, so I can help you with that."

He continued to stare at the floor. I nervously flipped through the workbook and found an empty page.

"Wanna play tic-tac-toe?" I tried again, hoping a game would pique his interest.

As the silence continued, I began to feel a combination of rage and failure: Why was this kid ignoring me and wasting my time? To distance myself from the emotions (and the desire to act on them), I sat quietly thumbing through the book until thirty minutes had passed, and then I guided him back toward the main building.

"See you soon!" the boisterous principal said, handing me back my paperwork with one hour of community service signed off.

Ninety-nine more to go, I told myself. *You can do this.*

I believed Da'Quan just had a difficult personality and I needed only to build trust and I'd get through to him. For weeks we did the same dance. I would try to make him comfortable by initiating games or a conversation, but there was no reciprocity. Eventually, I put the pencil and workbook in front of him and begged him just to complete one page. By the fourth session, I realized I would have to take a different approach. I defaulted to my mother's method of bribery: food. I used my lunch money to buy lollipops and packs of M&Ms, certain I could coax acceptance and participation out of him.

"You like candy?" I asked with a mischievous grin.

For the first time in all of our many interactions, he raised his gaze to meet mine and a tiny smirk crept across his face. I pulled my stash from my bag and dangled it in front of his eyes, which lit up at the sight.

"But nothing in life is free," I lectured. "You gotta start doing some work with me."

He nodded his head quietly, remaining completely silent. I grabbed his hand, intertwining his tiny fingers into mine, and led him toward the classroom. I sat him down and explained that he would get to pick two treats from my bag for every page we were able to complete together. He was excited now, so I eagerly pulled our desks together, rummaged through the cubby where I put the workbooks for safekeeping, and pulled out one for learning cursive letters by tracing them.

"This one looks fun and easy!" I said. "I want you to take home a lot of candy today."

I plopped the book down in front of him and searched through my book bag for one of the pencils the principal had given me weeks earlier. One of them was missing the lead tip and the other had never been sharpened. I scanned the classroom for a pencil sharpener and found an electric one plugged in on a long desk on the other side of the room.

"I'm really happy we are gonna finally start working!" I shouted over my shoulder and the whirring of the sharpener grinding down the pencil's wood.

When I turned back toward him, Da'Quan's head was buried in his arms, face down on the desk.

"What's wrong?" I questioned, carefully inching toward him.

I put the pencil down on the desk in front of him and placed my hand on his back.

"It's okay if it's a little hard," I tried to comfort him. "That's what I'm here for."

He raised his head, revealing his tear-stained face.

"Don't cry," I whispered.

My own eyes were blurred by tears, compelling me to instinctively turn away out of shame and fear of being seen. When I turned back to him, his face was twisted, screwed up, angry, and defiant. He maintained stern eye contact while his right hand extended toward the pencil and scooped it up. He fumbled with it in his hand, trying to firmly secure it between his thumb and pointer finger. Then he flipped to the first page in the book and poured his full will into tracing a lowercase cursive *a*. I watched as he struggled with the task, feeling broken and defeated, unable to mask my sadness and disappointment. Da'Quan was eight years old and barely knew how to hold a pencil. I marched out of the classroom to find the principal after the session was over, angry and outraged. I found him in his office, behind a sky-high stack of manila files.

"I can't do this anymore!" I exclaimed to him. "Why didn't you tell me he can't even write? How am I supposed to do anything with him?"

The principal's initial astonished look eased into understanding.

"Come with me," he calmly responded, rising from behind his desk with his arm outstretched, guiding me toward the door.

We made our way to the front of the building and he pushed open its doors. Bright sunlight rays pierced through the darkness, initially blinding me.

"Look over there." He pointed.

My eyes darted about the scenery.

"There."

He deliberately pointed toward a park across the street. I scanned the environment. The swings were broken, the grass overgrown. The playground was covered in haphazard graffiti. A woman sat hunched on a bench, her thin, feeble frame covered by a dirty, oversized T-shirt. She was too busy and preoccupied scratching her forearm and talking to herself to take note of us peering at her from a distance.

"You see that woman over there?" the principal asked. "That's Da'Quan's mom."

When Mom picked us up that day, I announced that I would not ever return.

"Yeah, it smells terrible in there," Stefan concurred.

On that evening, while driving home, I promised myself I would do everything in my power to never again risk being engulfed by such failure, despair, and hardship. I would do everything possible to avoid Black neighborhoods and schools. Only a couple years removed from all I had experienced in Houston, I couldn't confront the horror of that school and its surrounding environs. My heart raced and my palms became sticky with anxiety as memories of the constant fear of violence and the relentless fight to survive flooded my mind. I wasn't ready to reenter such a place. I couldn't help anyone there.

"I need to volunteer somewhere else," I told my counselor the following day.

"Well, what do you like to do?" she questioned.

I explained that I loved writing, teaching kids, and playing tennis on the school's team.

"You're on the tennis team?" the counselor interrupted, beaming brightly. "Oh, you should've told me that before, because the tennis girls have their own community service."

No one had ever mentioned this. But when I inquired later that day during practice, the coach told me that members of the team could get community service hours by volunteering as ball girls for a local tennis clinic.

"This Saturday, nine a.m., at Isleworth," she said.

I awoke early that morning and put on my freshly ironed tennis uniform. Mom punched the location into her phone's GPS and followed its directions down the long road that my school bus traveled every morning before dropping us off. When we arrived at the intersection where the bus would typically turn right, we made a left toward a neighborhood with huge mansions.

"You have arrived," the monotonous voice of the GPS announced as we pulled into the development's entrance.

Isleworth was a six-hundred-acre private golf club community that was home to some of America's richest and most notable names.

"We are here for the tennis clinic," Mom told the security officer, a Black man seated inside a cream-colored booth. Two huge gates swung open, revealing a winding road lined with palm trees, perfectly manicured lawns, and expansive estates. The man pointed us in the direction of the neighborhood's tennis courts. As we drove past the magnificent homes, I took note of the different cars parked in the driveways: Mercedes, BMW, Land Rover, Range Rover, Porsche, Lamborghini—there was every type of expensive car imaginable in its newest model.

"Wow."

We followed signs that read CLUBHOUSE through the neighborhood, marveling at the estates and the varied architecture. An enormous fountain stood in front of one home, topped by a marble statue. Another spread across at least five lots and had a guest cottage perched beside it. When we arrived at the tennis clubhouse, I was equally shocked and awed. The clubhouse looked like a modern-day castle, with huge bay windows and thick pillars covered in vines. I hopped out of the car and walked toward the entrance, looking all about for a familiar face. Patrons were walking between the nearby courts and the building, occasionally erupting in haughty laughter and patting one another's backs in full appreciation of whatever jokes they were exchanging, while trying to figure out their court assignments.

"Tiff!" a voice beckoned.

I looked around and caught sight of Colette, a teammate I had become friendly with. She was eagerly waving from atop the steps of the clubhouse. I rushed over to her and we locked hands and walked in together, looking for the rest of the tennis team. There were no other Black people in sight. The coach arrived and directed us to our stations. I was assigned to court seven, a clay court where clinic participants would be perfecting their forehands. I spent forty minutes collecting balls, running back and forth between the lines of the court, scooping them up into my skirt, and emptying them into the ball baskets as neon-green fuzz launched all about me. As soon as Colette was finished with her assignment, we took a couple balls from the basket and found an empty court and hit back and forth.

"Well, that was easy," I said in between forehands and backhands.

Then the announcement was made that it was time for lunch back at the clubhouse. I ran over to the building, urging Colette to pick up her pace. When I entered, I was mesmerized by a huge chocolate fountain and the many chefs stationed behind small stoves. Signs positioned in front of the food options read SALAD BAR, LOBSTER TAIL WITH GARLIC LEMON BUTTER, STEAK WITH CHIMICHURRI SAUCE, SHRIMP SCAMPI,

CHICKEN ALFREDO, and dozens of other dishes, all being freshly prepared by the order.

Pop!

The unexpected sound made me duck and cover my head in fear.

"White people love their brunch mimosas," Colette said with a chuckle, pointing to the bar where a man in a bow tie was pouring champagne into wineglasses already filled partway with orange juice.

"And look, that's Tiger Woods's wife over there," she whispered, nodding in the direction of a group of blond women.

The women all looked like replicas of one another: skinny, blond, and wearing visors that matched their skirts and tennis polos. They had straight white teeth and beamed at one another in quiet delight as they took turns speaking. When Nelly's "Hot in Herre" began to boom from the speakers, they bellowed gleeful cheers and began awkwardly shifting left to right while making strange motions with their fists. I gathered they were dancing by the way their heads bobbed up and down.

"White people," Colette laughed, shaking her head in disapproval as she scanned her dining options carefully.

I laughed and ordered a heaping plate of pasta and placed slices of garlic bread all along the perimeter of my plate. Colette and I stuffed our faces while swapping stories about pop music stars and our teachers. We were actually quite disappointed when our volunteer event was over. On the way out, my coach handed me back my community service paperwork. She had signed off on ten hours.

Well, that's more like it, I thought to myself.

The experience of volunteering at Da'Quan's school juxtaposed against my time at the tennis clinic only further cemented my belief that whiteness was good, rich, and worthy of aspiring to. Blackness was a condition to abandon and run from. My mind never contemplated Da'Quan's well-being as I handed out breakfast sandwiches during the neighboring town's annual 5K run during the next community service project. We community-serving tennis girls gave the mostly white runners—outfitted in their Nike shorts and sneakers—high fives, food, and Gatorades as they crossed the finish line. I spent only forty-five minutes engaged in the endeavor but racked up six more community service hours. I also accrued five community service hours for helping to decorate a clubhouse for the tennis team's end-of-season party, in an exclusive neighborhood where one of the players lived. By the time I was a junior, I was already halfway through earning all of the hours I needed to qualify for the scholarship, and I had managed to thwart the counselor's attempt to Blacken my experience of what "giving back to the community" meant. In my mind, there was a clear distinction between me and the other Black kids. I was Black, but in transition in the direction of whiteness. Though it would be impossible for me to arrive at that final destination, the reality of my skin color didn't stop me from trying to shift toward whiteness.

Welcome to the light!

As I walked past the hallways filled with Black and Hispanic kids, I felt a deep sense of superiority and pride in the fact that I would be joining the white kids in the higher-level courses. I was one of the "smart" kids whom my teachers adored. Though I stood out as the only Black girl in my AP classes and battled some self-consciousness, I much preferred the absence of full acceptance over the outright fear of violence and ostracism I had come to anticipate in Black spaces after Houston. Every time I passed by a rowdy, uncontrollable classroom full of students of color or saw a fight break out among the Black kids, I sighed with relief. I had escaped their fate and would no longer be subjected to such indignities or abuses.

I eventually joined my school's soccer team as a member of the JV squad. The varsity girls were mostly seniors and all were white, but the junior squad had one or two other girls of color, whom I welcomed. When we arrived at neighboring schools for games, we knew which teams would be easy to beat just by the state of their fields. And, of course, by the color of the other girls' skin. We could always feel confident we'd pummel majority-Black-and-brown teams.

"And look at their uniforms!" a teammate screamed when we approached one school where the team was warming up in plain T-shirts.

The entire bus erupted in giggles, the girls pointing and further commenting on the shortcomings of the other team, their environment, and their equipment. I laughed along awkwardly. Though the other girls looked more like me than my own team, I refused to identify with their circumstances.

"Settle down, girls," the coach finally interrupted.

We strode off the bus in a single-file line, our heads held high, and carefully placed our bags near our bench and put on our cleats before taking to the field to warm up. A ball rolled in my direction and I reflexively stopped it with my foot. A girl from the other team ran toward me to scoop it up.

"Thanks," she said with a small smile.

I turned away and avoided eye contact. We beat them 6–0 and spent the entire ride back to our campus laughing at their inability to juggle and shoot the ball and planning our team fundraiser. Though we had brand-new Adidas warm-up outfits, multiple silky uniforms, and matching bags with our individual numbers stitched into them, the girls wanted to raise funds to buy more equipment.

"My dad will probably just write us a check," one of the girls said.

He owned a multimillion-dollar cracker company and could "spare a few thousand dollars."

I knew my circumstances were nothing like those of the girls who were on my team, and around this time I also became obsessively aware of something that set me even more noticeably apart from the others: my body. After years of consuming Black female bodies via the media, I knew they looked nothing like the bodies celebrated by the "mainstream" media. The celebrated white Hollywood actresses, pop stars, and models of the time were all skinny; their slim waists, tiny hips, and flat behinds were coveted on magazine covers. The athletic white girls on the team resembled that prototype. I, however, had thick, strong legs with quad muscles that protruded whenever we sat in a circle to stretch. I looked around at all the other legs in the circle, and my pair looked fat and gross in comparison.

"I'm on a diet, because I got so fat over winter break," I overheard one of the girls from the team telling another during lunch one day.

The other girl nodded along in supportive agreement while scanning her friend's body from head to toe.

"Losing a couple pounds wouldn't hurt," she agreed. "Prom is coming up and I know you wanna look great for Brad."

If she was their definition of "fat," with her tiny frame and long, lanky legs, I was clearly beyond obese. My idea of what was a "normal" body had begun to shift, and all of a sudden mine was no longer a part of the norm. I looked like the hypersexualized strippers and video vixens used as props for the male gaze. The women who were coveted and protected for their beauty had nothing in common with my body. I began to run an additional two hours a day, on top of the two-hour daily practice I did for the team. I ate only salads. After a few weeks had passed, I scrutinized my reflection in the mirror for progress only to find more horror: my thighs had actually gotten thicker and stronger. I stared in disbelief and tried to accept that my body would never look like the body America wanted.

There was a distinct difference between being white and being white adjacent. Proximity to whiteness for thousands of Black people often changed with the flick of a single white man's wrist. In the 1960s, white bankers participated in redlining—discriminatory banking practices that restricted Black access to mortgages for homes in "good," white neighborhoods—which drew invisible lines around white suburbs Black families couldn't penetrate, leaving us to flounder in underfunded, impoverished communities where violence and hardship claimed the lives of too many. In my era bankers used the promise of access to home-ownership to lure Black families into predatory loans that would decimate Black wealth and eventually crash the whole system.

In 2006, the Florida housing market was right on the brink of disaster, yet developers all across the state were busy trying to cash in on a new trend: apartment-to-condo conversions. The promise of maintenance-free living was attractive to many prospective Floridian home buyers who appreciated the idea of "ownership" but didn't want to be burdened taking care of what they owned—mowing lawns or keeping up their own pools. The way the banking system had been structured, in the wake of many boom years and thanks to the gamified business strategies that permeated the zeitgeist at the time, it was possible for people to secure loans to purchase homes even though there was no documented proof they could pay back the loans. Minority families fell victim to this practice by a large margin.

When the banks said yes, they took the loans, and even families with low credit scores or who didn't even have enough money for a down payment were approved to pursue the ultimate American dream: homeownership. But the loans were calculated with high interest rates, and the fine print dictated that those rates would kick in as the mortgages matured. There was a high chance these loans would default, and while that would decimate individual families, that high-risk environment fueled the gamble investors were more than willing to take. Wall Street bundled these loans into complicated, risky products and sold them as assets throughout the global financial system. As long as the banking system stayed afloat, the government ignored these problematic but not technically illegal maneuvers. But such risks would have major ramifications, especially for people who looked like me.

Midway through my sophomore year, Mom got a notice from the complex where we lived informing her that the apartments would soon become condos and she could either purchase ours or move out. By then, it was hard for her to find stable work in our area, because the economy was struggling. In Florida, it was much harder for Mom to find steady full-time employment than it was in other states, and the financial crisis exacerbated her quest to earn a consistent income. Still, she refused to give up on her dream of making a life for us in the Sunshine State, no matter how far out of her way she had to go to do so. On weekends, she would enlist Stefan and me to accompany her either to Tampa or Clearwater, where she could make up for the hours she wasn't getting during the week in Orlando. We traveled up to two hours away from home, often for work schedules that would require renting a motel room for the weekend so Mom could try to grind out as many hours as possible.

"What's in it for us?" Stefan would always ask, scratching his chin, one eyebrow raised, when Mom would present us with the weekend's travel plans.

"Domin—"

"Sold!" we would both cry out in unison, before Mom could even finish her statement.

Mom knew just how to win our support. Even when we negotiated up from just a large Domino's pizza to a pizza and wings, it was still a bargain for Mom. We would stuff our faces and groan in delight while debating what to watch, as my mom crept out of the motel room at around 10:00 p.m. to go to work. I barely ever slept during those weekends. As decadent as we made it seem to eat pizza in bed, I was unable to rest. My mind was filled with worry for my mother—whether or not she made it to work safely, or if she was too tired to survive her shift after having to drive for hours just to get down to the motel. When Mom burst through the door on our last morning in the motel, a brown paper bag full of breakfast sandwiches in one hand and a cup holder with three cups of orange juice in the other, I knew she was happy and relieved to have survived another long weekend. For her, the sacrifice was worth it for us to maintain the comfort we experienced in Florida. For our burgeoning friendships to continue to flourish. For the promise of a free college education to be fulfilled.

"So where are we moving, and do we have to change schools?" I snapped at my mom when she showed me the notice from our landlords.

I knew that even in this real estate climate, with all of that magical banking happening around us, my mom still couldn't afford to purchase a condo. I got even more insight into our family's future when I ran into Colette. She approached me after school one day, her face streaked with mascara-filled tears.

"My family's moving, so I'm changing schools," she said. "I'm not finna go to Oak Wood."

Oak Wood was a nearby, mostly Black and Hispanic high school for kids who lived on the other side of our busy road and beyond. Colette's mom took her to tour the campus after her family got priced out of their neighborhood and found more affordable housing in the neighboring district. She told me that two fights broke out within moments of her arrival for the tour, the students were rowdy and disruptive, and the teachers clearly didn't care.

"We may have to move across the street," Mom confessed over dinner while discussing the changes happening in our neighborhood.

Even though I knew change was coming, the news was devastating. My hands began to tremble and shake as thoughts of Houston and of Da'Quan's neighborhood swirled in my head, as menacing and haunting as apparitions. I couldn't bear another fight. I couldn't withstand the pressure of not knowing: When would I be attacked again? Would there be a gun involved this time? Or a knife? Would I even make it to college? I broke.

"No, Mom, please," I begged in a whisper as I fell to my knees, pressing my hands together, praying to her as if she were God.

I began to sob uncontrollably. My family's life and the lives of my friends were all destabilized by a few bad banking practices, which would eventually crash the entire economy, resulting in 2008's great recession. Some 2.6 millions jobs evaporated. Families were even driven to homelessness. The price of oil tripled, driving up the price of food and goods.

We moved back to New Jersey a few weeks later—instead of risking a move across the street in Florida. It didn't take long before all of my friends left our Florida neighborhood as well. Karla moved to a town forty-five minutes away so she could continue going to a good school, and Michelle moved two and a half hours away to Fort Lauderdale. Dennis and his family moved north to Philly. The twins, Brielle and Rochelle, returned to upstate New York. We rolled Big Mama into a U-Haul and began the long journey back up north. Meanwhile, the government spent billions to bail out big banks. The CEOs and executives who were in charge of the banks earned millions. But normal families like ours were just uprooted and forced to resettle elsewhere. We were discarded.

CHAPTER 4

Calm

In every abusive relationship, there are moments of tumult when the abuser makes life unbearable for the victim. Then there are moments of calm, when things seem to be getting better and change seems to have arrived. These moments keep victims holding on, keep us thinking that our commitment, determination, and patience is paying off. For Black Americans, the Reconstruction era, from about 1865 to 1877, was just such a moment of calm. Newly emancipated Africans were finding empowerment through literacy and education, building schools and their own homes, cultivating their own land, and even becoming political leaders. The success by 1921 of Tulsa, Oklahoma's Greenwood District, known as Black Wall Street—a Black city that boasted its own airport, economy, school system, and safe neighborhoods—represents a similar moment of hopeful calm. The civil-rights-era crescendo, when laws and reforms were finally passed—including the Voting Rights Act; the desegregation of public spaces, schools, and institutions; the integration of businesses and neighborhoods; and more social and political power and representation for Black people—was also a moment when Black people could catch their breath. These moments are always used in history lessons as proof of the evolution of America's changing heart when it comes to recognizing the equity and equality of Black people. In the 2000s, the election of Barack Obama lulled America into the ultimate calm. If a Black man could hold the highest political position in the country, how could anyone argue there was anything that could be holding Black America back?

By the time I was a young adult, generations of Black people had realized Martin Luther King Jr.'s dream of integration. Many Black children whose families sought refuge from the country's Black ghettos never knew of a life beyond the safety of a white suburb. Thousands of Black children, like me, went to integrated schools, and some eventually went on to prestigious colleges. Assimilation brought respite for many Black children from the torments of life confined to ghettos, but not without sacrifice. For the generation no longer restrained by de jure segregation, our assimilation taught us there was much to be lost in the Black quest to access whiteness.

The moment of "calm" in my own life that lulled me into believing I no longer lived in the context of being Black in America came in my teens, when I was able to gain entry into white spaces in high school. As a young adult, for me access and acceptance came by way of "love."

Returning to North Bergen after so many years of being away was a relief. Mom rented a beautiful two-story home in a tiny subdivision that was at the bottom of the hill the town's high school sat upon, so Stefan and I didn't have to walk very far to get to class in the morning. Though the house came with a hefty price tag, it was among the few she could find that accepted pets. By then our dog, Sam, had grown from a tiny and timid black fur ball into a medium-sized, boisterous fur ball with the protective instincts of a mama grizzly, and he wasn't about to let us leave him behind. It was also liberating to return to urban life. On my first day back, I spent hours perusing stores along Bergenline and sat on "the Rocks" with a grease-stained brown paper bag stuffed with beef-and-cheese empanadas to watch the sunset in the evening. I was back home. As the air outside grew warmer and the season shifted from winter to spring, I looked forward to the embrace of school in this town, which I was sure would be just as I remembered it from childhood. By the looks of the busy streets filled with shoppers and buses still blasting Spanish music, not much had changed. But I was in for a surprise.

"Can you believe there's like forty kids in a class and they are still using chalkboards and old, dusty-ass books?" I relayed to my mom over dinner.

Niki enrolled in the local community college, and many of her classes were held in the basement of the old church where we had attended Sunday school many years earlier. Stefan was equally dismayed by the absence of the comforts and amenities we had grown accustomed to back in suburban Florida.

"Just give it a chance," Mom responded with a sigh.

But it was difficult to temper my expectations when they had so drastically shifted. The dark, dingy school hallways and classrooms had become offensive to my sensibilities. The overcrowded classrooms and apathy of teachers angered me.

"His mother doesn't even speak English. What do you expect?" I overheard the teachers snickering in their staff rooms about students who failed to adequately participate in class or pass tests.

I registered for honors and AP classes, but even those spaces required very little of the students. Without any rich white students for whom a higher standard and expectation could be set, the classroom became a boat that would no longer rise with the tide of privilege. The urge to abandon ship swelled within me. But then I received an unexpected lesson that taught me to see the beauty in the environment.

During my junior year of high school, I had a Filipino math teacher who wore his long brown hair in a ponytail and always kept his head bowed. Despite his timid and soft-spoken demeanor, he fought his hardest to instruct the class of rowdy teenagers. When he would approach the chalkboard to begin the day's lesson, many students would continue to carry on loud conversations. They would interrupt him without fear of retribution, because they saw him as a pushover. I often felt a sense of dread upon entering class. As a child, I was always instructed to respect my teachers, and I found the students' ill treatment of him—and my inability to do anything about it—quite disheartening. I simply could not stand to witness adolescents bully a grown man, a man who seemed to lack the guts to stand up for himself.

Then, on Halloween, as I walked toward the classroom, I spotted a tall brown princess with flowing hair, wearing a ball gown and glistening silver sandals with a small heel on them. When I got closer, I noticed this princess was my math teacher. Except he barely resembled the shy, unassuming man whom my peers ignored.

"Good morning, my students!" he said that day at the start of class, with beaming eyes and a huge, beautiful smile.

As Cinderella, he stood tall—his posture resembling royalty. He approached the chalkboard with confidence and hissed threats at students who attempted to interrupt him. He was another person in that gown, and his self-assuredness was hard to miss. The next day, our unassuming math teacher returned and students resumed their disrespect. But a few weeks later, Mr. Bolado disappeared. We, his students, became increasingly curious as to why. Gossip circulated that he had terminal cancer or had possibly gone to jail, but I shrugged it all off. Eventually, days became weeks and weeks became months. Christmas came and brought the gift of a two-week vacation, and all of the kids scurried home, still wondering if their teacher would return to teach, *ever*.

Upon our return from winter break, the school's counselor came to our classroom.

"I'm sure you have all noticed the absence of your teacher," he began. "Everyone should feel free to pursue a path that will lead them to happiness—that is their right—and sometimes that pursuit requires courage," he continued. By the end of his speech, we had learned that our teacher would be returning to instruct us as a woman, with a new first and last name: we would have to refer to her as "Ms. Samantha Melendez" going forward. For the first time that year, the entire classroom fell completely silent.

The next day, I entered to find a smiling teacher wearing a woman's blouse and a formfitting pair of pants. Admittedly, I felt a bit confused at first. I looked around for cues to show me how to react in a way that was acceptable. Then I remembered the insightful words of that counselor: *Everyone should feel free to pursue happiness—that is their right.* I knew all I had to do was respect that right. And that is precisely what I—and most of the student body—did.

Though there were a few students who were, from time to time, intentionally rude or disrespectful, they were outnumbered by the many who respectfully kept their opinions to themselves or outwardly showed support for Ms. Melendez.

"Oh my God, he's wearing a dress again!" one of the young boys in the classroom announced when our teacher entered in a loose-fitting, sleeved garment.

"She can wear whatever she wants!" a girl shot back from across the classroom, nipping any outburst in the bud.

I breathed a sigh of relief as I saw a tiny smile spread across my teacher's face. Our school environment made it clear that our teacher's dignity should never be compromised, setting a precedent for the rest of us and giving many students permission to act on a low tolerance for the outbursts of unruly peers. I'm certain our teacher recognized that some of her students were as brave as she was, willing to stand up to others in support of her right to just be. But many of us kids, including me, felt brave enough to do so only because the guidance counselor had given us a clear road map. The counselor's clarity helped us navigate the confusion of a novel event and arrive at a place of peace, love, and understanding. We were unknowingly mentored into standing for freedom, not for judgment or hate.

My school's acceptance of my teacher's transition signaled to me that America was changing, and I believed it would do more to accommodate me so that I might find my own place in it. I was so proud of and in love with my country—the one that would lead the world into a more embracing and respectful future.

Around this time, I came across a poster advertising the date for school soccer tryouts, and I felt emboldened: I'd always been able to find a place to belong on the field. On the day of the tryouts, I arrived in full gear. I still had my Adidas soccer bag and matching sweats from Florida and proudly strutted onto the school's blemished, patchy back field. The other girls at tryouts were mostly Hispanic, and I could see that many loved the sport but few had any previous training. They were impressed by me. And I accepted one of the most important positions on the field—center mid—and trained day and night, running up and down the town's hills, to prepare for our first game. I was disappointed at the sight of my new uniform, which the coach dug out of a bin of jerseys. The zip for the team bag I was given broke within hours of my receiving it. But I didn't let those superficial details dampen my spirits. I just wanted to get back onto the field.

Our first game was against a school in Bergen County. As we disembarked from the bus, I spotted the other team warming up in the distance. All of the girls were white, and their parents filled the seats of the stadium. The sight of their warm-up outfits made me shudder at the inferiority of our red cotton T-shirts. My stomach churned as I recalled the many times I had laughed at teams that looked like the one I was now on: Black and brown girls in cheap gear. We put down our bags near one of our team's benches and took to the field to begin our drills.

"Junkin' jacks: uno, dos, tres, cuatro," our team captain loudly called out, and the other girls chanted along in unison.

The white parents giggled and exchanged hushed, mocking jokes. I cringed and groaned. I was on the other side of the fence now—a poor kid worthy of ridicule, whose only practical purpose seemed to be to provide ego-building fodder through which the cheery white girls could boost their sense of self-importance and self-worth. Mere months ago, I'd have been drinking in this scene along with them. My eyes shot back and forth between my teammates, who were still proudly doing their warm-ups, and the white people, who had already decided where our team ranked. I wanted to sit the game out to avoid the embarrassment of certain defeat. I knew how whiteness and privilege converge to confer wins, but I failed to find the words to express my pain and reluctance to the coach when I approached him.

"C'mon, get out there!" he ordered, and I slunk back onto the pitch.

I positioned myself on the field and waited for the referee to blow his whistle and start the game. I scanned my team: our cheap red cotton T-shirts, each emblazoned with the school's name in yellow letters, tucked into red nylon short pants. And then I turned my gaze to the other team: their blond hair tied into high ponytails with ribbon, special gear for headbutting the ball, their polyester white shirts with their names printed across the back along with their numbers. I knew we were outmatched, and it didn't take long for the scoreboard to confirm my assessment. Within moments of the ball hitting the field, the other team gained possession and scored a goal. By halftime, the score was 8–0.

"STOP SCORING!" the other team's coach implored, turning to the blond white woman next to him, chuckling and shaking his head.

The humiliation was unbearable. I poured my anger and frustration into each kick, sending the ball flying wildly through the air and to the other side of the field or out of bounds. On the ride back to the school, I sat silently staring out the bus window as the other girls continued to laugh and giggle, despite the defeat. Unlike many of my teammates, I had been on both sides, and I understood that the burden of defeat was shouldered by disenfranchised minorities and that the prospects for slipping out from under that weight were not good.

After that game, I couldn't find the strength or desire to arise in the morning. I mourned the old me: the entitled girl with a matching Adidas uniform and soccer bag with the words "Olympia High School" and number 12 proudly stitched into them. I couldn't find the willpower to reconfigure or repurpose myself anymore. I felt isolated in my experience of the world of whiteness and unable to relate to the environment I'd always thought of as my home. I wanted to find a way to get closer to the privilege that was just within my grasp back in Orlando. I made a promise to live in pursuit of it from then forward.

"Love is for white people," I blurted out during French class one day. "I need to find a man who has money!"

My declaration was elicited by our teacher Mrs. Boguslavsky's fawning over French romantic movies and music. She was a sweet Russian Jewish woman who often wore red lipstick and taught all of the school's French classes. My outburst had a visible impact on her: her face twisted in disgust, and I knew she pitied me.

"Teefaneee," she began in her thick accent when she found the patience to respond, "I have been married to my husband for twenty-one years, and it was the best decision I ever made. I know one day you will find love too, and that is bewwtiful."

I secretly envied her certainty. But I refused to be swept up in the comfort her words sought to provide. By then, I was a high school senior who knew love and security were not guaranteed for Black women and were resources we had to fight for. I shrugged and rolled my eyes, making a cocky performance out of my disbelief. Jessi, a classmate who sat near me, grinned and mimed a supportive fist bump in my direction. I chuckled, feeling relieved that someone understood and could relate to my seemingly unpopular opinion.

Jessi was a white-skinned, Dominican Colombian American boy with a bright smile and deep desire to acquire the "better things" in life. Both of his parents were immigrants who barely spoke English, but that didn't stop him from coveting the trappings of "success" in all of its splendor.

"Yes, girl!" he declared when he brushed by me after class that day. "Get that money!"

Jessi wanted to escape into the bright lights of New York City, where he imagined acceptance and financial fortune awaited. I shared the dream and would spend much of my free time fantasizing about the life, full of art and adventure, that I would have when I made it to the city. We just needed to survive high school, start our careers (he wanted to become a doctor), marry rich (me), and sidestep out of second-class immigrant life. In the meantime, we spent our high school summers working the same shifts as lifeguards at the local pool and traveling to the city in our free time to walk around Central Park, shop in Greenwich Village, and peruse the four-story Barnes & Noble in Union Square. Jessi would arrive to pick me up at 7:45 every morning so we could be on time for our shift at the pool, which we would spend atop tall lifeguard chairs shaded by umbrellas or in the lifeguard room telling jokes or sharing gossip about the happenings in our small town. One summer evening after a typical twelve-hour shift, Jessi brought the car to a halt and turned to me with a look of urgency and concern on his face.

"I have something to tell you," he announced.

His abrupt delivery came as quite a shock and a surprise. I immediately wondered if he had developed romantic feelings for me after all the time we had been spending together.

"No, I'm not in love with you!" he said quickly, as if reading my mind.

The tension of the moment persisted, and he gazed down at the car's steering wheel, hesitating to speak—which was truly unlike him.

"I'm gay!" he finally screamed. "And I want you to come to the city with me tonight so I can meet boys!"

Though I admit I felt slightly disappointed that his romantic interest in no way included me, I was overwhelmed with joy that he felt open and comfortable enough to disclose his secret to me. He had been quietly concealing these feelings for his entire life up until that moment, fearful of the scorn and ridicule they could potentially spark. I reached over the gearshift and hand brake and pulled him into a tight hug. Our friendship was solidified. And I embraced my designation as his wing woman, the one who would accompany him as he pursued happiness.

"There's this place called Splash that I heard is amazing, and I want to go tonight," he said.

I went home on a mission to get dressed and have a night on the town. I felt invigorated by a sense of newfound purpose. When I burst through the front door, Stefan immediately sensed my busy intent.

"Going out tonight?" he questioned. "Where ya headed?"

Unable to keep the excitement to myself, but cautious not to reveal Jessi's secret, I told him about my plans.

"Jessi and I are going to a place called Splash in the city," I responded.

A smile swept over his face.

"Oh, I think I'll meet you guys there," he said.

I assumed "there" meant the city, and I told Stefan to give me a call when he arrived, then quickly changed into a cute shirt, jeans, and red pumps. I was already dressed and waiting when Jessi pulled up. He sped down the highway and through the Holland Tunnel like a bandit breaking out of prison. We cruised through downtown New York City, no longer in awe of the busy and crowded streets. We parked, fed the nearby meter, and then joined a slowly creeping line for Splash as a single bouncer checked IDs to make sure patrons were all over eighteen. Inside, the club was jam-packed and the gayness was both refreshing and fabulous. Men with chiseled bodies and perfectly square jawlines were bumping and grinding on one another, some without shirts and most carrying colorful drinks in one hand. The atmosphere was energizing and invigorating, and the men waved and blew kisses in my direction as I passed.

"Oh my God, aren't you so precious!" one random man squealed while cupping my face in his hands.

I swelled at the validation and began to whip my head around, twisting my hips in excitement. When beads of sweat began to drip down my face, I stood outside the bar and drank in the night air. My cell phone vibrated: it was Stefan. I stuffed it back into my pocket, uncertain what to tell him. Just as I was about to head back into the club, I caught a glimpse of a tall, handsome Black man strolling toward the entrance wearing skinny jeans and a sports jacket over a white V-neck T-shirt. He had a wide grin spread across his face and walked with both control and ease. As he came closer, a vague sense of familiarity swept over me.

"Let's go dance!" the man screamed at me over the music that spilled out of the club.

It was Stefan. In that moment, a veil lifted and I could finally see him as his whole self. My brother who sang Disney soundtracks with me to ward off moments of sadness, who was always there to anchor me in my experiences of the world as a Black girl, had come out. To me. It was my moment to bestow support upon him, and I wasted no time doing so. I grabbed his hand and we disappeared into the venue, where we spent hours dancing, shaking, and twirling to Beyoncé, Lady Gaga, and EDM. By the time we left, we were drenched in sweat and giddy over shared tales of our first night in the city's gay scene.

It didn't take long before Jessi found himself a boyfriend during one of our weekend escapades. His name was Dan, and he was a cute white boy from Brooklyn. They became acquainted on the dance floor, bumping and grinding to the bass of the music. The moment they swapped kisses, I squealed with joy. I was Jessi's proud fag hag, living vicariously through the love he so easily reached out to grab. It brought me great pleasure to watch as he and my brother lived their truth, but envy was quietly boiling deep within me. My own experiences with young love were far less giddy or romantic. I was surrounded by male peers who were mostly Hispanic, and it was rare that one would take a romantic interest in me. After repeated racist encounters that left me feeling helpless and worthless, I was wary, if not of them then certainly of their families.

"Why would you invite a Black girl to a Hispanic family's barbecue!?" one of Jessi's cousins, a man in his twenties, had asked one summer when I arrived at their aunt's house. It was clear he had been holding the question back, and it exploded out of him.

Everything froze for a moment and the *tink-tink-tink* of the guitar in the bachata music playing in the background reverberated through the now-empty air. Then the scene sprang to life with the power of a crescendo as Jessi's dad rushed the cousin. The scene unfolded in slow motion. Jessi's dad delivered the first blow to the cousin's chin, sending droplets of spit flying out of his mouth toward the trays of yellow rice, tostones, chicharrones, and pernil. Jessi ushered me toward the back door and we escaped through an alley to the car.

Another memorable incident occurred months before that, when the mother of my good school friend came to pick her up from our house. "You in this house full of Black people?" the mother asked when, upon arriving, she discovered to her dismay that my family was perhaps two shades more pigmented than she was.

"You will never come back here again!" she screamed behind my friend, who burst into tears and ran out of my front door in shame.

"Ay, negra puta," one mother announced upon entering her home and finding me comfortably seated, watching a movie with her son, a long-haired Puerto Rican kid from the neighborhood with whom I had spent a few evenings sitting on the Rocks and exchanging flirty looks.

Only moments earlier, he had slipped his fingers between mine and pulled my hand into his lap, as if claiming it for himself. I appreciated the gesture, hopeful that perhaps it meant a change in my dating fortunes. At the sound of his mother's voice, he jumped out of his seat and rushed toward the foyer to intercept her, but by then it was too late. I quietly made my exit as they argued back and forth in Spanish over my mere presence.

"It's not that serious. Don't be so dramatic," Jessi cajoled when I spoke of the pain of the repeated attacks on my Blackness.

Bearing the additional weight of "being too sensitive" forced my despair fully underground, while simultaneously it taught me to bury, even deeper, my concerns and anxieties about racism. Externally, I became hardened to the harsh, repeated blows, like a championship boxer accustomed to the violence of the ring. To cope, I learned to duck and dodge any attempts at undermining my personhood with poise and grace, often standing in the face of it and laughing or raising my eyebrow in contempt. However, beneath that feigned haughtiness, I was crumbling. And I wasn't the only one.

After falling out of contact for many years because of our many moves, Mom rekindled her relationship with my aunt Debbie, who vowed to send my no-longer-baby cousin Ashley to visit with us for a weekend. In our absence from the state, Debbie and my uncle had traded their three-bedroom house in Edison for a larger home in an even whiter neighborhood farther away from the city. They had also managed to purchase a UPS Store in a shopping plaza near the house, which they ran as a family.

"Pa has to lie to the white people and pretend he is just a worker," Ashley disclosed during her stay while telling us over dinner about the way her dad ran his business, her voice monotonous and lifeless.

He had changed his name from Darnell to Dave, so as to not offend the sensibilities of their customers, who were all white. My family and I listened to her tales from the burbs with equal parts shock and fascination. During her visit, she told us of one-sided friendships where white schoolmates would come to her birthday party but never invite her to theirs; of teachers who would accuse her of being too talkative or loud while failing to reprimand boisterous white boys; and of the loneliness of being left home alone while her parents ran the store. Her sister, Felicity, was already over eighteen and had run off with a boyfriend from Newark whom my aunt and uncle disapproved of because of his association with "the hood."

"We didn't work this hard to move out here for you to date a hood rat!" they would scold.

Felicity was of a darker complexion and maintained the same assertive and charismatic traits that had made her a leader back in our childhood neighborhood. In suburbia, she was a pariah, picked on by the white kids for having dark skin and, like her sister, called out by teachers for being too loud and abrasive.

Ashley had heard the older kids taunting her elder sister after school one day, "Monkey, monkey, monkey!"

Felicity eventually sought the companionship of Black children from the neighboring city, Newark—a hood known for producing the likes of drug kingpin Akbar Pray and legendary basketball star Shaquille O'Neal. In her escape, she found safety and embrace in the Black world, though participation in that world wrought its own hardships. Still, unlike Ashley, she found a place to belong. Aside from the occasional strip mall or church steeple where a few faces of color could be seen, there was very little in her suburb to remind Ashley that there were constructive ways to see herself reflected in the world. Or that she should be able to comfortably exist in the world as a Black girl. Hers was an identity conflict fueled by cultural isolation.

"Black people don't ice-skate," Ashley responded plainly when we excitedly invited her to go skating at Bryant Park in New York City.

We were confused by the statement, because we had made it a yearly family ritual during the winter holidays to travel to the city, cups of hot chocolate in hand, to don ice skates and glide across the rink together. Usually, there were many families of all races there. For Ashley (and many Black kids raised like her) the biggest danger of displacing her—a little Black girl—into the statistically white suburbs was the eternal conflict of assimilation versus self-love.

"Look at this!" I urged Ashley, pointing to an image of Surya Bonaly, the Black ice-skater who became infamous after having her score deducted at the 1998 Winter Olympics for perfectly executing a backflip, landing on one foot, on ice.

Ashley shrugged at the sight, still unconvinced. Even though there were many successful Black faces on television and in the media, for her, there was little substitute for real-life peers and activities when it came to actualizing a healthy sense of identity or cultural belonging.

"You can't really go anywhere without a car," Ashley reminded us when we incredulously questioned why she didn't just hop on a bus or train to come visit us.

Cultural isolation was further exacerbated by the limited autonomy of the suburbs. Many suburbs were built right on the heels of World War II, when cars became the dominant mode of transportation.[1] There were no subways or public bus routes, and it was just as rare to see a taxi. Her suburb simply didn't have the public transportation infrastructure to allow high levels of mobility. That hip-hop concert or Afro-American book club featured in the big city was accessible only via the benevolence of driver's-licensed friends or family members who found no need to go out in search of Black culture. Her friends were white and had white interests, so she dared not suggest wasting time or gas on a quest for Black culture. Her parents were already grounded in their Black upbringing back in their homeland and failed to contemplate whether or not her whitewashed upbringing conferred any sense of self, belonging, or identity.

Between 1960 and 2000—in the years following American integration—nine million Black people migrated to suburbs in search of a middle-class life, seeking safety and privacy and opportunity.[2] On paper, the justification made sense: enclaves like the white American suburb were, in many ways, a shortcut to the American dream. A luxurious life was more affordable and more plentiful away from cantankerous cities and metropolises or even the rural South. However, the siren song of a better life also had hidden pitfalls for Black people. What was promised in material goods was often lost in other forms of capital. By the 1990s and 2000s, Black youth, the demographic once thought to be immune to suicide, had increased their attempts at suicide by 73 percent.[3] I imagine this was not the dream Martin Luther King Jr. envisioned when he fought to end segregation.

To cope with feeling culturally adrift, Ashley lost herself in the animated computer-generated world of *The Sims*, wherein she cast herself as a blond-haired, blue-eyed white girl with white friends and a Ken-doll-look-alike boyfriend. As we watched her struggle to reconcile her fragmented reality with the presence of our multidimensional Blackness during her visits, we recognized the depths of her emotional anguish. Her cognitive dissonance was both real and debilitating in ways she couldn't articulate in the moment, except through declarations of what she had internalized was impossible of Black people. The peculiarity of it all—the whiteness she described and subscribed to and the figment of Blackness she created in her head—made us grateful for our "underprivileged" lives among people of color. Ashley's parents' "success" and their proximal whiteness didn't confer any additional status on Ashley, which left me confused and directionless. For the first time, but not the last, I was forced to wonder: What was there left to aspire to in a country where whiteness was the pinnacle of success?

By the time of my high school graduation, I was depleted and no longer had any desire to fight the current constantly pulling me toward disappointment and discontentment. The question of what I wanted to do with my life frequently arose, but I had no energy to engage with it. My guidance counselor spent most of our single session together trying to convince me to participate in the statewide "NJ Stars" program, which would give students who completed their associate's degree at a state community college and met the GPA minimum requirement a full ride to any state college. I shrugged and filled out the application for the program. There were no other tracks recommended to me, and I was too exhausted to seek out any other option. When graduation came around,

I didn't attend. I never went to prom or participated in any senior festivities. I just wanted to escape.

I met Alexei through the dating app eharmony. Unlike the other dating sites and apps on the market, users had to pay to use eharmony, and it touted that it had helped thousands across America make love matches. I imagined myself as one of the happy women smiling while casually holding the hand of my newfound love as we starred in one of the company's promotional videos.

"Tiff, yeah—she is definitely the greatest thing that ever happened to me," my imagined eharmony beau gushed.

It took two months of chatting with him online before I met Alex in person. He was a white boy who was raised in the suburbs of New Jersey by his Ukrainian immigrant parents. We met up in Hoboken at a pizzeria and immediately connected over our love of documentaries and our free-spiritedness. He was a deep thinker with a million and one theories about life and the origin of man. But it was clear to me that we came from very different backgrounds. I looked around his neighborhood and took note that I was the only Black girl in his mostly white enclave.

"Your parents pay for you to live here?" I asked in disbelief when he brought me back to his apartment on our fifth date.

Alex lived in Hoboken on Garden Street and First, only a ten-minute walk from the PATH train. The town was always busy, with residents and commuters shuffling between bars and restaurants and on and off buses and casually walking through the waterfront hub. I calculated that his monthly rent probably cost my semester's tuition at the community college. His dad, who had earned his degree as an engineer back in Ukraine, paid for everything, including Alex's apartment, car, living expenses, and tuition at Seton Hall. In exchange, he got passing grades and spent his free time pontificating about neuroscientific theories, smoking weed, and adding new prescription pills to his already robust inventory.

Our time together helped me feel as if I finally had some power and freedom once again. It also helped me feel less isolated, more secure, and more capable of realizing my dreams. At first, Alex was my biggest supporter. When I expressed the desire to lose weight, we signed up at a local Muay Thai gym and packed his apartment with fresh fruits and vegetables, chicken breasts, beans, and brown rice. For my birthday, he planned a weekend trip to Montego Bay, Jamaica, and let me pick any activities I wanted to do while there (I chose horseback riding and ziplining). When I expressed the desire for adventure, he told me, "Just spin the globe." I told my girlfriend Shirley that I wanted to travel somewhere distant and beautiful, and she told us her dad was planning a trip to Peru and would be happy to take us along and host us. Alex immediately booked us flights.

In Lima, we toured a magnificent cathedral with a gold-trimmed altar and a basement full of torture apparatuses that were used on the Native people when European settlers began their inquisition, which would last nearly three centuries and kill many for "crimes against the church"—like refusing to convert to Christianity. We rode motorcycles through Puerto Maldonado, a bustling but remote town a two-hour flight from Peru's capital over vast, clay-like brown plains where only a single house could be seen every few hundred miles, and spent time with an amazing family who wouldn't stop feeding us and offering us drinks. We trekked through the Amazon and set up camp with a guide who hosted tourists and offered to teach us how to brew coca leaves to extract the cocaine from them and kill a chicken by wringing its neck (I declined both offers). As the sun descended on our first night in the vast rain forest, I worryingly moaned to Alex about not having been able to get a yellow fever shot before leaving Puerto Maldonado. Workers at the airport had promised us we would be able to get the vaccine from the local hospital upon arrival in Puerto Maldonado, but it was closed in the middle of the day for an unknown reason.

"Symptoms: fever, chills, headache, vomiting, nausea, *bleeding, shock*, and *organ failure*," I rattled off to him, remembering the poster I had read in the airport about the mosquito-borne disease, which kills 30 to 60 percent of people who come down with severe symptoms.

"Look, Tiff," Alex responded, pointing to the window of our tiny hut.

When I turned around, the night sky exploded in my face, knocking the breath right out of me. The cloudless, dark, vast sky was completely speckled with glimmering lights and sprinkled stardust and looked like a painting crafted by a child recently gifted with a glitter set.

"Oh my God," I whispered.

All that time, I had truly been living Plato's allegory of the cave. The bright lights of cities polluted and blackened the skies back home, blinding me to the glory of the infinite universe. I spent that night staring up at the sky and completely forgot about mosquitoes and the diseases their tiny bites could harbor.

My moments of deep reflection and introspection were many while I existed in the comfort Alex bestowed. He created my sphere of safety and support with intention and the ease of a child gently blowing soapy water out of a tiny plastic ring to create a gigantic bubble. I practically moved in with him, and we spent the majority of our free time theorizing about our lives and our families' failures and indulging in thoughtful books and documentaries. *The Secret, The Power of Now*, and *The Alchemist* were some of my favorites, as a young woman who had spent her life so far feeling powerless and preyed on. The reading gave me a newfound, perhaps even overinflated outlook on myself and the world, which I imagined could be bent to my whims. The books helped me to reimagine myself and challenge the "self" I'd accepted over the years and envision one who had agency. They also quieted any notions that racism had any impact on my life or the outcomes of Black people, since all could be overcome if we simply put our minds to it. For my next semester in college, I registered for a calculus class as an elective, completely sure that I could defeat my long-held belief that I was somehow "bad" at math.

"All of this time I've just been holding myself back!" I exclaimed to Niki as I described to her my self-help-induced eureka moment.

She was unconvinced and refused to ignore my entire family's math handicap just to support my theory. So I set out to prove her wrong. I registered for Calculus 1, bought the big, expensive book with my college loan money, and counted down the days until the class was scheduled to meet. The first day should have been a reality check. Absolutely nothing that came out of the professor's mouth made sense. And the numbers and letters scribbled on the whiteboard might as well have been Egyptian hieroglyphs. But I pressed on in my grandiose, delusional reality, fueled by Alexei's support.

"It's gonna take a while to rewire the circuitry in your brain," Alex posited over a glass of wine. "You cannot become a math whiz overnight."

Six weeks into the class, I received my first grade: "19," marked on the top righthand corner of the test and circled in red pen.

My math skills were substantial enough to deduce that I was failing, dramatically.

All right, the jig is up, I thought to myself, prepared to pack my stuff and head straight to the registrar's office to drop the class.

There was only one problem: the date to drop a course without penalty had already passed. Which meant I would receive the failing grade on my transcript and lose my scholarship.

"Relax, relax, it's no big deal," Alex responded coolly when I told him.

My white knight with a shining pillbox was going to save me.

"Meet me at the library," he instructed. "Bring your book."

I sat at the library waiting for him with my stomach in knots, imagining how I would break it to my mother that I had lost my scholarship and could no longer afford to attend community college. I planned a new future for myself as a manager at Dollar General. Only weeks earlier, I had seen an advertisement for a management position there that paid fifty thousand dollars, which didn't seem so bad. I charted my new career path: work my way up from sales associate to cashier, then to store manager, and finally to regional manager. I buried my face in my arms and sobbed. Alex found me hunched over at the table in the farthest end of the nonfiction section and plopped down next to me.

"You're gonna be okay," he assured me. "Just get your book out and take one of these."

He pressed a tiny blue pill into my palm and handed me a bottle of water. He had secured these pills from a friend for twenty-five dollars a pop to avoid having to go to a therapist and be branded with ADHD—a lifelong label that he didn't want following him in his medical records. I had about twenty-five dollars total in my bank account at that time, left over from my lifeguarding pay at the YMCA. I hesitated for a moment, my eyes still blurry and heavy from my crying spell.

"Take it," he urged.

I popped the pill into my mouth and washed it down with the water.

"All right, I'll be back in a couple hours to pick you up," he said, and patted me on the back before making a beeline for the library exit.

I flipped through the book, waiting for a spark. And within moments, the fog of hopelessness lifted as I gazed down at the page and finally saw numbers and letters that I could decipher. The longer I sat with the text, the more it began to make sense and the less daunting it felt. I read through the first four chapters of the book in a couple hours, as if it were my favorite novel. A few months and a couple doses of Adderall later, I received a final grade of 92 in the class. The feat, however, did not come without sacrifices: many nights battling insomnia and sleep paralysis.

"I think I'll just stick to what I'm good at," I declared when Alex offered to get me a bottle of the magic pills from his street pharmacist.

"Welp, your loss," he shot back.

The nearing of the end of the semester brought with it bare trees and the stinging cold of the winter air. The season of family and celebration was upon us, signaled by the lighting of the hundred-foot-tall Norway spruce tree at Rockefeller Center.

"I want to take you to my family's house for Christmas dinner," Alex declared under the shimmer of its golden lights.

He wanted me to finally meet his parents, who lived in a white suburb an hour away. By then, he was already accustomed to sharing meals and laughter with my family, whom we frequently visited and even went on ski trips with. Though we could barely ski, Mom insisted that we should at least have the experience. Alex felt it imperative that I share the same comfort with his own tribe.

As we sped down the highway on Christmas evening, my hands positioned in front of the heat-blasting vents, he updated me on his family's background:

"My mom used to be an engineer back in Ukraine, but she quit to take care of me and my brother after we came along. Dad is into tech and likes talking politics, probably too much. They are good people, but where they are from, they are used to being around their own," he reported, like he was a general briefing an infantry soldier for war.

"It's gonna be fine," I offered, sensing his anxiety.

We turned off of the highway and onto a tree-lined street with spacious single-family homes carefully plotted along the stretch and pulled up in front of a colonial-style home that very closely resembled my aunt's house back in Edison. He shifted the car into park and peered off into the distance for a while before turning to me.

"All right, ya ready?" he asked with a deep sigh.

I nodded and gathered the wine and cake we had brought along for the festivities. The sound of the heels of my boots echoed in the air as I marched toward the front door with a steady, confident stride. He rang the doorbell and fidgeted as we awaited a response. The muffled sound of laughter and chatter exploded into a full chorus of voices and music as the door opened. A slender white woman wearing a black scoop-neck dress, with brown hair cut into a fashionable bob, stood in the doorway. Upon seeing us, her large grin softened into a look of confusion.

"Alex, w-we didn't even expect you," she stuttered, her voice thick with a Ukranian accent.

Her eyes fell upon me and her stare remained incredulous, but her lips spread into a toothy smile. I offered a nod but she turned quickly to walk away. Alex went inside and I followed. The home was well appointed and tastefully decorated with a black leather sofa set, a big-screen television, and carefully hung paintings on the walls. His family members were strewn all about, some perched on the staircase near the living room, others sitting at the dining table with plates of food and wineglasses.

"Come," Alex's mom said, waving us in the direction of a dark, empty foyer toward the back of the house.

She stood in its farthest corner.

"I can't believe you would bring a Black person here!" his mother hissed when we arrived within earshot of her.

Her words stirred no emotions within me. I was already quite familiar with such indignation. Alexei's mom was acting in the very same way that millions of European immigrants had for generations—those focused only on their quest for ascension into "whiteness" in America. She was laying a firm boundary to separate herself and her family from the likes of my Blackness so as not to risk being tarnished by association.

In 1995, Harvard graduate Noel Ignatiev blew the lid off the myth that the classifications "Black" and "White" were based on actual biological realities in his book *How the Irish Became White.*

He asserted the theory that America had a caste system and that "whiteness" was a designation created to safeguard the country's dominant class: WASPs (white Anglo-Saxon Protestants). "White" was an ever-shifting social construct with unclear boundaries that bestowed upon those graced with such a distinction full American citizenship. Encoded through law and economic and immigration policy, "Blacks" were positioned as inferior and "whites" as superior. Ignatiev used the history of how the Irish became "white" in America as a case study to demonstrate his point. Driven into exile by famine and political disaster, the Irish came to America's shores from their homeland in the mid-nineteenth century. Many were traumatized by the sights of the dead who had perished from starvation when the country's staple crop, potatoes, failed to provide the sustenance poor farmworkers had grown dependent upon. Tales of mothers clutching their dead infants while begging in the streets for food and the lips of the dead being stained green by the grass they desperately (and futilely) tried to eat were common in that horrific time. Still, it didn't take long before "white" (WASP) Americans branded the Irish refugees as poor, disease-ridden rapists and criminals who threatened to steal jobs and strain welfare budgets. Italian immigrant newcomers were subjected to similar treatment, being deemed as essentially "Black" in early America.

When they first arrived in America, Italians were met with a wave of literature that depicted them as "racially suspect" and were often relegated to Negro spaces. White America called the Italian immigrants "dago," "guinea" (an epithet used against enslaved Africans and their descendants), and other terms that more clearly exemplified their Black status, like "white nigger" and "nigger wop." The now-infamous Columbus Day holiday was birthed as a diplomacy effort between Italy and America after a bloody New Orleans lynching claimed the lives of eleven Italian immigrants and nearly pushed the two nations to the brink of war. Eastern and southern European immigrants, particularly those from the Balkans, were branded inherently inferior by Anglo-Saxons, who placed restrictions on their early attempts to arrive in America. For those who managed to successfully immigrate and survive the discrimination, the process of assimilation wasn't an easy one. It cost many white Europeans their entire cultural identity. Ethnic-sounding names like Anastasiya, Giuseppina, and Siobhan were changed to Emily, Jill, and Karen. Accents were neutralized and traditions like Carnevale and ceilidh dancing were replaced with consumerism, individualism, and, later on, Walmart, pop culture, and social media. Still, ultimately, for European immigrants, there was a path to "whiteness."

Assimilation demanded that immigrant newcomers to America, like Alexei's parents, aspire to "whiteness" and by the same token demanded that they distance themselves from and oppress "Black" people to climb the social order. So they, too, joined in the devaluation of Black Americans. During the New York City draft riots of 1863,[4] Irish and German immigrants in New York City turned their rage on Black people—they believed that Black emancipation would mean increased competition for work—and attacked Black city dwellers and burned a Black orphanage. Eleven Black men were lynched during the five-day riot, and by its end, hundreds of Blacks had been forced out of the city. Black men, women, and children were all assaulted, but attacks on Black men were the most vicious. Over the course of five days, the rioters hanged a Black man named William Jones and then burned his body, and beat Jeremiah Robinson to death and threw his body in the river, and a group of white men and boys murdered Black sailor William Williams while a crowd watched. Williams's murderers stabbed him, jumped on his chest, and riddled his body with stones as the crowd cheered and chanted, "Vengeance on every nigger in New York." From the 1800s on, European immigrants would play a significant role in the continued devaluation and oppression of Black people. They instructed their children not to play with Black children and refused to allow Black families to move into their neighborhoods. They burned Black cities, homes, and schools and murdered Black children, women, and men. And America rewarded this behavior by eventually allowing early European immigrants entry into society as "white" people.

By the time I met Alex's mom, I had already grown accustomed to the way I was treated by others because of my skin color. Uninvited, unwanted, and disliked was a standard state of being for me. Even the openness with which Alex's mom expressed such disgust and outrage over my skin's shade made no impact. Alex, however, was new to experiencing the indignities faced by Black people (even vicariously). Face reddened with embarrassment and nostrils flared in anger, he turned away and stomped off petulantly, grabbing my hand in his and barging into the kitchen.

"This is my girlfriend, Tiffanie!" he announced with bravado.

The room quieted as everyone's heads turned in our direction. They all mumbled welcomes and then turned back to their conversations. I chuckled a bit at the unfolding scene—his outrage at their lack of enthusiasm. Was he expecting a warm embrace? From white folks? For a Black woman? It was quite comical in a tragic way. Alex huffed, puffed, and dragged me toward the kitchen counter near the stove, where all of the food was set out. My eyes fell upon the potato salad, reddened with the stains of radishes' color, and I decided it most certainly was not worth the disrespect.

"Let's just go," I urged him.

He apologized profusely the entire ride home, but I assured him such apologies were unwarranted. After all, he had not done anything except love me and try to include me in his world. I could not blame him for the transgressions and indiscretions of his mother. There was also a secret I kept hidden away that protected me from such slights: in my mind, she was barely white, with her brown hair, dark eyes, and thick accent. I scoffed at her attempts to diminish my personhood based on race, when she barely occupied a higher position in the eyes of true white America.

But really. Was I supposed to be envious at the thought of losing my entire cultural identity just to fit into the confines of American white-ness? My pursuit of white adjacency was fueled by the desire to com-fortably exist in America, but the realization that it would come at the expense of my cultural identity forced me to reconsider my position. I loved my Blackness and my culture. Even the perceived benefits—the nice homes in the burbs, the expensive cars, the high-class education, the lucrative careers—struggled to outweigh the cost for me.

"There's somewhere really amazing that I wanna take you to on New Year's Eve," Alex offered on our ride back to his apartment.

He knew our relationship would crash and burn in the absence of something to steer us away from the thought of what his family's out-right rejection of me meant for our future. He reserved us a table at one of New York City's most exclusive nightclubs and took me shopping for a new dress and shoes. I chose a $127 black cocktail dress from Zara and matching heels from Aldo. Then we stopped in Macy's, where I was to get a free demo of how to apply makeup, which I knew nothing of at the time, in exchange for the purchase of foundation and a couple eye shadow and blush palettes. The gesture lifted my spirits, but his mother's words never stopped ringing in my ears.

I can't believe you would bring a Black person here.

I was only nineteen years old at the time, and the legal age to party was twenty-one in most of the city's big clubs. That meant I had to go back home, where I hadn't been for months, to ask Niki for her ID.

"Oh, didn't know you still live here," Mom reproached when I walked in the front door.

I mumbled something under my breath and darted to Niki's room. She was sprawled out on her bed reading Dean Koontz. She and Mom loved science fiction and books about magic, demons, ghosts, aliens, and the like. I made an exception for Harry Potter but much preferred literature that would give me insights into "the real world."

"Hey, can I use your ID to go out tonight?" I asked her.

I explained to her that Alex wanted to take me to a nice spot, but I was too young to get in. She dug through her wallet and whipped her driver's license out, rolling her eyes as she handed it to me. I made a beeline for the door.

New Year's Eve in New York was one of the most popular going-out nights of the year. Millions descended on Manhattan to stand in the freezing cold just to count down the seconds to midnight and watch the huge ball drop in Times Square. We squeezed through the crowds to get to a rooftop spot not too far away from the festivities. The wind was freezing that year and unrelenting, stinging like a whip as it repeatedly brushed past my face and legs.

When we arrived at the club's entrance, patrons queued in a long line that wrapped around the corner of the street. Those on the line were of diverse backgrounds, but everyone's dress followed a strict code: the women wore tall high heels and peacoats with thick scarves, and carried luxury-brand bags, and the men wore fitted dress pants, leather shoes, and similar winter wear.

"Come on," Alex said, pulling me past everyone on the line.

When we arrived at the front, two six-foot-tall Black men stood with their arms folded, while a white man with his hair pulled into a ponytail holding a clipboard spoke to those near the entrance, deciding whether or not to let them inside.

"Reservations only!" a voice boomed.

I stepped back as Alex charged forward toward the ponytailed doorman. When he caught his attention, they whispered back and forth a couple of times and the man looked down at his clipboard. Finally, Alexei waved me over. I hesitantly joined him. One of the Black men unclasped the velvet rope at the VIP entrance to let us in.

"Come on, babe," Alex said.

We entered an elevator operated by a Black doorman, who pressed "PH" for the penthouse, the doors slowly closed, and the elevator took off, building speed as it climbed dozens of floors. When it slowed and came to a stop, the doors opened onto a magnificent scene. The dimly lit lounge had dozens of bay windows overlooking the twinkling skyline of the city. The view was breathtaking. EDM blasted through the air. A skinny blond-haired woman greeted us at the elevator and escorted us to a table in the farthest corner of the room and removed a RESERVED sign.

"Can I take your coats?" she offered.

I removed my scarf and coat and handed them to her cautiously. Almost everyone in the environment was white, and I couldn't quite decipher how it should make me feel, but I certainly was not comfortable. However, my anxieties were tempered when two women arrived with bottles of Grey Goose vodka and Dom Pérignon rosé. At the stroke of midnight, Alex popped open the bottle of champagne and planted a long, passionate kiss on my lips, then poured me a glass. I was already woozy from having two glasses of vodka cranberry and stumbled under the weight of his affectionate display.

"Let's dance!" he urged, pulling me toward the center of the room and lifting the bottle of champagne to his lips and taking large gulps.

He found a suitable spot and stopped and turned toward me, awkwardly swaying side to side, tossing his arms up and down in the air. I tried to find the rhythm in the music, but Alex's dancing and the cacophony of the electronic sounds mixed with the alcohol and left me disoriented, stepping side to side in an awkward, poorly timed two-step. It wasn't long before my feet began to hurt and I felt the urge to sit. But then the familiar sound of bass and the calm of rhythmic rhyming filled the air. I closed my eyes as hip-hop music pulsed through me, sending my hips swinging left and right. Everything and everyone around me disappeared, and the world in my head was spinning, blurring my apprehensions.

The music twirled me about, its unseen magic guiding my steps. I was lost in the moment. Until a rancid smell infiltrated my nostrils. When I opened my eyes, a white woman was doubled over, throwing up on the floor not too far away from me. It was about 1:30 a.m. and my feet were killing me, so I sat at our table while the world continued to spin around me and Alex continued his offbeat flailing.

"No rush," the server said as she set down a black book with the bill.

I peeped inside and gasped at the four-thousand-dollar tab that stared back at me.

When Niki asked later how my night had been, I could only offer a shrug and a one-word answer: *expensive*.

I was equal parts enchanted and disillusioned. My first experience with *straight* New York City nightlife wouldn't be my last. Niki's ID opened a whole new world of access, and I didn't hesitate to take advantage of it. I began to frequent the city almost every weekend, exploring the most exclusive clubs and lounges, from the Meatpacking District to small, hidden speakeasies in Midtown.

When I hung out with my sister and my Black or minority girl-friends, extended waits in long lines were typical. Only after the door-man glanced at every single one of us from head to toe would we be allowed to pass. Sometimes we wouldn't even get in. Yet when I was with a group of my white girlfriends, we would glide by the velvet ropes with an ease befitting royalty, my averageness and Blackness masked by their presence. I drowned those dehumanizing nights in alcohol.

The environment afforded so much space to white, skinny girls—its main attraction. They were dancers who spent the night atop stages or bars, gyrating their hips while in bikinis or lingerie. Then there were the skinny bottle girls, waving firework-topped bottles whenever someone decided to spend five-hundred-dollars-plus on alcohol. And there were models who were just there to party, their slender hundred-pound frames and long legs giving away their status. I brought myself as close as my economically constrained reality would allow me to and tried to repli-cate the traits that made them all desirable. I went to the gym and exer-cised regularly to maintain the smallest waistline I could. I donned six-inch heels to appear longer and more slender. For *very* special occa-sions, I purchased a Michael Kors clutch to match my outfit, careful to tuck in the price tag, then returned it the next day.

"What a surprise, my friend got me the same clutch!" I would small-talk with the cashier in charge of issuing my refund.

The price of that single accessory was more than what I would spend on food for three weeks, so I made sure to sound extra convinc-ing to avoid any objection.

I leaned toward whiteness in a way that would afford me entry to exclusive spaces, but those maneuvers did not conceal the reality of my Blackness. Among our "average" group, my lighter or whiter friends always received the most attention or perks like free drinks. Despite the hierarchy of our appearance, one thing was certain: we were all there to be consumed. And get trashed. Maybe find a one-night stand. Definitely not to dance too much, because then your feet would hurt within a couple minutes of arriving. I learned the unspoken rules.

Yet something inside of me refused to be contained in that tidy box. I would always find myself shaking my booty to Beyoncé tracks or "doing the stanky leg" (if the music gods bestowed one or two hip-hop songs per night upon me). These moves were often met with stares, as if somehow I'd missed the memo. That particular kind of dancing was inappropriate, not high-class or upscale. I just wanted to hear music by people of color and feel free to express myself through dance, but my environment refused such an allowance.

Until I received an unexpected invitation to a completely different kind of party.

"Yuhall should come down for Carnival!" my aunt suggested to my mother that year.

We hadn't been down to Trinidad in years, and I had almost completely forgotten about the land I had once called home. Auntie Pat promised we could crash at her house, so all we needed to do was purchase flights. Mom urged us to take the trip, hoping it would help the family reconnect after we had all been pulled in different directions in pursuit of our individual lives. It was easy for me to agree to the offer. It was winter and I absolutely despised the cold weather.

When I stepped out of Trinidad's Piarco airport, the warm, humid air hit me as soon as the electric doors slid open. I still had my thick gray wool scarf draped around my neck, and it began to feel like an anaconda threatening to squeeze the air out of me. My boots felt as weighty as two bricks.

"Nah, ah," I stated aloud, "I'm gonna change. It's too damn hot."

I whipped a T-shirt, a pair of shorts, and sandals out of my luggage and changed in the bathroom. A weight was literally lifted from my shoulders as I floated out of the airport, rolling my luggage along, laughingly singing the Lord's praises for blessing us with summer in the middle of winter. It was evening and the sun was descending, turning the sky various hues of orange and pink. The mountains' high and low peaks created the backdrop of the gorgeous scene, stretching east to west as far as my eyes could see. I marveled at the beauty and warmth of my native land, which I had not returned to since childhood. My cousin pulled up and jumped out of his black-rimmed pickup truck, his arms outstretched to take our luggage.

"Allyuh reach!" he exclaimed.

Colin was one of my older cousins and I had met him twice before, once when he spent the summer at Debbie's house as a child and the other time when we came down to Trinidad for a mini vacation years earlier. Despite our limited contact, we always instantaneously picked up where we'd left off, and we shared many of the same interests and musical taste. I gave him a tight embrace and hopped into the truck's back seat with Stefan and Niki. Mom hopped into the front seat and we drove toward her sister's house in Trincity, where I'd spent the early childhood I could now barely remember. Along the way, the bass of soca music blasting from Colin's speakers rattled the car. Though I was no longer familiar with its tempo, I found my body naturally swaying to the sounds.

Trincity was a quiet Trinidad suburb where most of the families were Black and owned their homes. My aunt never put on the air conditioner, so it was impossible to sleep far beyond sunrise. I made good use of my early rising by taking morning jogs, listening to the sounds of chirping birds and marveling at the colorful flora. I loved the bright yellow buttercup trumpets, purple bougainvillea, huge red or yellow hibiscus, and magnificently colorful poui trees, which bloom in neon pink, orange, or sometimes red. I stopped to marvel at a tiny hummingbird hovering in front of a bush, fluttering from flower to flower collecting nectar.

"Mawning, mawning," a voice croaked.

My body tensed with anxiety as I searched for the greeting's origin.

"MAWNING," the voice more loudly insisted.

I turned my head around and caught sight of a woman pouring water into a dog bowl placed near a fence in her driveway. Then I scanned the street seeking the object of her greeting. We clearly didn't know each other, and I couldn't fathom the reason why two strangers would exchange words. Years of living in American big cities and towns taught me to avoid the gaze of strange passersby. I shrugged and continued my jog. But I couldn't run away from those discomforting moments, which seemed to follow me everywhere as I rediscovered my homeland.

"Mawning," a passenger greeted everyone as he climbed aboard a maxi taxi, which would travel along the country's bus route to and from Port of Spain and through Trinidad's eastern towns.

"Mawning," the other riders responded in unison.

I turned my body to the window to avoid him.

"Good day," workers greeted me as I entered local stores.

I rushed past them and grabbed the items on my shopping list hastily.

"Good night, good night," fellow joggers bellowed as they bounced and stretched past me, following the track along the local savannah.

I turned the music up on my iPod, blasting it so loud my ears rang for hours afterward.

"Yuh haddah learn some manners, eh," the same old dog lady from my first encounter chided me one morning.

Her criticism caught me off guard, pushing my defensiveness to its brink. My mind raced with a number of nasty responses, until we made eye contact and everything seemed to pause. She was staring firmly in my direction, her hands on her hips, and for a fleeting moment my grandmother's visage was transposed upon hers. I stumbled backward like someone had delivered a punch that set me off balance.

"Uh . . . ," I started. "I'm sorry, I couldn't hear you over my music."

"Oh, American," she responded, shaking her head. "No blasted respect."

Her disappointment sent my world spinning into disarray. Indeed, all humans with whom I shared a community should've been afforded the common courtesy of a greeting. Acknowledgment from the outside world is a basic way we can validate one another's existence. In that moment, I realized that I was deathly afraid of finally being seen. No longer being able to pass through invisibly forced me to recognize I had spent the vast majority of my life drifting through the outside world unnoticed. The following morning, I dropped my veil of standoffishness and muttered my first "Mawning, mawning" before the old woman could castigate me again. I felt exposed, naked, and uncomfortable for the rest of my run. I was coming undone and hated the feeling of my homeland tugging at the seams my American striving had so carefully sewn together. Little did I know my unraveling had just begun.

"Leh we go a fete tonight," my cousin suggested when he caught me on my way in from my jog. The suggestion gave me a moment of reprieve from my self-doubt. Partying was something I knew quite well by then. After all, I had been exposed to the best New York City nightlife had to offer. That night, I depended on my NYC nightlife savvy to guide me. I picked out the tightest, shortest dress I could find and a pair of matching heels, and I compared possible accessory options.

"What you gonna wear, Nik?" I asked Niki.

She had a similar minidress picked out, with heels that I had once tried but failed to shove my big feet into. I slammed the bathroom door shut behind me and wiggled my way into the dress, then scanned my face in the mirror. I smoothed down my hair with gel and water and applied some eye shadow.

"Whenever allyuh ready," I heard my cousin say from my position hunched in the mirror.

I finally emerged from the bathroom, stepping like a purebred poodle in a dog show. I was the New York pedigree and I was proud of that fact. Despite the reality that my dress likely cost twenty dollars from Forever 21 and had been sewn by tired, underpaid hands on the other side of the world, I felt like I was worth a million dollars. Fashion was something I understood. I was well versed in perfectly accentuating my curves and matching my outfit with high-heeled shoes and a clutch or bag. I was from the fashion capital of the world.

"Buh ya doh have a pair of sneakers?" a perplexed voice interrupted my vanity.

My confidence immediately faded.

"But I thought we were going to a party?" I responded, deflated.

"Ya better find a comfortable pair of shoes and some short pants," my cousin urged.

I changed my clothes, and all of a sudden I felt awkwardly vulnerable again. When I looked in the mirror, I saw an average Black girl, her self-esteem no longer propped up by high-heeled shoes. The anxiety of inferiority was bubbling from within me like a pot of corn-and-oxtail soup on high boil. I had learned to hate this version of myself during my years in New York. Gazing upon my reflection, I saw cellulite, dimples, and a girl many inches away from modelesque, and imagined this alone would be enough to get me turned away from the party, as it would've been back on the East Coast.

I didn't voice my concerns and instead plastered on a smile as if I were comfortable in my basic outfit chosen by my cousin, and I told him I was ready to go.

We arrived at a pier on the western side of the island, where the party called "Insomnia" was set to take place. The area was buzzing with life: thousands of people on the street, scattered among various venues, and food vendors sprinkled in between. Barely any police in sight. It was 2:00 a.m. and my eyes were already growing heavy with sleep. Bottles of alcohol in hand, I wondered if security would stop us and tell us to throw them out. Those thoughts were compounded by my fear that someone there would itemize my flaws and refuse me access to the party. But we just walked by after presenting our tickets. I learned that this was a "cooler fete," so whatever the heck you could fit in a cooler or in your two hands was good to go. And no one was expected to show up glamorous.

We entered into a huge arena with a stage set up, lights flashing everywhere, and girls handing out green bandannas and glow sticks. The bass of the music reverberated into the open air. My cousin motioned for us to follow him, and together we made our way to the front of the stage, plopped our cooler down, and started to have a few drinks.

Within moments, local artists made their way to the stage and the crowd started to move to the music, men and women alike rolling their waists to the beat of soca music. All shades and colors, but mostly Black and brown. All body shapes and sizes.

Soon the music began to take hold of me too, and I could feel myself losing control. My body swayed left to right, my hips shook. Nobody was watching. No one was judging.

By the time Machel Montano, the biggest artist in the country, took to the stage, the rolling waves of revelers were jumping up and down and swinging their bandannas and glow sticks over their heads. The air was electric and everywhere the sea of smiling brown faces beamed at me. The music continued to vibrate my entire being, bringing me to a state of euphoria. I barely noticed the sun was rising—it was already 5:00 a.m.—as it cast its warm glow on my face. As if the heavens had opened, cannons began blasting water from towers overhead. Everyone was drenched. Mud was everywhere. The bass boomed through the atmosphere. And for the first time I was there—actually completely present at a party. Excited and comfortable. The water was washing away any leftover feelings of insecurity or inferiority my American life had instilled in me over the years, leaving me complete, with a new understanding of my entire being. It was my baptism. My hair was plastered to my head, my eyeliner smeared. I was dirty, sweaty, muddy, yet I'd never felt so happy, so connected, and so loved. I locked shoulders with my cousin, my sister, and a few people we had never met before and created a tight circle, bouncing up and down in the muddy water and singing along to every song. When it ended, I collapsed from exhaustion on a nearby beach and came back to full consciousness only when I returned home and awoke in my bed hours later.

"Doh tell meh yuh tired already," Colin said, peeping through the door. "The bacchanal now start."

It was only Sunday morning, which meant the full week of festivities was still ahead of us. As if to undercut its harsh history, Trinidadians take Carnival very seriously. In the 1800s, Carnival was originally meant for white, French plantation owners to celebrate before Lent.[5] Enslaved Africans were unable to participate in the extravagant masquerades and balls indulged in by the planters. However, when emancipation brought freedom, Afro-Trinidadians created their own parallel celebration called Canboulay. They danced through the dark streets, carrying torches, beating drums, and singing songs with cheeky lyrics. They participated in stick fights and wore revealing, outrageous costumes.

Prudish Victorian-era white culture frowned upon the "obscene" nature of African Carnival. White aristocrats outlawed African percussion instruments in an attempt to stomp out the celebration, but then African perseverance birthed the steel pan—the country's national instrument. Plantation owners forced Africans to stop speaking in their mother tongue, but then Africans created calypso music to mock their "owners" and secretly communicate with one another. Canboulay was banned entirely, but it was reborn as J'ouvert, and spectacular costumes were created to represent characters from Trinidadian folklore. Even when suppression came in the form of outright criminalization, the ways of African people endured and eventually established the traditions now associated with the modern festival.

Despite every effort, white people could not restrain the indefatigable African spirit. Soca music empowers that spirit. Artists spend their entire year producing songs that they believe will energize crowds of thousands of revelers and sustain them through days of partying with little sleep. The music crosses all boundaries and unifies the entire country.

Leh meh see yuh jump! Leh meh see yuh wave!

The sound of Machel's voice filled the air as a car drove by, its music blasting and rattling the entire house, and I immediately found the energy to get out of bed.

"I'm ready!" I declared.

That Carnival marked the beginning of my journey into my Black womanhood—a womanhood that was not ruled by American respectability or decency. Where I could bend over and wine—gyrate my hips—on any man, but that did not mean he was entitled to my body. Or drop down into a split in the middle of the road on Carnival Monday and Tuesday in costume, for my own pleasure, not for others to stare. Where my thick thighs and curves would be coveted and celebrated, adorned with feathers and beads. Where men genuinely would want to enjoy my company, not simply get me drunk or into bed. Where I would be beautiful and far from average or mediocre. Where there would be no white gaze to diminish or commodify my self-expression.

Still on a high from my life-changing experience, I boarded the plane back to New Jersey at the end of our trip.

Alexei was waiting for me at the airport as soon as I touched down. I eagerly approached him, charged with stories of my visit to my native land. I felt invigorated and as expansive as Trinidad's northern mountain range, spreading my arms wide to embrace him.

"You're different," he said with a look of distrust and confusion.

I was. But I'd learn that it wouldn't last long.

"Let's go out to eat," he offered, cutting the tension.

I'd spent all that I'd earned at the YMCA teaching swim lessons on Carnival and on enjoying the vacation, so I knew I couldn't afford the expense.

"You know I got you," he said when he recognized my hesitance.

And just like that, I deflated.

Poverty and even intermittent brokeness are detrimental states of being. The sight of a negative bank balance when you are hungry between classes or in need of bus fare to get home after work late at night can trigger a whole cascade of negative thoughts and feelings of self-disgust. *Why didn't I do that extra shift at work? What am I going to do with all of this debt? What if my circumstances never change? Maybe they never will.* The thoughts buzz and hum like a swarm of killer bees. To be Black in America is to constantly battle to avoid awakening that inner voice, which grows more violent with each passing year, as you toil in the service of whiteness, begging for a return on the promise of inclusion. I was exhausted from my dependence on Alexei, and trying to break free of him sent me into spaces where participating infringed on my dignity. But when in America, do as Americans do. I sat in a restaurant of his choosing and contorted myself into the white-majority room, offering only whispers of my trip so that my voice and Blackness wouldn't take up too much space, making others uncomfortable.

I'm worthy.

Include me.

I'm not like the others.

Sure, you can touch my hair.

Each time I minimized myself to fit into the claustrophobia-inducing realm of whiteness, I found myself losing another piece of the big, vibrant confidence I'd found in Trinidad.

Are you Jamaican?

Don't be so sensitive!

There's no racism.

If I dared step too far out of line to question the invisible mechanisms making it necessary to minimize myself, there always seemed to be a retort that would dump the blame for my feelings back in my lap.

It was exhausting, especially after experiencing such Black freedom back in Trinidad. Alex was my partner, and he did make it much easier to execute the routine of existing while Black in white spaces. However, he also constantly denied my reality and my pain, downplaying the difficulties of my Black womanhood.

"See, I told you that all you needed was a break," he proudly declared when I returned from my trip more refreshed and relieved than he had ever previously seen me.

I shrugged and offered an uneasy nod of approval. He reached out to hold my hand and I immediately noticed his was quivering.

"Are you okay?" I questioned.

"Yeah!" he snapped, grabbing his hand back and concealing it in his pocket.

Up until that moment, I had felt like I knew everything about him. Especially because I had been so forthcoming with him about my family and my history. I knew we were from different backgrounds, but I thought that we saw eye to eye on almost everything. I especially believed that he saw me in my full humanity, as Tiffanic, not just another Black girl.

Then late one summer night, I received a message on Facebook.

"You looked so sexy," it read.

I stared at the computer, bewildered for a moment. I scanned the message and read it over and over again. The sender of the four-word statement was my father. At Alex's behest, I had reached out to him before going down to Trinidad. My dad still lived there, and Alex thought it was worth attempting to reconnect.

"Maybe he is a great guy and your mom just kept you away," he said.

I had told Alex about the abuse my siblings and I endured at his hands. I could still remember watching him throw my sister down a flight of stairs, but that did not soften Alex's insistence.

"How would you remember right?" he asked. "You were just a kid. Maybe there was more to it."

He had a point. By that time, I was already nineteen years old and had not seen my father in nearly a decade. Alex wanted to protect me from the status of a fatherless Black girl—just another statistic. To him at that moment, it didn't really matter what kind of man my father was. Only that I was not the type of Black woman who lived life without one. I gave in to his prodding, not wanting to destroy his perception of my exceptionalism. But as I stared back at the message on the screen, contemplating how to respond, I felt both exposed and exhausted. It wasn't the first time that my dad had made statements about my appearance. Before my trip to Trinidad, we had exchanged photos, trying to fill the gap of the time that passed. He had changed very little in the years that we were not in communication, but I had grown from a little girl to a young woman, and he made no effort to pretend he did not notice.

"I was expecting a beauty pageant queen," he said with disdain when he saw the picture.

The ten additional pounds that hung on my curves since my transition to college were obviously a liability. I was not as attractive as he had expected. And for that reason alone, he was terribly disappointed in the woman I had become, despite the many achievements won—obstacles overcome—in his absence. I decided not to pursue reunification after that exchange. I didn't see the point of attempting to rekindle affection for a man who didn't respect me.

By mere coincidence, I saw him at the airport on the day I was leaving Trinidad. When his eyes fell upon me, I noticed a gleam—a twinkle. In anticipation of Carnival and in preparation for bikini weather, I had run 2.5 hours every day with the intention of losing weight. Fifteen pounds lighter, I was something to behold, a daughter to be proud of, a woman who piqued the sexual interest of even her own father. We didn't speak that day. I was already late and did not want to miss my flight.

But now that I was back, he had sent this message. I wondered how my father could have possibly thought it acceptable to say this to his daughter. Why my objectification and sexualization was paramount in our relationship, while my achievements and personality fell by the wayside—unexplored, uncelebrated. I always knew that there was a certain delicacy to femininity that was a liability—that a pink dress turned gray by play would be unseemly. But I didn't anticipate that interacting with my own father would force me to reckon with the precarious nature of womanhood, a womanhood defined by the male gaze, intent, and desire.

When I finally showed the message to Alexei, he shrugged.

"Maybe he didn't mean it *like that*," he reassured me.

"I guess . . ."

I never fashioned a response.

The day Barack Obama was elected president of the United States of America absolved my father—and all men—of wrongdoing in my mind. Obama ran on a simple platform: "Hope." He promised change in America and spent $400 million on his campaign to convince us all that he was the man capable of bringing it about. It was hard not to buy into the dream. He was Harvard Law School educated, a father of two, and an apparently doting husband to a Black woman, and he spoke with equal parts conviction and passion. He had dedicated much of his career to organizing in Chicago's South Side, one of the country's most dangerous Black neighborhoods. He was the child of a Kenyan father and a white, midwestern mother. He could bridge the country's racial divide and heal the nation. It was not long before Democrats were unified in chants of his slogans, "Change we can believe in" and "Yes, we can!" For Black people, a Black man reaching the pinnacle of political success meant they could do it as well. For white liberals, his ascent to the presidency proved America was officially past its racist history.

"I never thought I would live to see the day," my grandmother said during his inauguration.

America's first Black president wasn't the only important man in my life promising change. Alex had hit an impasse in his life, tired of being bogged down by his family's expectation that he find a lucrative career in the midst of a gloomy recession. He wanted us to run away to an exotic world once more, but in a more permanent way.

"Let's move to Hawaii," he suggested late one night.

I toyed with the idea in my mind. I could take online classes so it wouldn't interrupt my schooling. And I knew I could depend on him to help us transition.

"All right," I responded. "Let's go."

"HAWAII!?" my mother cried in disbelief when I told her about my plans. "That's on the other side of the country, and you don't even know anyone there."

I shrugged and allowed her to scold me until she was tired. Finally, she rolled out her largest black suitcase and helped me pack my belongings. I wanted to take everything, because I had no idea how long I would be gone. I tucked away my high-heeled shoes, in case I needed them for a job interview, and several pairs of pants, jeans, shorts, sneakers, sandals, and sunglasses.

"Just be safe," Mom sighed in resignation.

On June 25, 2009, the plane bounced onto the tarmac in Honolulu. Alexei wrapped his arm around my shoulders and squeezed them in giddy excitement. As we walked through the Honolulu airport, my eyes caught a glimpse of a shocking news headline spread across a TV screen near a gift shop. I immediately called my mom.

"Michael Jackson is dead," I told her through tears.

I was in shock and disbelief.

One of America's greatest Black icons had fallen, leaving behind a legacy riddled with self-hate and self-destruction. In the few decades between his rise to music critical acclaim and his death, he had morphed into a white man via multiple plastic surgeries and even changes to his hair follicles. Controversy surrounding the births of his three children loomed, with many skeptical that they biologically belonged to Jackson, because of their white features and the unusual circumstances of the late pop star pairing with an unknown white nurse to conceive the children. When Michael Jackson appeared in public with his nose disfigured and destroyed, I was reminded of the warnings my mother had whispered years earlier while examining ancient Egyptian relics at the Metropolitan Museum.

White explorers shot the noses off so Black people wouldn't know their own history.

I was haunted not just by Jackson's death but by what the summary and trajectory of his life seemed to say about Blackness in America. A clandestine, unescapable force followed me all the way to the beautiful Pacific islands, islands that had been ruled by a Hawaiian monarchy— before being stolen and claimed by white men for America. Alex and I found a relatively affordable place to stay in Waikiki so we could take in the tourist sites before finding a place to rent longer term. We walked along Ala Moana Boulevard and Kalakaua Avenue, the city's busiest waterfront streets, lined with magnificent hotels and luxury retailers like Louis Vuitton, Chanel, Gucci, Saint Laurent, Moncler, Bottega Veneta, Miu Miu, and Golden Goose. The streets were teeming with tourists, mostly Americans wearing colorful Hawaiian-print clothes, cameras in hand. Pan music and reggae bellowed from the insides of stores as people entered and exited. When the buildings ended, we caught a view of the beach. It was various shades of blue and green and almost entirely covered with beachgoers on the sand and surfers bobbing up and down in the sea.

"It's so amazing, babe," Alex said, squeezing me tight while we gazed out at the beauty of the island.

It didn't take long for us to settle into life. I imagined finishing my degree online, getting a job, and never leaving. Alex put a down payment on a small apartment twenty minutes outside the shopping district and purchased two scooters that we used to zoom up and down the city's busy streets. I found a job at a jewelry store and worked during the weekdays. On the weekends, we toured the island and relished its stunning details. The island was one that could've been crafted only by a thoughtful and meticulous God. Its mountain ranges served as the backdrop to an ocean of dolphins, colorful tropical fish, sea turtles, and other exotic marine life. As I became more settled in our little routine, I noticed Alex failing to establish one.

"Ya gonna go get a job?" I asked one night over a dinner of poke, one of the island's famous raw fish dishes.

He shrugged and downed a glass of red wine.

"Yeah," he responded dryly before shaking the last drop onto his tongue. "Imma go get another bottle of wine."

I ironed my uniform and went to sleep early to make sure I would awake in time for my shift at the jewelry store the next morning. Venturing into the streets of Honolulu alone felt both scary and liberating. The transience of the people in the environment made it impossible to ever settle upon a familiar face, but I enjoyed my job, which gave me the opportunity to encounter so many people from all across the U.S. I was treated well, as exotic as the environment I was living in, by the white tourists, who struggled to confine me to an ethnicity on an island where brown-skinned, bushy-haired girls who looked like me could possibly be Hawaiian.

"Oh my God, your hair is so beautiful!" an older white woman said, rushing toward me upon entry to the store.

"Are you a Native?" she asked.

I told her I was from New Jersey, but the answer proved insufficient.

"Nooooo, where are you *from* from?" she continued.

"Trinidad?" I responded, unsure what type of answer she was seeking.

"I knew a beautiful girl like you had to be from somewhere exotic!"

As she detailed her recent trip to Tahiti for her daughter's wedding and the fact that her son was studying marine biology at the local university, I sold her two opal-and-diamond rings with matching earrings that rang up to over ten thousand dollars. She begged for my boss to snap a photo of the both of us, and I obliged. She held the bag proudly and clasped her hand around my waist. The interaction felt intrusive, but I brushed off the feeling and relished the pay increase my sale would generate. I was working on commission and would be entitled to a percentage—white tourist fascination and preoccupation with my appearance had its benefits. I felt proud to be able to afford my portion of the rent and even put aside money to buy my mom a beautiful pearl earring and necklace set I spent hours gazing at through the showcase's glass. It was priced at $9,975, but my employee discount meant I would be able to afford it after only a couple months of working. The jewelry would serve as the perfect consolation gift to my mom, who was now disappointed that I had left her and almost everyone I knew behind for my new island life.

"Come home, baby," Mom urged during our daily phone calls.

She was like a broken record that I eventually learned how to ignore. I enjoyed my newfound sense of independence and freedom. I ate lunch on the beach and went sightseeing on my moped in my free time. I picked mangoes off of the neighbor's tree and quickly drove away with them, as if I had stolen diamonds. I even rented a longboard and took it out to join the sea of surfers. While bobbing up and down as the waters ebbed and flowed, I watched how everyone else laid their bodies along the length of their boards and paddled toward the open sea with their hands, and I did the same. I took note of how they turned to carefully position themselves in front of a wave, paddled even harder, and then popped up into a crouch, riding the wave to the shore. After watching for a few minutes, I positioned myself accordingly and waited for the tug of the ocean's current, signaling a coming wave. The board felt stable beneath me, but my legs quivered as I paddled to build speed. The sea gently carried the board and I hopped up onto my feet, like a wobbly toddler taking her first steps. It felt exhilarating.

"WOOOOOOO!" I screamed into the air.

On the ride home, I sang Bob Marley to myself aloud while cruising on my scooter, the wind blowing through my hair. I had "Buffalo Soldier" stuck in my head after hearing it on repeat in the retail stores, where the reggae artist was beloved. But when I arrived at the apartment, something felt wrong. I walked inside and it was completely dark. I peered through the darkness and found Alexei sprawled on the sofa, an empty liter bottle of vodka on the floor next to him.

"Alex," I whispered.

He didn't move. I tried to shake him awake and he mumbled incoherently under his breath. He smelled sweet and sour, like a pile of trash left in the hot sun. I crept into the bedroom and flicked on the light switch to look for a blanket to cover him with. Something wedged between the mattress and the bed's box spring glittered under the overhead lighting fixture. I tugged at it, and it quickly came loose, revealing a magazine. On its cover a Black woman sat naked on a chair, her legs sprawled and her belly round with pregnancy. My mind struggled to make sense of the image. I continued to flip through the magazine's contents. Page after page revealed pictures of naked, pregnant Black women in various poses. As I flipped through them, Alex's comments over the course of our relationship began to beat in my mind like a percussion instrument.

"I love mixed kids," he often said.

"I know our babies will be cute, because they will be mixed," he would chime in during discussions about our potential future together.

I lifted the mattress and several other magazines spilled out onto the floor, all displaying varying shades of pregnant Black bodies. I collapsed onto the bed and stared at the ceiling. After what felt like an hour, I mustered the strength to collect the magazines from the floor and push them back under the mattress and then went to bed. I'd barely fallen asleep when Alex stumbled into the bedroom and lay down beside me, the sweet smell of alcohol clouding the air.

"I didn't know you were home," he whispered.

He stretched his arm around me and I struggled to refrain from cringing at his touch.

I went to work the next day, but all of a sudden the gazes of white people felt like a violation. I immediately declined the requests to touch my hair or take a picture with me. Customers complained I was rude and unfriendly.

"Please wear your hair in a bun," my boss requested upon my arrival one morning, urging me to adhere to the dress code in the employee handbook, which specified "neat hair."

I pulled my hair into a tight bun but took note of the fact that the young white woman who worked my shift continued to wear her hair freely flowing, without any complaints from management. I began having a hard time getting out of bed and arrived to work late frequently. I struggled to find the desire to take to the ocean and ride waves. I stopped eating lunch on the beach, instead opting to sit alone in a nearby mall's food court.

One day, a hippie-looking white woman wearing a tie-dyed shirt and yoga pants sat down next to me.

"You look like you need an adventure," she offered after a few quiet moments passed.

I shrugged.

"You need to go on a spiritual quest," she continued, disregarding my lack of enthusiasm. "You should go to the Big Island."

"I'll look into it," I muttered.

Her suggestion was like a seed that had been planted, but it would take weeks before it sprouted. I dragged between work and home, failing to see the beauty and welcome that had once felt so embracing. The bottles of wine and vodka continued to pile up at our apartment, and Alex looked increasingly disheveled. And though I never told my mother about any of the things plaguing me, she could sense the dread in my voice whenever she would inquire about my day.

"Come home, baby," she continued to pressure me.

But I wasn't ready to go home yet. A quiet thought had begun to grow louder, pulsating through and revitalizing me. I did have to leave. While riding my scooter home from work, I stopped and pressed my face against the window of an "outdoors and adventure" store and saw a huge backpack and tent staring back at me. I went home and checked my bank account. I had saved half of the money I needed to buy Mom the jewelry set.

"Sorry, Mom," I whispered.

The next day, I bought the backpack and tent and booked a flight to the Big Island. There was no choice more difficult than the decision to end my relationship with Alex and accept that I had to move on. The fear of the unknown paralyzed me. And I was scared I would never find someone better. I had grown so dependent on the security he provided, even if it had come at the cost of my own dignity. It must be human nature to seek comfort and stability, even sometimes in absolutely the wrong places.

I woke up early one morning and began to pack my things into the backpack. I had acquired flower-print dresses and "I heart Hawaii" shirts, which added to my already extensive collection of personal items. I dumped it all onto the bed and scanned my stuff. Then I got a large trash bag and threw the high-heeled shoes, the sandals, and the majority of the clothes into it, making a mental note to drop it off at the local Salvation Army on my way to the airport. I never even told Alex I was leaving.

I arrived at the Big Island's Kona airport and the sun was blazing. I grabbed my backpack and walked toward signs promising EXIT. I had no idea where I was going and had not booked a hotel. I marched down a long road, taking in the scenery. Kona looked like a desert. Its mountain ranges were brown and only sparsely covered in greenery. The air was so hot and dry that it made my throat feel itchy as I trudged farther and farther. Forty minutes into the hike, I wondered if it would ever end. My shoulders had already begun to ache under the weight of everything I was carrying, and I was exhausted, thirsty, and hungry. I stopped and tied the tent to the bottom of my backpack, leaving my hands free to squeeze my thumbs between its straps and my shoulders to relieve the pressure from its weight. Then I spotted a random garbage bin like a mirage in the distance. I jogged up to it, dumped my backpack on the ground next to it, and let out a long sigh of relief. After ten minutes of rest, I reached out to grab the bag and my entire body buckled under its weight. I unzipped it and dumped more things out, inspecting them one by one for necessity. By the time I was finished, only a couple T-shirts, short pants, and my sneakers remained. I continued down the road with a smile spread across my face. Shortly afterward, I stumbled upon the main road and could see a diner in the distance. I plotted my next move over a huge breakfast of pancakes, bacon, eggs, and an extra-large orange juice.

"Um, can you recommend somewhere I could go to stay the night?" I asked my waitress, a brown-skinned woman with round hips and a friendly demeanor.

She scanned me up and down, took a glimpse at my backpack, and raised one finger in the air.

"Sistah, I know the perfect place for you," she said before walking off back toward her cash register.

She scribbled on a colorful sheet of paper and returned to my table.

"Ever hitchhike before?" she asked, extending the paper in my direction.

It was a map with two places circled—the airport and Ho'okena Beach—and a line tracing the highway between them.

"Nah ah," I responded.

"Well, good luck!" she laughed.

I paid the bill and made my way to the side of the highway, holding the map in my hand. Then I extended my thumb in the direction of Ho'okena. A truck crept to a stop in front of me.

"Where ya heading?" the driver asked.

I pointed to the spot on the map, unable to pronounce its name.

"All right, jump in!" he said.

Robert was a white guy from the Midwest who had visited the island a decade earlier and never left.

"What brings you here?" he asked.

I hesitated, then allowed the truth to slip off my tongue.

"I got tired of being the only Black person everywhere I went in Oahu," I finally admitted. He shrugged his shoulders, slightly annoyed by my statement.

"Why do you even care, anyways?" he said. "We are all just people."

It was the response I'd expected from him. I knew that Barack Obama's presidency had given America permission to think of itself as colorblind, an old tool white people used to deflect complicated conversations about race. Any admission of being a color-seeing person was readily dismissed as bigoted, unprogressive, and outdated.

Yet it was only days earlier—when I sat next to a local vendor who wove baskets, hats, and flowers out of palm leaves—that an enthusiastic middle-aged white woman had requested that I be the "local" subject of her photography session.

"I love getting pictures of locals. Do you mind?" she asked in our direction, camera in hand.

I shook my head no and shifted away from the brown-skinned, sun-kissed local man with a huge, protruding belly and jolly demeanor. He looked like the Hawaiian Santa. He spread his arms wide, as if beckoning the camera toward him for an embrace, then plastered a huge grin on his face as she snapped a couple of photos then scurried away.

"Well, now that I know that you are cooperative, I'd like to get a picture too," another white woman chimed in, stepping up to take her place as photographer. It was as if we, "the locals," were a part of the scenery to be captured. Like a tropical fish or brightly colored indigenous flower: a prop in the perfect portrait of island exoticism.

If, by any chance, either of those women mistakenly captured my facial expression in one of the photos, it would be no surprise to me that stories of "unfriendly," "poor" locals would accompany the slideshow images of her vacation. My brown skin was still a liability in Hawaii, as it was in all of America. It left me vulnerable to the degradation of white fetishization. For Robert, as for most, my admission of that truth was more damning than the truth itself.

"Ever camped before?" the truck driver asked.

I welcomed the subject change and confirmed that I had not.

"Well, this will be the perfect experience," he assured me.

The tone of the conversation quickly shifted to excitement as he recounted all of his experiences on Hoʻokena, zooming past miles of desolate land.

"That's all lava fields," he explained, pointing to the expanse of black rock all along the highway. "Up near the beach is greener."

He told me about the nightly jam sessions where campers gathered along with their guitars and drums to sing songs around campfires. Of the pods of dolphins that frequented the bay and the caves that you could hike to that overlooked it. And that he met his wife, a Japanese astronomer, during his first camping trip there.

"That place is magical."

The highway turned into a two-lane road that climbed up a mountain and twisted along a cliff overlooking the island's shoreline. After nearly forty-five minutes of endless storytelling, we arrived at a sign that read HO'OKENA and pointed down a sloping hill.

"I live up that way, not too far away," he explained. "But I'll take you down."

He dropped me near the beach's entrance and promised to return a few days later with his wife to check up on me. I welcomed the kind gesture.

"The guy who collects the nightly camping fee can be a real asshole, so be prepared," he offered as a last piece of advice before driving away.

"Hey!" I called, but he was too far off already to hear me.

I realized I'd become so accustomed to city life, I had forgotten to take cash out of the ATM to keep on hand. The beach had a few tents already set up next to empty park benches and barbecue pits. I found a spot at its farthest end, unfurled the tent, and erected it with the black rods that came in its package. When I finished, I sat in the warm sand, marveled at the ocean surrounded by huge mountains, and congratulated myself for having the balls to move on from Oahu: for trusting that what came next could be better. But as the sun descended, bringing the darkness of night, I encountered the "asshole," who approached with authority.

"I'm here to collect camping fees," he announced in a deep Hawaiian accent.

"Um, I didn't know I had to pay. I'm not from here," I explained, peeping through the darkness at a husky-looking man wearing a headlight, with his face buried in a chart.

He stared at me for what felt like forever.

"You braid your own hair like that?" he finally asked, gesturing to the cornrows I had styled after getting fed up with the heat my Afro was attracting.

"Yeah," I responded uncomfortably. Back on the mainland, I always felt self-conscious sporting the obviously "ethnic" look.

"It's real nice," he said with a bright smile.

We exchanged stories about ourselves and it felt like our connection was instantaneous. I told him about the hardships of finding my way as a young person. He warned me about all of the locals to steer clear of and told me where to get the best "grindz."

"You remind me of my wife," he finally said with a smile. "She's a tough Hawaiian woman."

I gave him the couple dollars I had crumpled up at the bottom of my bag, and no one bothered me the entire time I was there. When Rob came to visit to check up on me a couple days later, I told him about my interaction with the rule enforcer, and his jaw dropped in disbelief.

"Well, I guess I shouldn't be too surprised," he said. "It's the white people who they don't like."

"Whatever, I don't see color," I retorted.

"Touché," he said.

He then offered a change of scenery.

"We are headed Puna side," he said. "You should go see more of the island."

I accepted the ride. Then I was alone again, but on a black-sand beach on the other side of the island, trying to muster the bravery to do something I had never done before. I lifted my shirt over my head, took a deep breath, and pulled the strings of my bathing suit top loose.

Immediately, my mind began to race.

What if people stare at me?

I wish I would've spent more time at the gym.

I hate my thighs. . . .

I waited for a moment, took a deep breath, and tightly gripped the strings that remained clasped in my hand, then looked around to take note of any wandering eyes that were possibly staring in my direction. The other beachgoers were all casually sunbathing nude, splashing one another near the shoreline, or bouncing up and down, carried by the rhythm of the sea. No one even looked my way. The only person making me uncomfortable was me. I had to get over myself and my insecurities. And being publicly nude on the beach was the next step in my "mind over matter" approach to becoming more comfortable with my body.

As a Black woman in her early twenties, I had struggled with my body for most of my life. I remembered my mother bringing home a bag with two white training bras and presenting them to me when I was eight years old.

"These will help you feel more secure," she promised. I hadn't yet realized the reason why I should feel insecure, but I accepted her gift and squeezed my body into one of the garments. The bra fit snugly around the sides, providing support for my breast buds, which had just begun to sprout.

"It fits?" she asked.

"Yeah," I murmured with a shrug. Then I ran out of the house to play. When I came back inside some hours later, I stared into the mirror at my chest covered in what seemed like an odd, unnecessary contraption and hoped I wouldn't have to wear it every day. By the time I turned sixteen, those sentiments completely changed: I couldn't go a moment without wearing a bra. I loved how perfectly round and perky my breasts looked with one on and hated the idea that gravity would somehow cause them to sag or droop. I spent the years between that moment and the one on the beach in Hawaii trying to alter my appearance.

Diets. The gym. Running. Swimming. Low-carb. Zumba.

Psychologically, I was at war with a pathological set of standards that found fault even in "perfection." I did not understand that I could not fix what had already been made perfect. A delicate process stitched together the patchwork of tiny traits and characteristics that predetermined, with precision and ease, my weight, my height, my skin color.

When I stepped onto the nude beach and looked around at the other bodies peacefully bare, I didn't let the insecure thoughts that rushed through my mind deter me. I was accustomed to and refused to be controlled by fears of imperfection. Perhaps six-pack abs would make me feel more confident. Or perfectly perky breasts. But all I had was my perfectly imperfect body, and I had to be okay with that. I released the strings of my bathing suit top, letting my breasts bounce freely as I stepped out of my shorts and bottoms, then threw my clothes aside and stretched my arms up wide, letting the sun kiss every inch of my skin.

You are naked. . . . Now what? Better reach for the towel and cover up before someone sees, my mind urged.

I laughed at the thought and slowly began taking small steps—*left foot . . . right foot . . . left foot*—toward the ocean, the curves of my body bouncing with every step. I paused when I reached the shoreline to watch the waves crash against the sand, then took a deep breath and dove in. The cool water rushed over my naked body, sending chills up and down my spine. I splashed and swam carelessly, and when I finally grew tired, I lay floating on my back in the water, my nipples erect, peeking out of the water. The warmth of the sun caressed my face. The chilly ocean rhythmically moved my relaxed body up and down to the beat of the current.

And my mind was completely silent.

You are so pretty for a Black girl, an imaginary whisper intruded.

I dove deep into the water to escape it. I walked for miles. I climbed mountains. I hitchhiked. I slept on black, green, red, and white sandy beaches. I encountered other travelers and spent nights sleeping in caves or out under the stars. I swam with pods of dolphins and learned how to scuba dive. I marveled at the sight of miles and miles of lava fields and the oddity of houses built atop them. I laughed and told jokes and cried recalling the pain of far too many heartbreaks. I learned of the history of the Hawaiian people and how a coalition of businessmen from the United States invaded their homeland and staged a coup d'état against its then-monarch, Queen Lili'uokalani. I ate more poke bowls and groaned in delight as the taste of fresh tuna, soy sauce, and avocado titillated my taste buds.

And I got to watch as a mama whale gave birth to her baby. People gathered all around—some with binoculars, others with camera phones or other techie gadgets—to catch a glimpse of the majestic miracle. I imagined the long journey ahead for that whale and her newborn. To-gether they would travel thousands of miles, aided by the currents of the vast Pacific Ocean, to Alaska. Sharks, boats, and debris could threaten their mission. Yet every year, whales made the journey to this distant Hawaiian island to give birth near its shores and then returned after a few months to feed in the cool Alaskan waters. I, too, found myself yearning for home. There are no words to describe the humbling beauty that is the Big Island. A beauty that makes all of life's hardships seem trivial and insignificant. But Trinidad and Tobago was drawing me home like the ocean's current.

"It's time to end your walkabout," Mom joked—referring to the Aboriginal coming-of-age ritual—during one of our calls, but I knew she was concerned that I was so far away.

Niki called with a surprise the next day. "I got you a Carnival costume!"

Mom had put her up to it, knowing just how to tempt me away from

Hawaii. I wanted to parade down the streets, eat bake and shark on Ash Wednesday, and then pass out on the beach. And most important, I wanted to feel at home.

"Go with the flow!" friends and acquaintances in Hawaii often urged—calling back to the lava that slowly creeps down the sides of gigantic erupting volcanoes. I booked a flight and left a couple days later, waving goodbye to the land that had delivered on its promise to reawaken me.

I arrived at Trinidad and Tobago's Piarco airport with a newfound sense of confidence and pride. I was ready to step into my new womanhood—to be free in and proud of my own body. Niki had chosen blue-and-yellow bikini-style costumes for us that were covered in rhinestones and came with large feathered headpieces. We decided to stay at the Hilton—where five of us (Niki, my mom, Stefan, my aunt, and I) packed into a room with one king-size bed—to have better access to the street festivities that bring the nation's capital to a standstill. During Carnival, all streets in Port of Spain are closed and vehicles are redirected, causing major traffic jams. Area businesses and government buildings are shuttered and boarded in anticipation of the two-day unofficial-holiday mania.

The Hilton provided the perfect headquarters for us, nestled in its own tropical oasis on a hill, a short walk down to the Savannah. Although all of Port of Spain is a Carnival stage, the Savannah is dubbed the "Home of Carnival" and is the heart and center of the action. On the morning of Carnival Tuesday, the anticipation was palpable, and revelers swarmed the hotel. Costumes adorned melanated bodies of all shapes and sizes. My mom and my sister helped me get prepared for "the road." Mom helped me secure and fasten the bikini-top ties to my elaborate ensemble. Then my sister carefully traced my eyes with eyeliner and covered my eyelids with blue eye shadow. The finishing touches of colorful glitter and face gems were added to give pizzazz. I pulled on a pair of sheer, nude-colored tights and then carefully wiggled my way into the bottom of my bikini and secured the two strings attached to it at each side. When I gazed at myself in the mirror, I was stunned by my regal reflection. I donned my headpiece as if it were a crown, solidifying the majestic sight.

Then the sound of an unfamiliar voice and bass came crashing through our hotel room.

Jump up, jump up
Jump and put your hands up
Paaaalaaaance

A Carnival truck blasted music that thundered and vibrated the floor beneath our feet. My heart was pounding in excitement. Without exchanging a single word, Niki and I grabbed our fanny packs, stuffed them with some money, and rushed toward the door. This was our second time partaking in the festivities, so we were more familiar with exactly what we would need to keep the party going all day long.

The "bacchanal" had begun.

Revelers were already flooding the streets of the Savannah, creating an ocean of glittering colors, making their way to the stadium, where judging points were erected along a stage in the center in preparation for the festival competitions. We scanned the crowds looking for costumes that resembled ours to help us distinguish our band from the others, but our attention was quickly diverted. Two bare-chested men in short pants emblazoned with "Tribe" were barreling toward us, their hips rolling as their feet fell to the rhythm of the music with each step. Their arms were extended in invitation and we didn't hesitate to take the cue. I turned toward one with chiseled abs and dark-brown skin that shimmered in the sun and rolled my hips in time with his. Niki shrieked in surprised delight as his friend lifted her from the ground as he continued to dance and gyrate. It didn't take long for us to locate our own band, YUMA. Each band varies in size and provides its patrons with its own unique "on the road" experience. Big trucks not only provided the music but also served as mobile clubs for Carnival bands and their consumers. Bar service, meals and snacks, live performances, lounging areas, and even bathroom and powder-room service were all part of the mobile package. YUMA—a large-scale band of about ten thousand members—was known for its young, uninhibited crowd, which embraced the wild, carefree abandon that my sister and I had grown to love. We soon found our rhythm, chipping and wining in cadence with the music alongside a moving truck labeled BAR, and I ordered two rum-and-pineapple drinks.

"Make it with love, sexy," I suggested, cajoling the cute male bartender into making the drinks extra strong.

Although drinks were free, too many would mean constant trips to the moving "potty truck," which could become a chore in a band this size. And frankly, I just didn't want anything to take me out of my zone. My souped-up drinks were handed over with a wink, and I passed one to my sister before turning to get swept up in the crowd. The frenzy heightened as it was announced that the band would be crossing the biggest judging point, at the Grand Stand in the Savannah.

As we entered the gates of the arena, thousands of spectators were cheering us on as we waited to ascend the stage. Security formed a barrier, preventing us from entering before it was time. On their cue, hundreds of masqueraders charged forward as confetti erupted, cascading and fluttering like sparkling butterflies. The experience was surreal. Emboldened by the crowd, the masqueraders brought out their best tricks. Our fellow revelers knew how to put on a show. Waists gyrating, feet bounding, hands reaching for the sky, faces elated, we cast aside the heavy robes of respectability and self-control and lost ourselves in moments of pure joy. Too soon we started our descent off the stage and back onto the streets, but only to continue celebrating our liberation well after the sun went down. The sound of Destra's song "Bacchanal" was stuck in my head, playing on repeat:

> *It's in my blood, it's in my veins*
> *Can't wash it off, I'm forever stained*

CHAPTER 5

———

Moving the Goalposts
and Gaslighting

During the Revolutionary War, around nine thousand African Americans became Black Patriots and fought beside white men to secure the country's freedom from Britain.[1] Many were lured by promises of freedom and the hope of first-class citizenship in exchange for bearing arms. But postwar America conferred little reward on Black Patriots. Many enslavers reneged on their promise to free captive Africans who fought in the war. And after the war, some states in the North and South even restricted Black participation in the military. In 1792, Congress outright banned African Americans from military service. The goalposts—access to the elusive American dream—always seem to move out of reach for Black people.

By the time slavery was outlawed, respectability became the manual that instructed generations of Black Americans on how to finally find a place in the white world. We were told how to coif our coils and bring them under control with texturizers, perms, hot combs, curlers, and flat irons; how to speak in a way that brought about the assumption of our learnedness; and how to wardrobe ourselves in white symbols of success like pearls, cocktail dresses, and tailored suits. We were told to aspire to obtain a higher education to secure opportunity and wealth by becoming doctors, lawyers, politicians, and CEOs. We were lectured on how to appeal to the moral righteousness of the white man and vilified for our own failures, which had allowed us to fall prey to America's systemic racism. We were given a religion that literally cast images of a white man as God. These were the rules of respectability reflected in Bill Cosby's famous "pound cake speech," given in 2004 during an NAACP award ceremony to commemorate the fiftieth anniversary of the *Brown v. Board of Education* Supreme Court decision, which integrated schools. In the speech, Cosby ridiculed the Black community and blamed single-parent households, the use of African American Vernacular English, lack of personal responsibility, and a whole host of other behaviors for the failure of Black America. He even blamed Black people for the police's use of deadly force against them.

His solution to the dilemma of the Black struggle was a simple one: hard work and education. Much of Black America agreed with his assessment. They urged their children to be twice as good as white children. They told us to go to college, that obtaining degrees would solve the problem of inequality and racism. Despite the full implementation of all of these rules of respectability, the Black people of my generation still somehow fell short of reaching the "promised land." For many young Black people, it felt like no matter how hard we tried to get ahead, an unseen force was always moving the goalposts.

As a young adult, I was constantly reassured that by obtaining a higher education, I could somehow summon the perfect middle-to-upper-class life, like a magician pulling a rabbit out of a top hat. America promised that a college education was the surefire way for Black people to bootstrap themselves out of hardship, and we obliged. The federal government made it easier than ever to secure loans to pay for "higher education," and I made sure to squeeze every dime I could get out of the system to buy my way into a good life. I managed to secure all of the necessary credits to complete my associate's degree, so my time at community college was officially over and I had to figure out what to do next. I was back in New Jersey with my mom, and according to the plan laid out for me by the state, I was supposed to go on to the local state college.

"But where do you *want* to go?" a counselor asked me. "You look like an artist."

No one had ever asked me that before. And no counselor had ever seen anything in me before either. She handed me a pamphlet for a school she thought would be a good fit. It was a liberal private school in the heart of downtown Manhattan that touted students' freedom to design their own curriculum and branded itself as a home for intellectuals and freethinkers exiled by the mainstream. I identified with the brand and immediately applied. Weeks later, I received my acceptance letter from the school and stared at it, mouth agape in disbelief: I was going to go to school in downtown New York City. I beamed in great delight until my eyes settled upon the cost of tuition: $1,200 per credit. The most joyful moments for a Black woman are often riddled with anxiety and uncertainty. *How will I pay tuition? Where am I gonna live? How am I gonna afford to travel? I know Mom isn't gonna like this price.*

"Don't even worry about it. I'm sure they will give you a scholarship or something," Alex responded coolly when we spoke on the phone.

He had moved on from our breakup and also left Hawaii, taking up residence in California and registering for master's classes at Berkeley, which his parents promised to pay for as long as he finished the degree. But I knew there was no way in hell I could disclose the cost of the tuition to my mom or sister. Mutiny and outrage would certainly ensue. As would the warnings about student loan debt.

"Don't ruin your life before you even get to start it," Mom would lecture.

Stefan, however, shared my desire to escape into the bright lights of the city, drawn to them like a mosquito to a bug zapper. I sought him out for words of encouragement.

"That's perfect!" he exclaimed. "One of my friends is looking for someone to take over her apartment in the Lower East Side while she travels with her husband."

The LES was one of the oldest neighborhoods of the city, where white immigrants had made their homes in crowded tenement buildings. It later became an iconic art scene and was home to some of America's most notable photographers, poets, and musicians, including Lady Gaga. I fell asleep that night dreaming of the new life I would have in the Big Apple. One full of artsy, intellectual friends who still loved to shake their asses to hip-hop and display their empty ring fingers when Beyoncé called all the "Single Ladies" to the dance floor at the club. Maybe I could even find an amazing boyfriend to ride the subway with hand in hand and who would become my husband in front of my legions of aforementioned artsy, intellectual friends. More than anything, I imagined my life in NYC would be one where I would finally feel at home and fully embraced. America had won me back.

The apartment was located in a building on Ludlow, a bar-lined street with tiny boutiques that sold expensive leather boots and fashionable trench coats and ran between East Houston and Delancey, which served as the last outlet onto the Williamsburg Bridge for cars. I arrived an hour before our appointment, just to take in the scene. It was a cool, comfortable summer day, and millennials were busy buzzing all about, pouring in and out of storefronts like bees swarming a hive. A group of fashionably dressed young Black people emerged from one of the bars, a trendy spot named Pianos, so I figured it would be hospitable to me, a hard-to-miss Black woman sporting a gigantic curly afro. I sat by the bar, bobbed my head, and mouthed the lyrics to Biggie's "Juicy" as the roomful of twentysomethings of every color danced and conversed all about me. I wondered who among us would be the next big artist.

My phone buzzed and broke my trance: it was my brother's friend Pam texting me that she was ready for me to come pick up the keys to the place. I rushed out of the bar and sped down the block toward the address, two blocks away according to my GPS. When the robotic voice in my phone declared, "You have arrived," I figured I must've put in the wrong address, because there was no entrance to an apartment building anywhere in sight. I stumbled into a Thai restaurant, with a completely open storefront and outdoor seating, for directions.

"Right next door," the young server assured me.

I stepped outside, searching for the door as if I were on Platform 9 ¾ and I was a lowly Muggle unable to perceive the boundary that protects the magical world from intrusion. I paced between the bodega at the top of the block and the restaurant two more times before my eyes fell upon the old, dingy door covered in moldy, grimy-looking steel. I pushed the button beside a faded label that read "Apt 21."

"Hey, come on up!" A cheery, staticky voice erupted from the intercom, and a loud buzz followed. I pushed the door open onto a long, dark hallway barely illuminated by fluorescent bulbs. The walls were dirty and gray, so I pressed my arms close to my body to avoid contact and booked it to the stairwell. I had been warned that the apartment was a fourth-floor walk-up, but nothing could've prepared my lungs for the workout. I triumphantly arrived in front of the door, heaving, my excitement still intact.

"Come on in!" Pam said as she flung open the door.

She was a biracial girl who wore her straightened hair up in a ponytail and a big comfortable shirt and jean shorts. We exchanged quick greetings and embraced each other like longtime friends. Then I entered what appeared to be the kitchen, based on the fact that it had a stove and a sink—nothing more. The room was just big enough for me,

Pam, and her husband, Tom, a scruffy, blond-haired guy from England, to crowd into.

"It's a little quaint, but the neighborhood is so amazing," Pam offered. My opinion of the space must've been quite apparent on my face. I scanned the rest of the room to discover a large wooden workman's table with drawers overflowing with papers and covered in nails, with a hammer, mail, and magazines rounding out the scene.

"Let me show you the room!"

The bedroom had vaulted ceilings and four huge windows overlooking the busy street below. It was decorated with a loft bed and a large TV mounted to the wall right beneath it. I was sold. The deal was I would pay $600 per month for the room and share the apartment with Michael, a Puerto Rican guy from the Bronx who had a heavy New York accent and loved to cook and laugh. The place was a steal by NYC standards. The average rent in the area was $3,300, but Pam's apartment was rent stabilized—a law enacted in 1969 to help New York natives continue to afford the forever-increasing cost of living. She had inherited the apartment, locked in at a relatively discounted price, from her mother, who had moved in decades earlier and left her the apartment to retire to Florida. I knew there wouldn't be another opportunity to secure an affordable place. In 1993, under the influence of real estate industry lobbyists, New York City legislators passed bills that would make it easier to flip rent-stabilized apartments and condos back into profitable housing by increasing the price after each new lease agreement.[2] Attracted by the allure of the big city, which their parents had escaped for the safety of redlined suburbs, younger whites provided an influx of prospective tenants who could afford the price increases. Over the next decade and a half, the city lost over 152,000 rent-stabilized apartments. Fortunately, Pam's was not one of those.

"Mom, I got an apartment in the city!" I announced while walking through the LES on the way home.

"Oh," she responded.

Worried by her lack of enthusiasm, I pressed her further.

"Aren't you happy?" I asked.

Mom feigned excitement, but I knew she was hurt. Months earlier, a FOR SALE sign had been erected on our North Bergen rental house's front lawn by the landlord, forcing Mom to spiral into fear over housing insecurity once more.

"I need to buy a home for us," she told me when I caught her desperately scrolling through online real estate pages one night.

Mom understood that homeownership was integral to the American dream, which could be easily stolen by a landlord with grand ambitions. She needed to find a place for us to settle, and by then we were all too exhausted and wary to contemplate another interstate move. Though she was making a comfortable salary as a hospice nurse for a top agency, it still wasn't enough to afford the cost of living in the Northeast. To balance her monthly expenses, she depended on credit cards and loans, and she sometimes failed to pay them on time, resulting in penalties to her credit score. She didn't have the finances to afford a house, and certainly not one in the neighborhoods we had grown accustomed to. But one day she stumbled upon a saving grace: foreclosed homes and FHA loans.

The government-backed program was a lifeline for first-time home buyers who wouldn't otherwise qualify for mortgages from big banks. With eased credit requirements, applicants who qualified could submit smaller-than-average down payments. Mom immediately found a house well within her purchasing means: a two-bedroom, two-story, single-family home in Greenville, Jersey City.

"So you aren't going to move in with me?" she asked when I told her about Pam's apartment.

I stumbled over my response.

"N-no, Ma, I—I can't live there," I stuttered.

Only weeks earlier, she had asked Stefan and me to accompany her to view the house. We turned onto JFK Boulevard and drove through the long intercity stretch, watching as the street numbers descended and the faces crowding the streets transitioned from white to brown and then finally Black. When we arrived at the corner where the house's street name intersected with the boulevard, we turned left along a public park where two drug addicts were slumped on benches as children rode by on bikes and boys and men played basketball in the fenced-in courts. I didn't need to see more of the neighborhood or even view the house to know there was no way in hell that I wanted to move there, but Mom remained steadfast in her mission to nab a stable living situation. The car cruised down Dwight Street past Bergen Avenue, a street filled with shops, hair salons, and boarded-up buildings, and onto Martin Luther King Drive, where I pointed out a building with a sign that read FRIENDS OF THE LIFERS YOUTH CORP. There were Black people everywhere—mothers pushing strollers with their older children walking beside them, men standing idly on corners chatting in large groups, and teenagers loudly exchanging jokes and laughter. At the top of the block on which the house was situated, a group of fifteen or so Black men congregated in an empty parking lot. Their eyes locked onto our vehicle, following it down the street as we passed. We pulled up to the front of the house and Mom offered words of encouragement aloud.

"This looks nice," she said.

The house had an orange brick facade and was tightly nestled between homes on each side, separated only by tiny alleyways. A group of children walked by loudly chastising one another and peered into the car as they passed. The neighborhood conjured memories of Houston— the insecurity, ostracism, fear, and uncertainty. My hands became sweaty and began to tremble, so I stuffed them in my pockets so Mom wouldn't notice. I didn't want to ruin her big moment.

The real-estate agent let us into the house. It was cozy, with wooden floors, walls painted in burnt orange and red, and a newly renovated bathroom with modern-looking gray textured tiles. The house also had a deck that overlooked a tiny backyard where a lily magnolia tree bloomed pink flowers. Mom was immediately sold.

"I want the house!" she enthusiastically told the real-estate agent.

"We can't move here, Mom," I whispered when the real-estate agent turned his back, shuffling through his briefcase to find the paperwork. "This is the hood."

Still, she left that day application in hand and intention set. That house was the piece of the American dream Mom could afford to call her own, and she refused to let the opportunity for stability slip through her fingers. At that point, we had very different worldviews and priorities. Unaware of the violence and trauma her kids had endured back in Houston and overwhelmed by the constant anxiety of being pushed out of the rentals she made into homes, Mom just wanted to plant roots for our tiny family. Exposed to the torments of Black life in America in a way she was not, I merely wanted to survive, and I knew living in an urban neighborhood could mean more exposure to violence, trauma, and possibly even death. To sway my mother's well-settled opinion, I inundated her with crime statistics about the area. I warned her of the increased likelihood of getting robbed, carjacked, raped, or even murdered. I hoped exposure to the numbers would arouse fear, anxiety, and hopelessness. It did, but not enough to dissuade her. Our paths had finally diverged, cutting the proverbial umbilical cord.

"Mom, please be careful," I warned her from the safety of my NYC apartment.

I half jokingly told her to wear a bulletproof vest while walking Sam, but she didn't laugh.

"I hear the gunshots at night," she replied.

I felt sick.

I pushed aside my anxieties and headed to my new university's campus to register for classes and figure out by what miracle I would find a way to pay for it. To save some money on travel, I got around the city on an adult-size kick-push scooter. I felt like a star shooting across a universe full of endless possibilities as I flew past cars stuck in traffic, my large, curly Afro blowing in the wind. The New School's main building was located on Fifth Avenue between Thirteenth and Fourteenth Streets, and I felt so proud and important walking through its front doors. I had finally made it to the city—the place where I could realize all of my dreams.

Alex was right: I did find a way to pay for the first semester.

A combination of government grants, loans, and the school's scholarship program ensured I could register as a full-time student. With the simple click of a mouse, I secured thousands of dollars from the government to pay for my higher education, believing that I would most assuredly be able to get a job to pay it all back after I graduated. Though I had no idea what type of career I wanted to pursue, I knew I loved to read and write and also desired to find my place in America. I desired acceptance and to feel like I mattered, just as much as I wanted to feel intellectually challenged. When I learned that the school's students also had access to NYU's Bobst Library, I perused every floor of the twelve-story building, basking in the splendor and vastness of the world of millions of thoughts that I could effortlessly leaf through. I sat for hours in the computer lab scrolling through JSTOR, an online database of academic studies. I was on a search for something, but I couldn't quite quantify or qualify precisely what it was.

Then the recurring dream started. In the dream, I would be standing on the other side of the Hudson River in the park where I watched fireworks as a child. Planes would begin to descend from above, zooming by in the direction of New York City. And then, one by one, they would start dropping bombs on the unsuspecting city. In the dream, I would feel an acute sense of shock and horror. As I looked around at my environment, I would recognize that I was all of a sudden no longer in New Jersey but actually back in my childhood home in Trinidad. I would awaken with my heart racing, drenched in sweat. I tried to work through the dream with many of my friends and family members.

"I just feel so on edge now every time I'm outside in New York," I told my mom on the phone.

"Just come home, baby," she coaxed, her usual refrain.

But I had no home. Mom had moved out of the North Bergen house, dumping the things that wouldn't fit into the smaller Jersey City house. Niki had moved back to Trinidad after failing to find secure employment, despite completing her bachelor's in counseling and nearly finishing her master's. Stefan had joined her right after he finished his degree as well, and they were sharing an apartment atop a high hill in the lush green mountains of Maraval, not too far away from the country's popular Maracas Beach.

"It's impossible to find a job and these New York gays are so racist," Stefan had lamented before booking his one-way ticket back to his native land.

Sam, our family dog, had died shortly after Mom moved into her new home. I sold my newly (credit-card) purchased digital camera to pay to put him down after doctors diagnosed him with cancer and he couldn't get up or walk any longer.

"He looks like he is sleeping," I whispered to Mom as the vet injected the deadly serum into one of Sam's legs.

I held my body stiff and erect as we exited the vet without Sam and put on sunglasses to conceal the tears filling my eyes. Then I locked myself in my room back in the city, buried my face in a pillow, and cried for an entire day. Mom had realized her dream of finding a place where she could anchor her family, but by then it was too late, because we had all set sail on our individual quests for self-fulfillment. The chapter of our all living together as a family had officially closed with Sam's death. And there was no way that I would steer my life in the direction of Black pain and suffering.

"Just come home," Mom urged again not too long after Sam's passing.

"That place isn't my home," I shot back.

The silence on the other end of the phone made me immediately regret my words.

"Okay, baby," she said.

I could tell she was choking back tears. I muttered, "Goodbye," barely getting the word out before she hung up. I fell back onto my bed, devastated. Mom had cast her anchor, but by then we had all set sail in search of brighter horizons. It felt like I had abandoned her at sea on a boat with no motor, surrounded by sharks and all manner of threats to her safety, in the dark of the night. I quelled the shame, anger, and anxiety bubbling within me by making a single promise: I would eventually return to save her and tow her to safety. I just needed to beat the system first.

I was equipped for the task. I had spent my life quietly taking notes about navigating America as a Black woman, and it was finally time to put my hacks to the test. I was going to be Black and successful, and I knew just how. I needed to look the part—Black and exotic, but not too Black or too exotic in a way that would offend white sensibilities. I kept my hair wild, bushy, and untamed but made sure to use a texturizer to soften its kinky texture. I wore African prints and clunky jewelry but shopped only at Forever 21, Zara, Urban Outfitters, or H&M. I needed to maintain a 3.8 GPA or above or risk being "average," which was unacceptable for Black women. Macintosh had swept through universities, becoming the gold standard of computing, so I invested in a MacBook to familiarize myself with the brand that had become the computer of my generation. I had to fund all of my "needs," so I opened multiple credit cards. Every swipe brought me one step closer to achieving the acceptable self I knew my environment would deem most worthy. I sauntered into class, fashionably attired and eager to participate in every discussion. I turned in my papers early and spent hours reading and studying in the library. I researched internship opportunities to get myself "through the door" at big magazines and newspapers in the city. I worked forty hours a week teaching swim lessons at a gym, including early-morning shifts on Saturdays and Sundays. I got drunk every evening to help my racing mind find peace so I could fall asleep at night. I traveled for hours every day, cruising on my scooter across dozens of blocks and avenues or bouncing among subway cars, buses, and light-rails. I was sprinting a marathon, propelled by the fear of falling and being left behind.

I carefully crafted my identity around the idea of meritocracy and "climbing the ladder." My dreams and aspirations were all tangled up in "success"—in escaping the conditions of Blackness. Yet although I could name my destination, I couldn't really define success. And I hadn't thoroughly investigated what I would have to sacrifice in pursuit of it. One class changed that: Economic Stratification in the U.S. Economy. I registered for the class after its description in the school's course book promised it would reveal the secrets of America's economic racial hier-archy. Reflexively, I scoffed at the class's goal of examining racism, as if it were far-fetched.

What racism? I thought to myself, still spellbound by the myth of meritocracy that promised anyone could be as successful as they pleased, regardless of their skin color.

I donned my fashionable costume and hopped aboard my scooter on the class's first day, almost certain that there would be little to glean from a professor who was clearly stuck in America's past—but unable to resist the lure of the description.

"Why do you think we see all of these disparities between white and Black outcomes in America?" Professor Darrick Hamilton, the first Black man I ever had as a teacher, asked us on the first day.

"Because niggas are lazy," I casually responded, prompting quiet chuckles from my peers, who were mostly white.

I felt pleased with my retort and a smug look swept across my face.

"Well, that is one theory," Professor Hamilton responded, unfazed by my remark.

He then proceeded to distribute a class syllabus that would change my life and finally force me to confront my own role in America's hierarchical caste system. Week after week, Professor Hamilton slowly uncovered the hidden reality of the system of white supremacy and Black oppression, forces that had been acting on my life for years. He explained that race was a social construct and that in America, a social hierarchy exists that positions whiteness at its pinnacle and Blackness at its dark depths. What began as a justification for the enslavement of the first African people who arrived on the country's shores as free laborers for European settlers, who had escaped their homeland to chart their own destiny and find religious freedom and economic success, grew into the bedrock of America's economy and stability. How else could God-fearing men and women brutally shackle, torture, and force the labor of millions of Africans but to relegate them to a social standing similar to that of animals and beasts? Over centuries, that system, created for economic gain, corrupted the entire social fabric of the country. It was embedded in laws, culture, language, and schools. Professor Hamilton lectured on redlining, the wealth gap, school tracking, income inequality, and even colorism. In coming to that realization, I was relieved of so much guilt. I finally understood the hidden lessons in

African American music that spoke of the inescapable struggle. And why I had fought so hard to distance myself from Blackness. Systemic racism was a force clandestinely acting upon the lives of Black people like gravity compressing us into a tiny box of hardship and pain. I could forgive myself for simply wanting to break free of that box. But I was exhausted. Navigating the twists and turns of redefining myself and my understanding of my relationship to America as a Black woman had left me dizzyingly disoriented. Racism had begun to reveal itself in much of my own thinking and the circumstances that surrounded my life. I became increasingly cognizant of the many ways in which race was entangled in all of my friendships and relationships.

I leaned on my old friend Jessi for support as I tried to catch my breath after classes ended that summer. I couldn't even begin to explain the pain of confronting the damaging truth of what it meant to be Black in America.

"You found your rich boyfriend yet?" Jessi asked over a Colombian lunch.

I hadn't even come close, and it had everything to do with the color of my skin.

"Don't be so dramatic," Jessi said patronizingly when I tried to explain how finally confronting racism was weighing on me.

But what I had once thought was America's "dark past" was now casting a noticeable shadow on my present. It was growing increasingly apparent to me that there were no heights to which a Black woman could climb without the very real threat of a single shove or kick sending her violently tumbling down and crashing into hardship.

It was 2013, less than a year after Whitney Houston, the country's eighties and nineties music icon, was found dead, drowned in the bathtub of a Beverly Hills hotel room after an apparent cocaine-induced heart attack. She was only forty-eight years old. Her death coincided with that year's Grammy Awards, which commemorated her career with a nearly hour-long tribute. I watched the celebration of her life, captured in a montage of videos and images of her greatest performances as other stars gushed over the singer, with equal parts sadness and relief. Her death signaled the end of a heartbreaking saga—the great rise and fall of one of America's most visible Black female pop stars. Before her death, the spectacle of Whitney's life—her tumultuous marriage to Bobby Brown, her drug use, her declining career and erratic interviews—had begun to overshadow her talent and success. "Crack is wack" had become infamously associated with the singer after she made the declaration during a 2002 interview with Diane Sawyer. Her husband was charged with battery after he assaulted her, leaving visible cuts and bruises on her face. Bravo earned its highest ratings by airing *Being Bobby Brown*, a reality TV series that documented the couple and broadcast many of the singer's most unflattering moments for public consumption. Her vulnerability pained me, a gut-wrenching reminder of the status of Black women in America. If Houston, a multimillionaire American sweetheart, could fall prey to domestic violence and predatory commodification, how could I believe America had better plans for me—a poor, Black immigrant girl?

I listened to Oprah Winfrey's interview with Houston's daughter, Bobbi Kristina, and wept as she described the last day she spent with her mother before her death. The late icon's daughter described lying beside her all day and night, snuggled in her embrace right before she died. In 2015, Kristina was found unresponsive in a tub, just like her mother. She died a few days later in a hospice. A medical examiner concluded her cause of death was "immersion associated with drug intoxication." Hope that Whitney Houston's entire decades-long legacy would live on through her daughter ended on that day.

"But that doesn't have anything to do with racism," Jessi argued when I lamented Whitney Houston's fate.

I was only just beginning to process for myself how much it did. Though I never wanted to admit that racism was negatively impacting my life, it was almost impossible to avoid all of the negative depictions of Black women and relationships that were still rife in the media and pop culture. The toxic relationship between pop prince and princess Chris Brown and Rihanna publicly ended in tumult after violence between the pair erupted and images of a badly beaten Rihanna circulated in the media. The idea that a Black woman should be forgiving of infidelity, abuse, and mistreatment from her spouse or boyfriend was commonplace—embedded in songs, movies, and music videos depicting Black men as "players" and women as their trophies. Reality TV shows like *Love & Hip Hop* where Black women engaged in constant violence and drama, often over a man, had become a mainstay in American culture. The death of Whitney Houston forced me to question what success even meant for Black women. Could money, degrees, mansions, or lucrative careers save us or render us worthy of respect or protection? Would they offer us the status and power of less-pigmented women or white men? If Whitney could not have a healthy, committed relationship with a man, would I ever be able to find one?

During my first few months in the city, I felt very hopeful that a chance meeting could lead me to love. At that time, when people asked me whether or not I wanted to have children, I instinctively shot back a resounding *no*. But the truth was that the ideas of marriage and motherhood were deeply woven into my notions of "happily ever after." Well into early adulthood now, the prospect of "settling down"—finding a husband and starting a family—felt like it should be on the horizon. In a bustling city of millions of strangers, it was very hard to find intimate moments to become acquainted with anyone, so I figured online dating was my best bet. Every time I created a new profile on sites like Plenty of Fish, eharmony, and Match, a barrage of messages from potential suitors would ensue. I enthusiastically opened them, hoping at least one would contain romantic words from the man who would eventually become my husband and the man of my dreams. Instead, each click revealed a picture of the penis of a stranger or an unthoughtful single-word greeting.

"I never had a black girl before," a white man in his early twenties wrote.

"I'm not really looking for anything serious" was the standard line used by men.

My white girlfriends assured me that they were experiencing similar dating difficulties.

"Haven't you heard of hookup culture?" one asked.

She explained that apparently all of New York City (and many of America's young adults) had decided they no longer wanted to share meaningful attachments. They were living for the moment—a casual encounter at a club or bar, a movie back at a random stranger's apartment that could lead to sex, or the exchange of naked selfies. She argued that I should embrace the culture and just "have fun."

"I don't think anyone is into the hetero, monogamous thing right now," she said with a shrug.

And yet it was not uncommon for these very same white women who once promised we were in the same struggle to later announce, via social media, that they had found a new beau. Or to see them walking about the city or lounging in Union Square or Washington Square Park with their hand clasped in the hand of a white, brown, or Black man. It wasn't uncommon to see successful white marriages (and even interracial ones between white women and men of color), even if some ended poorly. By then, the notion that white women had free rein over the dating market was a common one.

In Kanye West's hit "Gold Digger," he warned a Black woman,

whom he castigated for using men for their money, that her man would leave her for a white girl. The statistics bore out the truth of West's assertion: since the 1980s, Black men had been two times more likely to marry a woman outside of their race than Black women had been to marry outside of theirs.[3] Many of these men traded their success and status for access to white women. And that meant fewer dating options for young Black women like me.

For one of my classes, I interviewed a group of very "successful" Black women in their forties and fifties, desperate for insights. Would I ever find love? Was there any hope? I quickly realized one trend among them: they had never married and none of them had children. Their careers were their lives, and most seemed rather proud of that fact. It wasn't until the third or fourth interview that I found the courage to ask why.

"It just never happened for me," my subject, who worked at the White House during Obama's presidency, responded.

As I dug deeper into the dark reality of dating while Black and female, I would quickly understand more. I stumbled on a book by Ralph Richard Banks called *Is Marriage for White People?*, which unflinchingly spelled out the truth. In it, the Stanford law professor argued that "single is the new black," because Black women's chances of finding love were marred by the statistical realities working against us. With the normalization of online dating came an onslaught of data that revealed racism would become a significant barrier to any chance at love for me. User data found that Black women were rated as the "least desirable" in the online dating world, and it's not hard to connect that lack of desirability to society's stereotypes about Black women. Men outside of our race were unlikely to date us, so our best chances for love were within the Black community, where the high school graduation rate for Black boys hovered around 50 percent in the early 2000s; one in six Black men were incarcerated by thirty years of age, many more were branded "felons" or spent time behind bars, and many were locked out of the labor market, leaving very few with the means to provide for a family.[4] By the time I made it to college, Black women were outpacing their male counterparts in both education and career advancement.[5] The relationship between Black men and women was strained and broken, in large part by the pressure cooker of living under white supremacy: The decayed school system that failed those boys. The war on Black people, disguised as the "war on drugs" and "war on crime," which led to mass incarceration and stripped millions of Black men of basic rights like voting or finding employment. For Black women, a college degree couldn't ameliorate the irreparable damage caused by those injustices. That paper made us no more valuable.

America tried to blame Black women for their circumstances and for our single Black motherhood, but the system had long been rigged against us—especially those of us who "bettered" our circumstances with education. If the women I interviewed were any indication, as an educated Black woman oriented toward "success," I didn't have the right to have kids or start a family. And I didn't want my future family to end up a statistic—similar to the 70 percent of Black families headed by single mothers in the eighties and nineties.[6] I didn't want to raise my children constantly on the verge of economic insolvency or housing instability. So I reasoned it was simply better to not aspire to marriage or having a family at all.

Shortly after the realization of the grim reality that would make it unlikely for me to find a "suitable partner" to marry, my best friend from Florida, Karla, called me with news that she was having a baby. Then only twenty-four years old, she had already married a man she had fallen in love with, finished college, and purchased a new home and a car.

"I'm very lucky," she said, explaining that her parents and her in-laws were both supportive and helpful.

They helped put a down payment on a home. And even though Karla worked incredibly hard, she knew she had people to turn to if anything serious happened. Days before Karla was scheduled to deliver, she told me that her daughter had Down syndrome.

"And she has fluids all over her body, so we aren't sure what's going to happen," she said.

Anxiety came in waves for me as my best friend breathed through contractions and brought her first child into the world. A beautiful fighter, her baby girl battled for weeks for her life before she was finally released to the care of her mother at home.

As I watched the emotional, psychological, and financial hardships that Karla endured play out, I wondered: How would I have survived such circumstances? If I did find a suitable partner, what would be the likelihood that his family could help us through hard times, since I already knew mine couldn't? Would they be able to provide us the financial support young people need to start a family, buy a house, and/or pay off student loan debt?

My sister, Niki, took the first leap into Black motherhood. Her partner, a Black man named Mark, lived in a project building in Brooklyn and had few to no prospects for bettering his circumstances. Niki met him during one of our partying escapades in the city when he worked security at Hudson Hotel's lounge, a swanky Midtown spot we frequented. He was already in his late thirties and didn't have the millions of dollars necessary to afford housing on his own, so he resigned himself to living in the Section 8 apartment he had inherited from his mother, who died when he was only sixteen years old. Niki decided to come back to America and move in with him so they could be a family unit until they saved up enough money to return to Trinidad together. By then, she was already in her thirties and understood that the prospect of meeting the "perfect one" or somehow managing to have financial security before venturing into motherhood was unlikely. Despite having degrees, she still struggled to find stable employment.

"I'll use Medicaid and WIC to help out with the baby," Niki told my mom.

Mom was both disgusted and horrified.

"I worked this hard for you to be on welfare?" she exclaimed. "For you to end up with a man from the ghetto?"

Niki had her beautiful baby boy, Marcus, and moved in with his father in Brooklyn. Over dinner when we would visit with Mom, Niki reported stories of people on crack trying to sell her stolen merchandise, the smell of the drug seeping out of the building's elevator, where people gathered to smoke it from pipes, the smell of urine in the hallways.

"At first, I used to shoo her away when she came to the door," she said of a drug-addicted woman named Latasha who often knocked on her door to sell perfumes and women's clothes. "But I got a pretty good deal on these, so I'm not mad at her anymore."

Niki showed us her new sneakers and we all erupted in laughter. Still, my mother's disappointment was palpable. And secretly, though well aware of the odds that were stacked against me, I hoped that family life for me would start in a place of comfort.

Fortunately, birthing babies was not at the top of my agenda at that time. Instead, I felt it necessary to change America and its treatment of Black people. I was convinced that if I offered education to Americans, as my professor had taken the time to educate me, the country and its people would make an about-face and admit to and eradicate the disgusting reality of racism. By then, Occupy Wall Street was in full swing, bringing thousands of people to the streets to protest America's economic inequality. I rode my scooter for blocks and blocks between lower Manhattan and Zuccotti Park, where protesters had set up an entire campsite to "occupy" (literally sleep in and never leave) the financial district.

"We are the ninety-nine percent," I chanted along with seas of thousands of people.

In America, there was a chasm-like division between the 1 percent of citizens who held a vast majority of the wealth of the country and everyone else. I, like many Americans at the time, was finding the voice to speak up against cruelty and inequality.

I stumbled upon another illuminating class that promised to demystify the pathway to breaking into New York newspapers and magazines. It was taught by Professor Susan Shapiro, a middle-aged Jewish woman driven to the city in her twenties from the Midwest by dreams of making it big as a writer. By the time I sat down in her classroom, she had already authored several books and published work in most of the nation's prestigious publications.

"My goal is for my students to get their book deals when they are young, because no one wants to look old and tired in their author photograph," she would joke.

But she never joked when it came to the success of her students. Many had broken into mainstream publications, and some even used her lessons to go on to get major book deals. I squandered no minute in her classes and dutifully participated in every critique session of other students' work and attentively took note of every recommendation uttered to better my writing. Armed with my learning—studies and statistics that revealed the truth about American racism—I set out on a quest. I became a social justice warrior, armored with thick skin and wielding knowledge like a sharpened sword. To flex my writing muscles, I registered for the school newspaper.

"There's an event this evening and Junot Díaz will be there to receive an award," one of the editors piped up. "Anyone want to volunteer to write a story?"

"It's pronounced 'Ju-Know,' and I want that story," I quickly shot back.

Surviving a white-dominated environment was like traversing a desert with no water. The celebration of a person of color for their literary work felt like a waterfall oasis in the midst of the dry, arid vastness of whiteness. As I walked into the auditorium, I felt a surge of pride. Díaz was the headliner of the event, scheduled to receive an award: a twenty-thousand-dollar check and an engraved silver bowl. He was a Pulitzer Prize–winning author and a Dominican-born immigrant raised in Parlin, New Jersey, not too far away from my hometown. He took to the podium to read a chapter from his book, which was laden with expletives and references to nineties pop culture. His realness was refreshing. His vernacular, his swag, his message: it was as if he were speaking for and directly to me.

"There ain't fucking nothing special about me," he said to the crowd, many of whom were college kids of color, urging us to strive to be in his position.

His words gave me some much-needed sustenance, but my thirst was far from quenched. I needed more of his honesty, support, and direction. I needed him to divulge the secret of surviving and thriving in whiteness.

"Can I interview you for my school newspaper?" I anxiously inquired at the event's conclusion.

"Sure thing, sis," he responded coolly.

It was the most exciting moment of my college career. When the school newspaper met the following week, I pridefully announced my journalistic feat.

"I got an interview with Junot Díaz," I stated confidently.

The whole class oohed and aahed.

"Harrison can help you with the questions," the professor piped up.

The assertion that I needed "help" was offensive to me, but I was too swept up in the daunting task to get caught up in the slight. I knew exactly what I wanted to ask: How does a person of color survive and thrive in America? When an email titled "Questions for Junot" from the paper's editor popped up in my in-box a few hours after class, I opened it.

"How was it to be raised without a father?" the first question read.

Quite white, I thought to myself with a chuckle.

I closed the email and avoided the editor's request to go over the questions. For white people, the consequences of minority status always seemed to be of more interest than how those people were systematically oppressed to end up in that position: the hardships of the Black single mother; fatherless life in the "hood"; the struggles of an undocumented student. I was more interested in understanding and unveiling the system that *created* those consequences: the discrimination; his opinion on undocumented students; his thoughts on then-president Barack Obama; unfair policies and how to navigate racist spaces, especially those that claim to be "liberal." That conversation, I would eventually learn, was far less welcome.

Díaz agreed to a phone interview and scheduled our chat in the early evening. The day of the call, I was so anxious to finally execute my first journalistic interview. I repeatedly checked the time and set multiple alarms to make sure I wouldn't be late for the call. I busied myself running petty errands as a distraction.

You got this! I encouraged myself while dialing his number.

He answered after only two rings. "Hey, sis!"

I almost burst at the seams from the thrill. The interview went on for about forty-five minutes. I carefully led him through my list of questions, ranging from how it felt to be raised in America as a first-generation immigrant and his thoughts on the then-controversial DREAM Act (a piece of legislation that would've afforded undocumented immigrants who arrived to the country's shores as kids conditional residency) to his opinion on Barack Obama and whether or not he felt isolated in the white-dominated world of literature.

"I was the first kid of color in my New Jersey high school's honors program," he recalled. "When I was in high school, I already knew what it meant to be selected out by an arbitrary criteria. Being identified or being selected out has less to do with me and more about the way this country likes to crown individuals but oppress communities."

In that moment, my pain was validated and legitimized, stirring hurt feelings. The rage within me was only quieted by the sense of relief that I was not alone in my experience. On that day, I was released. From the feelings of guilt for building "success" on the back of African American institutionalized failure. From the burden of aspiring to whiteness while toiling under the weight of inferiority. I had begun to sense that embedded in the status of the "minority" was the inherent absence of power, but during that phone call I was no longer a minority. In Díaz I saw myself, and in that reflection the faces of millions of Americans of color sprinkled all across the nation, rendered voiceless by the majority rule of whiteness. I marched into class with conviction upon completion of the interview. I printed the five-page document at the campus library and carefully held it upright, in both hands, as if it were a precious artifact.

I entered the professor's office with quiet confidence, resolute in my desire to be heard and understood for the truth of what I, and people like me, endured for our taste of the American dream.

The professor accepted the five freshly printed pages with enthusiasm in anticipation of the interview with the famous writer. His chest puffed with pride as he fixed his glasses to gaze upon the text. Insecurity threatened to break my composure, but I maintained my upright posture, watching resolutely as his eyes scanned each line. The moment felt stifling and protracted.

"These pages aren't numbered," he finally said. "No editor in the real world would accept it like this."

He pushed the papers back in my direction. I sat frozen, unable to muster a retort; the fragility of my newfound confidence was made glaringly real by one white man's rejection.

"I like how he answered the questions," he finally offered. "They just flowed together."

It didn't seem to occur to him that I had written the questions with that intent. In a span of five minutes and with only two statements, the professor had managed to reduce days of my labor and years of my experiences down to the inferred wordsmanship of Junot Díaz. When it came time to respond to edits for the piece and have it published, I could barely muster the desire.

That brand of racism, dismissal, denial, and exclusion at the hands of my white contemporaries had become a part of my everyday life experience. This undermining force stalked me like a relentless phantom as I progressed through the institution—shunned and castigated for every speech on Black female hypersexualization by the media and my critiques of income inequality. I got my first opportunity to write professionally when I met the editor of a webzine aimed at young women during one of Susan Shapiro's classes and begged for a chance to intern at their office in Midtown. The site granted me free rein over what I wanted to publish, and I began by penning a flurry of essays that focused on my experiences in America as a Black girl and woman.

Commenters of the white liberal variety flocked to the pieces I wrote detailing the insidious nature of America's structural racism to decry *my* "bigotry" and deflect my anger. White feminists called me divisive for pointing to the continued marginalization of minority female voices in the wider feminist movement. Patricia Arquette called for solidarity from POC and WOC to rally against gender wage inequality, yet I couldn't help but point out that the biggest wage gaps were unmistakably race based. This white liberal audience insisted that it was *I* who needed changing—my self-defeating perspectives and irresponsible "preoccupation" with racism needed reframing. They pointed to class, not race, as the problem—yet thanks to two generations of cyclical discrimination, disadvantage, and inequality, class ascension is a dream for most African Americans, and so race and class are tightly intertwined. Many white people preached love and acceptance but grew silent when faced with facts regarding racial inequality. The rarefied air of white condescension was oftentimes stifling for me. As a woman of color, I was frequently out of breath from offering constant explanations that fell on deaf ears.

Liberalism allowed whites to maintain a sense of self-righteousness; to claim higher moral ground and standing, which bred arrogance and enabled ignorance and inaction in the face of deeper issues. When juxtaposed with the gun-toting, "nigger"-hating, religiously obsessed folks who often identified as conservative, it was easy to understand why white liberalism seemed so miraculously progressive. However, both ideologies exist on a spectrum of white political and ideological supremacy. A supremacy infrequently fought against or even acknowledged by most whites, regardless of their "political alignment." Even liberal spaces dispensed Eurocentric materials, curricula, histories, and reading lists. Clichés like "Music is universal" or generalizations that Black women aren't "classically beautiful" and the persistence of labels like "thugs" and "savages" reveal just how segregated society still is. The myths of meritocracy and hard work, despite the cushion of inheritance from generational wealth, continue to keep race and class inextricably bound.

By the end of my college career, I had realized most whites were implicated in the continued dominance of white supremacy. But white liberals had the slippery advantage of being able to scapegoat conservatives to avoid culpability. As a person of color, I found that dodge as dreadful and painful as being faced with the overt, clear-cut racism of the Right. I preferred to be immediately rejected rather than be accepted under the pretense that I was welcome, only to later be ridiculed or dismissed. I preferred knowing exactly where I stood. I did not have the emotional strength to continually battle the guilt-ridden, aggressive, spiteful subconscious of the white liberal who is intellectually well intentioned but psychologically fragile, fragmented, and frustrated. America still had no space for me.

I went to college because I believed it would help me be more successful and award me higher social standing. No one ever told me that as a twenty-five-year-old Black woman and first-generation college graduate, "success" would often come at the cost of my happiness and emotional well-being. That being educated to the reality of America would leave me feeling lost, lonely, and bewildered. And that people of every race and background would deny me the right to express my feelings and opinions, forcing me into an isolated, often self-loathing, depressing corner. I was finding that a Black woman's social circumstances may very well be worsened by higher education.

As my debts piled on and I became increasingly aware that obtaining my degree wouldn't necessarily put me any closer to securing the life I dreamed of, I began to regret my decision to go to college. What was the point of a forced reckoning with societal realities when I had no power to shape society? I was over thirty thousand dollars in debt and once again became a cruel statistic. Black women held two-thirds of the nation's student loan debt and were more likely to default because of nonpayment.[7] By the end of my college career, I couldn't even find the money to pay what I owed on my tuition directly to the school, so they decided to withhold my diploma. What was the point of all of my hard work?

Then I sat down and thought about the women who would never feel a sense of entitlement to independence or respect because they saw themselves through society's lens, which labels them unworthy. I thought about all of the Black people who sacrificed their lives to award me what I took for granted. I watched some of my friends struggle through a life of low wages and long workweeks. I imagined how much more vulnerable women and people of color were, especially while unknowingly existing in a predatory society. And I realized that more than anything else, I was thankful. Thankful for the chance to believe I deserve better. And for the opportunity to fight for it. Even if all I contribute to that fight is conversation or a perspective that everyone may not appreciate.

From then on, I vowed to safeguard myself from constant invalidation and assault. I didn't know it then, but years later, I found the word to describe those constant attacks on my intellect: gaslighting. In an abusive relationship, the abuser uses this form of emotional abuse to manipulate their victim and force them to question their own thoughts, their memories, and even the events they have experienced. Victims of gaslighting can sometimes begin to question even their own sanity. Unwittingly, I was protecting myself from America's racist emotional abuse by refusing to allow others to rewrite my own story.

CHAPTER 6

Healing

After the War of 1812, thousands of African Americans who served on behalf of the British fled the U.S. Black American soldiers, who had been lured to fight for the Brits in exchange for their freedom, boarded boats destined for English-ruled territories throughout the Caribbean when the British lost the war. By 1816, many had settled in Trinidad, the southernmost island of the Caribbean and the land of my birth. They became known as "Merikins," and their legacy of economic prosperity would endure for centuries. Merikins were among the tens of thousands of Black refugees who escaped the U.S. for freedom, gaining that freedom even after fighting for the losing side in a war. Others made their way to Canada alone or in small family groups, and many settled in Nova Scotia and New Brunswick.[1]

Fighting to wrestle back our freedom and dignity from the system of white supremacist abuse is a repeated trope in any stretch of Black history. Revolts by the enslaved erupted all across the Western Hemisphere during the 1700s and 1800s, the most successful of which, the Haitian Revolution, led to the emancipation of Haiti from France. The fight is also expressed through the splendor and fashion we see in photos taken during the Harlem Renaissance in the 1920s and 1930s, when the Black city was a cultural mecca and suits, ties, minks, and furs were the standard dress code. The Black power movement in the 1960s and 1970s loudly declared that "Black is beautiful" and prompted the popularity of Afros and the worship of Black hair and skin. That struggle to reclaim footing is articulated by the politics of Marcus Garvey, the Black separatist movement, and the proclamations of independence made by African Americans who journeyed back to Africa after the Civil War to establish Liberia.

Black emancipation has always been about more than just being physically free—the fight for freedom included the freedom to write, narrate, and create our own destinies. To find our voice and speak aloud without fear or concern of reprisal. Our healing is captured in the words of Black authors, poets, singers, and songwriters. In Maya Angelou's telling of "why the caged bird sings" and Frederick Douglass's *Narrative of the Life of Frederick Douglass, an American Slave.* In the haunting melodies of Negro spirituals and the rhythm of blues, the boisterous belting of gospel music and the smooth flow and cadence of rap music.

In an interview during the eighties about rap artists who "pushed the envelope in terms of exercising their First Amendment right" and became "the voice of the streets," Detroit rapper and activist Royce da 5'9" said, "It was that voice that America couldn't control. . . . It was that voice of the streets that they didn't know what the next line is gonna be and that scared them. Because we spoke our own unapologetic truth. We spoke about environments that were overlooked, that didn't have a voice, you know, that didn't have a say, that didn't have pretty much anything."[2]

Black liberation and healing come in the form of Black friendship, kinship, marriage, and love—in spite of constant hardship. In the way we help one another reckon with the struggle of oppression. My decision to leave America was born of the same tradition of trying to break free to chart my own future. To heal from my abusive relationship with America. And to finally find my voice as a Black woman, to speak about my trauma.

For the two years I spent at the New School in the city, I felt exhausted, like I was running on a hamster wheel as fast as I could but going nowhere. I was an A student, had an internship, and worked teaching private swim lessons even during the winter. I somehow made it to every class on time and even managed to complete all the necessary credits for my bachelor's. I felt like I had done everything right, but the balance on my school's bill told me differently. I still owed thousands of dollars for my last semester in college, and it was the school's policy to withhold diplomas from students who failed to pay their balances. America had dealt me one of its harshest blows. The thought of smiling through a graduation ceremony to receive an empty case marked "diploma" that I had no means of filling was a degradation I couldn't find the courage to endure.

On the day of my college graduation, I told my friends and family the news: I was leaving the country I had lived in since childhood.

"I just need a change," I told them, but they knew there was more. Was it some romance gone awry? they wondered. Some impulsive response to a broken heart? I *was* running from heartbreak. My relationship with the United States of America was the most tumultuous relationship I ever had, and it ended with the heartrending realization that a country I loved and believed in did not love me back.

For a long time, I survived by holding myself together with the labels I'd accumulated over the years. I plastered each one to my body with superglue, as if the labels could assert to me that I was someone. Sports fanatic (hot pink). Feminist, beautiful, writer, comedian, fashionista, friend (fuchsia, yellow, blue, purple, red, green). I hid behind and I leaned on them; they were my only shields.

My green label softened my view when a childhood friend's family banged down my front door and demanded their daughter get out of a house full of Blacks. Blue protected my heart when my Black peers ostracized me for my enjoyment of complete, complex sentences. Yellow blocked my ears when whispers floated through the air at my white American boyfriend's home like haunted ghosts: *I can't believe he is dating a Black girl.* I thought that those otherwise painful words could pass through me like a gentle breeze barely creating a flutter if I had my identity labels to hold on to.

I felt I existed on the fringe of ugly, ignorant, and uncultured. Black but not Black enough for my positive attributes to be unjustified. "Where are you from?" potential dates asked when they met me. "I am from Trinidad and Tobago," I learned to answer. "Oh, that's why you are so beautiful and exotic—I knew you couldn't be all Black."

"Black people don't really know how to swim," my coworker once told me when I worked as a swim instructor at my neighborhood's pool. "What about me?" I asked. "Oh, you aren't Black. You're from Trinidad," she replied.

"The Black children don't like to read very much," I overheard one librarian telling another while I sat reading a book a couple feet away. They passed by me with smiles.

I was the perfect victim: I was told that I was the exception to my race, but no matter what kind of striving I accomplished, I could never truly transcend it. I was isolated and always on my own, an easy target. I was the yardstick by which other minorities were measured. If I could finish high school and college, why couldn't so many African American people find their way out of their hoods? If I could speak English without using Ebonics slang, why did others call themselves "niggas"? If I managed to make it through twenty-three years without contracting an STD or getting pregnant, why did Black women have the highest statistical risk of disease and teenage motherhood? Daddy America looked to me to prove that he had done something right. The others must simply not be trying.

But I know I survived because I was never able to make America my home. I never watched my childhood neighborhood illuminated by helicopter lights in search of criminals or inundated with hipsters in search of apartments. No state, city, or town has been a mother to me, cradling generations of my family, only to see them destroyed by unemployment or poverty. No school system had the time or opportunity to relegate me to "remedial," "rejected," or "unteachable." I learned to reject the misogynistic, drug-infested messages and imagery of hip-hop culture that are force-fed to Black youths through square tubes. I am not a product of a state of greatness. I am a by-product of emptiness.

In that empty, dark space where I had to struggle to define myself, alone, I found my Blackness. I stripped myself of the labels, painfully peeling them off one by one. Beneath them there was a wounded, disfigured colored woman who refused to be faceless anymore, to remain hidden any longer.

Still, I count myself lucky. Where my open cuts remain, eventually scars will take their place, and those scars will fade with time. For many, their wounds will never heal. Gunshots bore coin-size holes into their chests that will never close. Their chained wrists and ankles will continue to bruise. Their minds have collapsed under the weight of a failed education system.

I was already back in Trinidad and Tobago when the Trayvon Martin verdict came down in the summer of 2013. I wasn't surprised, but I was still speechless. I hoped that his murder would force Americans to reexamine their "postracial" beliefs. A friend of mine posted on my Facebook page, "You made the right choice." I think I did too.

I found freedom at last by leaving the land of the free.

Trinidad welcomed me back with open arms. On my first few days back in my homeland, I lay in bed in the early morning with tears in my eyes as I listened to the birds singing their melodic tunes. I journeyed outside to find an entire nation of Black people living beautiful daily lives unrestricted by the stifling confines of whiteness, and I was in awe. I boarded the maxi bus and excitedly called, "Mawning!" to its passengers in anticipation of the chorus of greetings that would come in response. I went into groceries just to hear the sound of reggae and soca music humming in the background. I went to job interviews in search of employment and was astonished when I landed a job with a local paper almost immediately. I wrote about my journey to liberation and was thrilled when the piece was published in a popular American online magazine and read by millions, many of whom related to my experience. I was so proud that I sent the piece to Junot Díaz, hoping that my success would make him proud.

"When you get pregnant, remember Francophone names are the best," he responded.

I stared at the message in disbelief. My oasis was just a mirage. I was absolutely crushed and sought Niki's support.

"Can you believe what this asshole just wrote to me?" I asked after relaying the exchange.

"Tell him: Ju know what, Junot, Ju no know shit," she casually responded.

I shot her line back to him in an email.

"I was just kidding!" he replied.

Though my literary crush did not respond to the piece as I had imagined he would, I found solace and support in the eloquent comment of an unknown man from the Midwest. He left a message in the comments section of the piece that bewitched me. It spoke of my humanity and pressed others to validate my experience. I had skimmed through so many comments at that point, most of which existed in a binary world of right or wrong. The comments never spoke from a place of understanding. I wondered who this person could be who saw me as, above all, a human being.

"Please contact me on some kind of social media," I requested of the unknown writer. Soon afterward, I found a message in my in-box on Facebook from Justin. He introduced himself with a brief, simple paragraph. His profile picture was of a blue altocumulus-cloud-filled sky.

We exchanged messages about our dreams, goals, passions, and pasts. He told me he was an animator by trade, but he wrote because he felt it was the only way he could express himself. I told him about my new life outside of the busy one I had left behind in New York City. We traded our old writing and shared new pieces, inspired by each other. Each exchange was a tiny snippet of ourselves, cut out along imaginary lines, folded up digitally, and delivered thousands of miles by cables and satellites.

One day, a tiny photo of a smiling young man popped up beside one of his messages. I clicked it frantically, wanting to finally meet this stranger with my eyes. The picture was blurry and small; him smiling heartily with dimpled cheeks and caramel skin. I stared at the photo, my heart and mind racing at the sight of his face. *Is this really him? Does he have any more pictures? He is really cute. Am I crazy?*

He was a thoughtful, passionate twenty-eight-year-old Black man who had spent the majority of his life in a mostly white suburb of Ohio. His family, as he described it, was the "go-to" Black family. Growing up, he felt isolated by his skin color, trapped in a world of whiteness that he could never fit into.

"I remember one day my brother and I were playing with a group of kids," he said, "when one asked, 'What race are you? Because I am white.' I hadn't really thought about it, even though I knew my skin was brown. I thought everyone was white."

That was the beginning of the realization that he would never be included or accepted.

"Do Black people have tails?" he remembered a peer asking when they were both children.

When fathers in his town warned that he should not date their daughters, that was only further validation that he would always be othered and diminished. After five months of intense, vulnerable exchanges, we made plans to spend Christmas with my family in New Jersey and then New Year's Eve back in Trinidad. I bought my plane ticket a month in advance and we anxiously counted down every day together. I was excited to show someone my homeland, especially a Black person who could experience the same freedom I had by escaping America.

He drove eight hours from Ohio to meet me at Newark International Airport on the day I arrived to shepherd him to my island oasis. I spotted him immediately in the distance. He stood tall and confident. I walked up to him and we stared awkwardly at each other for a long moment, our minds unable to process each other's presence. His eyes softened first and he pulled me close, embracing me tightly in his strong arms. I breathed in deeply, taking in his scent for the first time. He held my hand, grabbed my bag, and led me to the exit. I watched him intently as he walked: his big, soft lips, his brown skin, his eyes focused ahead. To me, he was perfect.

He escorted me out the airport doors to his old Buick.

"Oh God, I didn't miss the cold or these gray skies," I moaned.

"I promised my mom I'd do her a favor and drop some things off for my grandparents when I got here," he interjected.

Justin's grandparents lived in Bedford, a town in upstate New York, in a wealthy neighborhood full of huge estates, each with acres of wooded land. Rich and famous white folks, including Tommy Hilfiger, were new to the neighborhood—driving up prices there, building mansions, and flooding the local town with expensive, exclusive boutiques. His grandparents had moved there decades earlier to raise their three children in what was then a rural town. They sought refuge from both the racism of the South—where his grandfather was born and raised and where he witnessed public lynchings—and New York City's ghettos, where fears of being robbed or shot loomed.

"Living up here in the middle of the woods made them pretty *interesting*," Justin warned.

Fear crept into my psyche as we sped past the miles of woods. Most American horror movies start in the woods, and it began to feel like we were in an opening scene of one. Justin turned off the main road, and as the car slithered up a winding dirt path, I peered at a house coming into view in the distance. The wooden home looked older but well maintained and was surrounded by an immaculate front yard with perfectly arranged outdoor furniture. As we neared the end of the path, something made my heart sink and then begin to race: a tall Black man with broad shoulders, wearing overalls, a plaid shirt, and tall black rubber boots, was standing there with a blank face, holding a pair of shears. His face remained deadpan as Justin inched toward him, the sound of rocks crunching beneath the tires as we drove. The car stopped right in front of the man and Justin shifted it into park.

"Ummm . . . Justin," I started, only moments away from a shriek.

The man continued to stand there holding the shears, his lifeless face unchanged by the surprise presence of other people. Then he abruptly turned away and marched like the walking dead toward the wooded area off to the right of the house.

"That's my uncle," Justin plainly stated, as he pushed his car door open and hastily jumped out of the driver's seat, rushing toward the trunk.

Still frozen in fear, I could barely mutter a response. I turned in my seat and watched as he popped the trunk open and disappeared beneath its hood. He slammed it shut with one hand while balancing a huge black plastic bag between his chest and his other arm. He started toward the passenger side of the car and then balanced the bag again as he popped open my door.

"You look like you saw a ghost," he said with a chuckle. "C'mon, it'll only take a couple minutes."

I wanted to decline the offer but, well, love. I cautiously followed Justin toward the front door, secretly hoping the garbage bag did not contain body parts. He rang the doorbell and the front door cracked open.

"You got the bears," a woman's voice hissed from inside.

I couldn't see the woman, because Justin's body was blocking my line of sight.

"Yes, Grandma, I got the bears," he responded.

The door remained open only a crack and silence emanated from inside of the house. After a few awkward moments, Justin pushed the door open the rest of the way and entered. I stood just outside but peeped in, hesitant to follow. From what I could see, the house was decorated with porcelain figurines, white and pink lace, and vintage-looking furniture. His grandmother, a dark-skinned Black woman wearing a long nightie (also covered in frills and lace), peered down at us from atop the flight of stairs that led to the second floor.

"Grandma, uhhh, this is Tiffanie," Justin awkwardly began.

Her stare did not soften. I waved shyly.

"That's the one from the islands?" she began. "You betta watch out if she tryna just get a green card offa ya."

Justin let out an embarrassed sigh, his entire body slumping forward with the exhale.

"Grandma, I brought the bears," he said.

Justin's grandmother was actually from "the islands" herself (Barbados specifically), but years of Americanization had taught her to harbor a distrust of immigrants. She first landed on America's shores as a little girl with dreams of becoming a classical piano prodigy. Eventually she enrolled at Juilliard, where she acquired a taste for the finer things, and when she married Justin's grandfather, he squandered no opportunity to spoil her. A southern-bred, light-skinned Black man who came of age at the height of Jim Crow, Grandpa was equal parts rage and determination. After watching the lynching of a Black man down south, he migrated north and established a drilling company in the then-Italian-mob-run New York construction industry. The Italians weren't thrilled by the competition, but when they came looking for trouble at the business one day, they had no idea they would encounter a nigga with the might and anger of the Hulk. As the Italians approached, Justin's grandfather grabbed a brick and ran up to their leader, pummeling him with it until nearly all of his teeth were knocked loose and his face was a crushed mess of blood and bones. Stunned and horrified, the crew of Italians backed off and never returned. And that is how Justin's grandfather was able to establish a multimillion-dollar company in the midst of the height of New York City racism and mob rule. With his wealth, he moved his beautiful wife away from the dangers of the city to the woods of upstate New York. They established a popular Black church together and bought land to start a summer camp that would serve hundreds of Black children as they frolicked and played in the local lake during the summers while learning about Jesus and the sacrifices he made to relieve us of all sin. Whenever she would complain about missing her life, family, or friends back in the city, Justin's grandfather would shower his grandmother with gifts—mink furs, sparkling diamond rings and bracelets, and expensive collectible figurines. By the time the last of her three children—two boys and a girl (Justin's mom)— was born, she barely ever left her room and stayed in bed most days. Only during special events at the church would she doll herself up to make an appearance, a smile plastered onto her face and her ears and neck covered in sparkling diamonds.

"You can put the bears over there," she ordered before retreating to her room.

Justin plopped the large black garbage bag onto a nearby chair and ushered me into the house. He untied the bag and its contents were finally revealed: teddy bears his mother had sent from Ohio to donate to his grandparents' church. We spent a couple minutes touring the old home where Justin had spent his childhood summers before his dad relocated the family to Ohio after graduating as a doctor from Columbia. Both of his grandparents were proud Republicans who watched Fox News, which they blasted from the living room while eating dinner at the adjacent dining room table.

"The day I take you back to Ohio, I'm pretty sure you will break up with me," Justin said, laughing.

I rolled my eyes and sarcastically laughed along: nothing could get in the way of how I felt about him. Not to mention that, according to my plan, he would never have to return. So any issues with his family wouldn't be a problem. We had only about a week until our scheduled departure from Newark back to Trinidad. We were right on the brink of freedom. I knew going to Trinidad would bring him healing in the same way that it had for me. I was thrilled to share a life with him, un-inhibited by the scrutiny of white people.

On New Year's Eve, we packed into my mom's car with our luggage, headed for the airport. She dropped us at the departures terminal and honked as she pulled out to return home. The New Jersey sky was gray, and the wind was so cold that my face and fingertips stung even though they'd been only briefly exposed to the elements when I'd dragged my bag to the curbside check-in. My mind raced with endless possibilities of what could go wrong and hinder our departure. I held my breath as we checked in, anxious that I had somehow made a mistake with my book-ing or that my passport had expired. When I was handed my boarding pass, I worried that we would not make it to the terminal in time. When I sat on the plane, I worried that our escape would be thwarted by an accident during takeoff. As the plane glided above the Atlantic and then the Caribbean Sea, I imagined its engines failing and how it would feel to fall from the sky and crash-land in the ocean. By the time the runways of Piarco International Airport came into view, I was drained and ex-hausted. I closed my eyes and imagined deeply breathing in the smell of the tropics, allowing my body to finally relax. I turned to Justin. He was absently staring off into the distance.

"C'mon, let's go home," I interrupted, breaking him out of his trance.

We deplaned and hailed a ride to my apartment, which sat high atop a hill in Maraval. We collapsed into bed when we arrived, and by the time I gathered the strength to check the time, it was already 11:45 p.m. There were only fifteen minutes until the New Year. I shook Justin awake and told him we should go look for festivities in Port of Spain. We quickly put on T-shirts and shorts and rushed out the door, eager to get to the fun. When we stepped outside into the night's breeze, it was filled with the sound of crickets and laughter.

"Buh where allyuh going?" one of my neighbors, a stocky dark-skinned man with perfectly straight white teeth, inquired as we passed.

I explained we were going to town to look for a party.

"Well, the vibes now start," he responded, stretching his arm across the unfolding scene.

All of the neighbors and their children were out, screaming, laughing, and dancing to soca pounding from a huge speaker nearby. A pot of pelau was bubbling on top of a makeshift outdoor stove: a rubber tire over a wood fire. Everyone had brought out their favorite bottle of rum and lined them up side by side on a high wall that served as the bar.

"Grab a drink!" he offered.

I looked to Justin for his approval and he gave an ambivalent shrug. The decision was mine to make. I grabbed two plastic cups, poured us both drinks, and then found a comfortable spot near the pelau so I would be perfectly positioned to be first in line for a plate when it was ready. The cool mountain breeze blew, carrying the scent of the sweet coconut milk and fresh seasonings, making my stomach grumble. The sight of bright lights and the sound of loud bursts from fireworks interrupted my food-obsessed train of thought. Everyone paused their joke telling and dancing to watch the sky light up with a grand display as fireworks erupted all along the street and throughout the valley. I grabbed Justin's hand, squeezed it tight, and offered him an ecstatic, toothy grin. We sipped our drinks, ate, and laughed out loud at stories told by rowdy old men until the wee hours of the morning. There were no lurking eyes set upon us from a distance, threatening to spoil our happiness by calling the cops. There were no complaints that our music was too loud—the socially acceptable code for saying that there are too many Black people congregated in a space. For those moments atop that tiny mountain on a very tiny island in the middle of the vast Caribbean Sea, we were both free. And the fun had only just begun.

I wasted no time plunging Justin into my world in my new home. I showed him how to get around the country on maxis via the bus route.

"Mawning!" I proudly announced, and the choir of other riders responded with its regular greeting when we boarded the bus.

I showed him how to eat doubles and roti with his hands and instructed him to order only "slight peppa" or run the risk of a bathroom explosion after the meal. We walked around the Savannah, the largest roundabout in the world, which encloses a green space filled with exotic trees and plants, and planned a picnic in the nearby botanical gardens. I was filled with hope and excitement for our future then, envisioning the family we would one day have as I watched a mom and dad kick a ball back and forth with their two kids. Trinidad offered a life we could never attain in America—a nice, affordable apartment with a mountain view in a safe neighborhood. A life free of racism and the white gaze.

Justin was a gifted thinker and writer, so I imagined it would be a breeze to teach him how to navigate the online writing world, so that we could make money to sustain our new life. I spent hours showing him how to communicate with editors of magazines, newspapers, and news sites to land stories. At first, he claimed to be interested, but no action followed that declaration.

"What do you wanna write about?" I asked.

He shrugged. Justin was like a windup doll that refused to spring into action no matter how hard I wound him up. He was the most articulate man I knew, and yet somehow he was still battling to find his voice.

CHAPTER 7

————

Hoovered

How many unkept promises has America made to Black people to keep us invested in the American dream? In our relationship with a country that has proven itself over generations to be committed to our devaluation and destruction? To reel us back in after dealing us constant blows and abuses?

The white lie began with the unrealized promise of emancipation and oath of "equality" for all. It was perpetuated by the diversity programs and initiatives—invitations to "integrate" white spaces, social, corporate, political—that were supposed to give us "access." More promises were made by the banks that leveraged our social networks—our communities and church leaders—to gain our trust to buy into higher-cost, higher-risk loans to secure mortgages and degrees that would make us more "successful." "Work opportunities" in factories lured Black people from the rural South to the North, Midwest, and West during the Great Migration. The full rights of citizenship had been promised to those who fought in wars.

I cannot fault Black America for falling prey to the promises of the rest of America; I did too. An abuser seldom allows a victim to simply leave and will always resort to hoovering to keep a gainful dynamic intact—sucking the victim back into the relationship by making pronouncements of love, with grand gestures or assurances of change. And that is precisely what happened in my relationship with America. I repeatedly found myself drawn back to the country in pursuit of the fulfillment of its promises.

It wasn't too long before Justin's money ran out. We argued every day about the future of our relationship and, most pressingly, where we would live. He wanted to return to the U.S. to help his grandparents with their business, which was on the verge of collapse.

"Come on, Tiff," Justin softly urged. "We can always save some and come back."

Almost simultaneously, America cast its net about me once more, this time luring me with promises of a career opportunity. A close friend thought I would be perfect for a job in Baltimore and promised me the salary would be enough for me to finally pay back my student loans and officially get my life started. Even if I wanted to return to Trinidad, working off my debts in the U.S. gave me the chance to do so more freely. So I obliged Justin's request. I left my soul safely tucked away in those Caribbean moments of freedom. My soullessness anesthetized me to the usual pain and hurt of departure as the taxi zigzagged through Maraval's mountains and then barreled down the highway toward the airport. I boarded my flight and returned to the States as a hollow woman. By the time the plane zoomed over the Atlantic Ocean, destined for New Jersey, the sight of Newark's gray, stale skyline had no impact on me. I arrived with a simple mission: survival. Justin and I just needed to save enough money to go back home to Trinidad together.

We boarded the PATH train in Newark Penn Station and then parted ways at the train's first stop in Jersey City. Journal Square was the closest stop to Mom's house. I waved goodbye to Justin as the train pulled out of the station, headed for New York City. He responded with a small affirmative nod. The train disappeared into the dark tunnel and I was left to navigate America alone once again. I dragged my bag toward the bus terminal and hopped on the first bus I saw digitally emblazoned with the words "6 Ocean Ave." I scrambled a couple dollars out of my pocket and fed them, one by one, into the fare box. I breathed deeply and steadied myself as I walked down the aisle toward an empty seat near the bus's back door like a programmed automaton, rigidly executing each step. From the corner I could see a woman slumped over in her seat, her gray-speckled black hair frayed and her hand resting on a cane.

"He don't be paying his child support!" The voice of a woman filled the bus. "That nigga ain't 'bout shit."

The bus's journey down Ocean Avenue was both depressing and enraging. I gazed out of the window as we sped past old, boarded-up buildings, liquor stores, and people who looked like the world had left them behind. When I arrived at the top of Mom's street, a cop car was parked in the middle of the road, blocking traffic, while the officer was busy patting the pockets of a Black man who was pressed against a vehicle. I rushed past the scene, trying to remain invisible. I rang Mom's doorbell and the door immediately swung open. She greeted me with a tight, warm embrace, but not even the sight of Mom's bright eyes and smile could stir my emotions. I dropped my suitcase onto the floor of the living room and took a seat on the sofa. After a few minutes, she called me into the backyard and unveiled a meticulously set out dinner spread that included one of my favorite dishes: oxtail and red beans. We ate our food and exchanged stories to catch each other up on the past few months. By then, Bill Cosby was making national news after dozens of women broke years of silence to accuse him of drugging them and of sexual assault. We mused over how the iconic father of Black America had fallen so low, especially after preaching respectability for Black people for all those years.

When the sun descended and gunshots began to fill the night air, we retired to bed. Comfort and sleep evaded me that night.

Though I had physically returned to America, my spirit hadn't joined me and the walking dead never slept. When the sun arose, my eyes were heavy and deep black rings encircled them, but my mind still refused to rest. I rolled over and punched dates into my phone on a website selling bus tickets. I needed something to make me feel alive again and hoped the trip to Baltimore would present new, worthwhile opportunities. One of my mentors, Ben, had scheduled a meeting for me with a woman in a top position at a nonprofit organization dedicated to fighting for social justice. She was a Black woman who worked at the White House during Barack Obama's tenure. Ben wanted to convince me that I should remain in America and commit myself to the fight. I never turned down any opportunities, so I agreed to the meeting.

On the day of my arrival in Baltimore, an altercation happened between police and a young Black man that spurred protests. Fox News reported that the man had been shot in the back while running away from police, at the same junction where, months earlier, Freddie Gray Jr., a twenty-five-year-old African American man, had been arrested by the Baltimore Police Department and charged for possessing a knife. The officers who arrested Gray cuffed his hands behind his back but did not secure him in the police van before transporting him. During the ride, he sustained multiple injuries to his spinal cord, and he died days later as a result. Many were outraged that the police would kill another Black man in the same place where Gray had been apprehended. The energy of the protest lured me like a mosquito to light.

The taxi ride from downtown to North Avenue and Pennsylvania sank me deeper into depression. Huge high-rises became abandoned, boarded-up row houses. Thriving chain restaurants and businesses were replaced by liquor stores on every corner. And the busy, diverse swirl of people became large groups of Black people crowded onto the sidewalks and protesting on one corner of the intersection, with news trucks on another and the media—mostly middle-aged, well-dressed white men— off to another side. By the time I arrived, the police were addressing the media, guarded by officers armed with riot gear, batons, and pepper guns. They released the details about the altercation: supposedly, a gun fell out of the man's pocket and went off while he was running away from authorities after being approached for no apparent reason in the first place.

"I don't believe none of that shit," a tall Black man with braids said to me. "They shoot us down in the streets like dogs and always tryna cover it up."

He then pointed to a case of water sitting in the middle of the sidewalk.

"It's hot out here, sistah," he said, offering me a bottle. I took it and gulped the water down and thanked him, then moved through the crowd trying to find someone who had seen what happened themselves. Everyone was confused, and most of the original witnesses had already dispersed. I stood there a bit longer, then I decided to leave.

As I walked back through the neighborhood, looking for the subway station, it became clear to me that this was more than simply a scene: it was a neighborhood. A neighborhood full of people struggling to keep a semblance of normalcy, to carry on with their lives in spite of all of the confusion and chaos. School was letting out and children were parading the streets—the teenagers walking in small groups, the children walking hand in hand with parents or other adults. An ice cream truck parked on the side of the road in front of a completely burned-out establishment with broken windows and boarded doors. I watched a mother order from the truck and hand her daughter a sprinkle-covered ice cream cone. The little girl's eyes lit up in excitement as she took the first taste of the sweet treat. I smiled. The little girl returned my smile with a wave, her face practically glued to the ice cream. I thought of the many Fourth of July celebrations where my brother and I had stood as happily and eagerly in front of a Mister Softee truck. But the song that emanated from the truck's speakers haunted me, now that my college research had uncovered an article that revealed the racist lyrics that accompanied the popular tune for decades:

Nigger love a watermelon ha ha, ha ha!
Nigger love a watermelon ha ha, ha ha!
For here, they're made with a half a pound of co'l
There's nothing like a watermelon for a hungry coon[1]

When I finally made it to the train station, I realized I had absolutely no idea where I was going. And I had only an hour to get to the meeting on time.

"Which train do I take to go downtown?" I asked a little African American boy about twelve years of age. He pointed to the line with a TRACK 2 sign hanging above it.

The train arrived within moments and we boarded together. He sat across from me with a bag of goodies that I could tell were recent purchases. The first thing he pulled out of the bag was a combination lock. He toyed with it, muttering the numbers under his breath and concentrating intently as he tried to unlock it. I immediately thought about my middle school and high school years, when I did the same exact thing, and I smiled a bit. When he had accomplished his task, he put the lock away, then pulled out a pair of plastic handcuffs. My heart sank. I wanted to stand up and snatch them away from him and throw them into the garbage. With so many young Black men ushered into the prison system via the education system,[2] it felt like his future was being foreshadowed to me with those two items.

As gun violence in schools increased over the course of the 1990s and 2000s, claiming lives in spaces that were supposed to be safe havens, schools adopted zero-tolerance policies and hired school resource officers (SROs) to put an end to the violence. But these practices also resulted in an incarceration surge for Black youth. Harsh disciplinary actions taken by schools for behavioral infractions where violence and guns were concerned resulted in the suspension and expulsion of hundreds of Black and minority children from school, and also put them in early contact with the criminal justice system via SROs. While policies dictated ways American schools could "protect" children, data and studies revealed a far different result: the criminalization of Black youths.

"Why do you have a pair of handcuffs?" I asked the boy on the train.

He shrugged and continued to fiddle with the toy, pushing the tiny key into the lock and releasing the cuffs, then pressing them back into the secure position. The school-to-prison pipeline became more than just a theory supported by numbers and statistics for me at that moment. Thousands of little children of color who are shuffled through that system finally had a face. That boy and his two possessions made it all feel far too real for me. I feared that he, and so many innocent children just like him, might not survive the system unscathed. I felt not only saddened but powerless and angry. I felt like I needed to do something, to say something. But I couldn't find the words. As the train rolled into the next stop, he shoved the cuffs back into his plastic bag and exited. I did not say anything to him or warn him. I couldn't do anything to protect him. I could only hope that he would not become a statistic, that he would beat the odds. But I also felt guilty. Had I stolen his innocence with my questioning and harsh stare? In other, lighter hands, would I have viewed the toy as just that? A simple toy?

The train lurched forward and the boy disappeared into the distance. The magnified feelings, however, stayed with me. Feelings that, in years prior, I could usually roll up all tightly and shove into my depths like an overstuffed suitcase. The seams of my consciousness that held me together were coming undone. The return to the pressure of Black American life threatened to make me burst.

When I arrived at the building where the meeting was set to take place, I was escorted into a huge, silent office space filled with white faces. I felt the weight of that overpacked suitcase on my chest, and my hopes sank. I couldn't contain the dread and the certainty that there was nothing worth pursuing there, so I did an immediate about-face and walked right out. I knew I would never be a "good fit" there, and I was too exhausted to muster the energy to even pretend otherwise.

Americans at this time were all trying to process the murders of Black people at the whim of a racist police state: Delrawn Small, Alton Sterling, Philando Castile, and many others. The public promised "No justice, no peace" to the victims' family members, but the public had no means by which to keep that promise. The police who murdered a twelve-year-old boy, Tamir Rice, while he played at a neighborhood park faced no ramifications. No one was found guilty in the shooting death of John Crawford, whose only crime was shopping in Walmart while Black.

How could I convince myself that Black Lives Mattered when the country was built on the dehumanization, commodification, and destruction of those very lives? The enslavement and incarceration of those bodies? How many public executions needed to be nationally broadcast before Americans arrived at the collective agreement that racial injustice continued to plague the land of the free? Where was our police-brutality Rosa Parks? Could America promise that were she to rise and stand against injustice, she wouldn't find herself in a police car or with five bullet holes in her back? Decades after the assassination of Martin Luther King Jr., the government released documents that revealed King was spied on and abused by his own government, which hoped to discredit him through revealing his extramarital affairs. Signs erected on dilapidated roads to honor the great civil rights leader were still haunted by the spirit of a dream unfulfilled, Black blood pulsing through these streets—the veins of America's racist body. Black deaths became grotesque spectacles, feeding the country's appetite for our suffering and pain. As those deaths are shared and spread widely on social media, the energy and excitement spurred by that voyeurism rises and falls like a tide, and in the aftermath, the bloodstains are washed away from public view. *Black blood clandestinely nourishes America*, I thought.

My phone vibrated, interrupting my thoughts. It was Justin.

"I got into a fight with my grandpa," he said, his voice shaky and breathy. "I gotta get out of here."

I was surprised. I couldn't imagine Justin getting into a fight with anyone, let alone his elderly grandfather. When I pressed him for details, he only pushed forward.

"What should I do?" he asked.

We couldn't afford a life together back on the East Coast; the chances of our both finding well-paying jobs were slim to none. I had bailed on my meeting for the potential job opportunity. Justin had graduated from Ohio State University in 2009 and had never found stable employment, and I was beginning to realize that it was unlikely that would change. I was already sunk into the despair and hopelessness of coming into contact with so much Black pain. The trip to Baltimore had affirmed so many things I already knew about American life: there was little room for Black people to truly be happy or free here. I checked my bank account. I had $960.

"Let's go anywhere we can afford," I responded.

Within days, we were on the daylong flight to the other side of the world. We had decided to visit his brothers in China, where they were studying Mandarin at a college on an island called Xiamen. I wanted to return to Trinidad, but I needed Justin to feel supported in deciding our next steps if we were to be in a relationship together. His brothers offered without hesitation to host us. We stayed with them for a few weeks while I found extra work writing online to fund the next leg of our adventure: a backpacking tour around Asia. Over the course of three months, we slept in and trained at a Muay Thai boxing camp on Phuket. We rode mopeds through the busy streets of Ho Chi Minh City and bought crab from an old woman vendor who cooked it for us right on the sandy shores of Nha Trang Beach in Vietnam. We stayed in beachfront accommodations and elegant high-rises for under twenty dollars a night. We ate at fresh seafood buffets where we indulged in strange offerings like crocodile meat and snake blood, and the chefs plucked shrimp, fish, and crabs out of huge tanks right before plopping them onto the grill and serving them to us. I spent the entire day at the spa, receiving a manicure, pedicure, full-body deep-tissue massage, and facial for under forty dollars. In Southeast Asia, our fortunes had drastically shifted from being underclass peasants to being lords of the manor, though Justin's meager savings had begun to dwindle and I was only making a thousand dollars a month writing.

"Why don't you just start writing with me?" I asked one evening while on our way to a tour a group of high school students had recommended during one of our visits to a local park in Ho Chi Minh City.

I didn't want to return to America, and I knew our life in Asia was unsustainable if we didn't have a combined income.

"This place is really cool, and you will learn a lot about our history," one of the students chimed in, drawing my attention away from the heavy conversation.

CU CHI TUNNELS, read a sign erected in front of an expansive wooded area.

As soon as the bus shifted into park, Justin hopped out of his seat, grabbed my hand, and pulled me toward the exit. We joined a line to purchase tickets for entry and then were escorted to a covered, empty area with old metal chairs facing a small TV.

"We need to talk about this," I whispered.

I was consumed with the unwanted thought that we would be drawn back to America and once again have to separate in order to survive, and I wanted his assurance that he would do anything to ensure that didn't happen.

"Later," Justin said.

"But . . . ," I began, but the TV flickered on and a commanding voice emanated from the front of the room, silencing me.

I turned my attention to the old-school box as subtitles translated the message being delivered in Vietnamese by a voice that sounded both robotic and emotionless.

"The evil, devil white man . . . ," read the subtitles spread across the screen.

That introductory declaration gripped my attention. The scourge of white supremacy had found me in the farthest reaches of the globe. The video explained that about a century earlier, the French had colonized Vietnam and, as a result, by World War II the country had become both ideologically and politically split. A treaty signed during the 1954 Geneva Conference divided the country along the latitude known as the seventeenth parallel and put Chinese-and-Soviet-communism-inspired leader Ho Chi Minh in charge of the North and French-educated and Western-leaning Emperor Bao Dai in charge of the South. When the Cold War intensified worldwide, the United States hardened its position against communist sympathizers and allied itself with the South's subsequent leader, the oppressive and tyrannical Ngo Dinh Diem, to crack down on the Vietcong (communist/North Vietnam sympathizers). The United States wanted to stop communism from spreading across the world and stepped in to eliminate the ideology before it firmly planted roots in the Southeast Asian country. With training and equipment provided by the American military, Ngo Dinh Diem arrested some one hundred thousand people, torturing and killing many of them. In 1961, America sent its troops to the region and shortly afterward began its bombing campaign on North Vietnam and its neighbors. The North Vietnamese fighters were woefully outnumbered and lacked the resources of their Southern, American-backed foes, but they refused to give up fighting. With shovels and pickaxes, they dug the underground system called the Cu Chi Tunnels to move about and attack unseen, and created booby traps in the vast jungles of the region. By 1967, there were five hundred thousand American troops stationed in Vietnam, engaged in what felt like endless warfare. Though the American forces were better armed, they were outmaneuvered by the Vietnamese troops' guerrilla tactics. As images of the death and devastation that resulted circulated in the media, Americans became very critical of their country's involvement in the bloody war, and the government decided to pull out of the region. By the conflict's end, more than three million people had been killed, including over fifty-eight thousand American troops. More than half of the casualties were Vietnamese civilians.

As I lowered myself into a five-by-five-foot hole that was an entry point to the tunnels, I was awestruck by the sacrifices of the Vietnamese soldiers who fought side by side with their countrywomen and countrymen to secure their freedom. After the initial descent, I squeezed into a room that the tour guide explained was used as an infirmary, and envisioned bloodied bodies begging to be mended after exposure to the ravages of war. How many nights of terror were endured in those dark tunnels? How did it feel to be finally liberated from the torments of the country that boasted of democracy and freedom? By the end of our tour, the implications of my tourism in the region were laid bare: armed with the U.S. dollar, I was the beneficiary of white colonialism, imperialism, and war. The cloud of that realization followed me for the duration of our time in southeast Asia. The commodification of Asian female bodies in red-light districts, established during the war as "rest and relax" areas where American military men sought out female "companionship" in exchange for pay, finally made sense. The ubiquity of young people in the city's parks who spoke perfect English looked more like colonialism than higher education.

Where did I fit into it all, as a Black American woman? The privilege of my Americanness connected me to a dreadful history of Asian exploitation and oppression. But my Blackness forced me to carry the heavy reality of my inferiority.

"Let's go back," Justin said one night.

I reluctantly agreed and we booked two tickets to Ohio. Christmas was nearing, and Justin's parents were excited to play host.

Justin's parents lived in Mansfield, Ohio—a small, rural, mostly white town where Confederate flags regularly adorned cars—in a huge colonial-style home next door to a cornfield and adjacent to a barnyard that could have served as the set for a horror film.

"Y'all brave," I laughed as we pulled into the driveway.

The weight of rural whiteness was heavy in the air, causing me to feel like I was stifled and struggling for oxygen as we walked toward the front door. I took each step carefully and deliberately, as if any tiny sound could awaken some scary creature lurking in the environment. When the door swung open, Justin's mom's smiling brown face greeted us. Her hair was braided into two ponytails with bows tied to their ends, and she was wearing a denim dress with a flowery-print cotton shirt beneath it. Justin's mom spared no effort in creating the *Little House on the Prairie* lifestyle she idealized for herself and her children. Stories of his upbringing were proof: She homeschooled Justin and all six of his siblings, most of whom, by then, were in college or teaching English abroad. She raised her children in the church and allowed them to indulge only in pastimes sanctioned by her evangelical Christian belief system. Justin's family was the picture-perfect image of American success by most quantifiable measures: They owned a large home that boasted all of the trappings of Americanness—an immaculately manicured lawn and expansive backyard, multiple cars in the driveway, a spotless kitchen with new appliances, and an eight-seat dining room set where dinner was frequently eaten. They went to church every Sunday and listened only to Christian music. The only thing that weighed on them was the burden of their Blackness.

"Welcome!" Justin's mom said with a wide smile.

She showed me to the guest room, and then we all sat around the kitchen table exchanging pleasantries as 1940s Christmas tunes sang of white Christmases and frightful weather. After we settled, Justin's mom urged us to take a tour of the town. It was a cold, gray, cloudy day and everything in sight appeared to be on the cusp of death, from the bare trees and brown lawns to the empty street and storefronts. Mansfield was a mostly dilapidated town with three main attractions: a sprawling state penitentiary called the Ohio State Reformatory, which offered daily tours (one of which boasted the opportunity to have a "paranormal experience" and another where participants could walk through the area where *The Shawshank Redemption* was filmed), a rubber factory, and an indoor carousel. It was late evening and both the rubber factory and the prison were already closed, so Justin's mom pressured us to ride the carousel.

"Mom, Tiffanie doesn't want to ride a carousel," Justin roboti-cally said.

"Come on, it will be fun!" she urged.

He reluctantly acquiesced. I secretly poked him with my elbow to exchange an inside look of equal parts humor and disdain, but he re-fused my eye contact.

"Just humor her," I whispered.

He wasn't humored.

We all entered the building that housed the ride and walked into a gift shop where a young white woman was selling tickets. Justin's mom giddily purchased one for each of us—Justin, his dad, me, and herself. We stuffed our tickets into a box and then pushed through the turnstile that allowed entry into an adjoining circular room that housed the hand-crafted wooden zoo-themed carousel. There was a horse with a mer-maid tail, a black-faced kitten that much resembled a llama, an extra-large bunny rabbit, panda bears, ostriches, and some other more classic op-tions like horses with four legs and a carriage. A large white family was in the midst of hanging birthday decorations for a child's party as we entered. The men resembled characters I had only ever seen on the popular reality show *Duck Dynasty*. They wore green-and-black camou-flage and heavy-looking black leather boots and had long beards, and the women had dirty-blond messy hair and wore jeans and T-shirts. As we made our way to the carousel, their gazes shifted in our direction and the stink of silent revulsion and outrage filled the air. I scurried onto one of the nearby horses and crouched down, trying to make myself as small and invisible as possible, and then I looked to Justin and his fam-ily for guidance on how to brave this new white world. His parents both sat erect, their faces frozen in delight like mannequins. Justin's shoulders were hunched forward and his hand firmly grasped the pole that ran down between his legs to steady his mechanical horse—a black stallion with a blue saddle. The music began and the room blurred as the carousel whipped around in its orbit. The horse I rode gently inched upward and then descended to the sound of organ music. Every time the carousel made its revolution, the *Duck Dynasty* look-alike family came into focus. Their mouths were agape and some had begun to whisper and point in our direction. I shuddered and shrank more and more with each turn, praying for an end to the experience that would not include an assault on my person. Or utterances of any racial epithets.

"Want to ride again?" Justin's mom asked when the ride came to a halt and we shuffled toward the exit.

I shook my head no but couldn't manage to say a word. I was horrified by the discomfort of the moment and wondered why anyone would possibly subject themselves to such scrutiny and contempt. But I guess Justin's family had grown accustomed to trading their dignity for their piece of the American dream.

Justin's parents moved to Ohio in the eighties, after his dad took up an offer by the government that would wipe away the debt he had accrued in pursuit of becoming a doctor in exchange for his working in an "underserved" community. He imagined "underserved" was a euphemism for a Black city or town and was excited by the prospect of "giving back" while simultaneously being able to pay off his student loans. When his first assignment listed "Jackson, Ohio" as the town that was home to the clinic he would lead, he pulled out a map to find the city nestled in the woods of Appalachia, where poverty and racism were both widespread and overabundant. He knew it would be a challenge to overcome the prejudices of the local populace in Jackson, but he was up for the task. Without any debt, it would be much easier for him to create the life he imagined for himself, his son, and his then-pregnant wife.

"They stopped coming to the clinic when they found out my dad was going to be the new doctor," Justin explained while showing me clippings of an article the local town's newspaper had published upon the arrival of the new Black physician.

When the refusal of the white clientele in Jackson to come to the clinic to receive his care forced it to close, he took the next offer that would confer a clean economic slate, from a neighboring town, Gallipolis, where he was hired to oversee the opening of another clinic.

"We can take a ride to the first town where we lived when we first moved here!" Justin's mom genially offered.

"Oh God, Mom, no," Justin begged.

But her mind was already set. In the morning, we would make the three-hour trip to Jackson and Gallipolis. And I would finally get to see what life was like growing up for Justin.

"Do you take tea or coffee?" Justin's mom asked when I arose from bed the next day.

"Uh, what's that noise?" I asked her in between heaves, still struggling to catch my breath.

Moments earlier the bursting sounds of gunfire had come ricocheting through the guest room and I had jumped out of bed to rush downstairs, scared of what might have happened while I was sleeping. In my mind, anything could happen when too many Black people occupied a house in a land of Confederate flags.

"Oh sweetie, that's just the boys in the back with their guns," she replied.

"Morning, Tiff," Justin murmured as he entered the kitchen.

I stared at him wide-eyed.

"Whaaaat?" Justin asked, irritating me with his patronizing tone. "Who doesn't like the sound of gunplay on a beautiful, sunny morning?"

He explained that the neighborhood folks all had guns and they sometimes enjoyed using them in the woods. The purchase of a semi–assault weapon at the local Walmart was actually a commonplace occurrence.

"They take a bunch of old nineties computer monitors and TVs back there and then shoot them up," he sardonically continued. "But some of them are just stockpiling for when the next Civil War arrives."

I laughed, because his insights were delivered like jokes, but I was terrified. I spent my morning seated as far away from the windows as possible. I knew the dangers of a stray bullet. By the time we were ready to begin our journey south to Jackson, I was relieved to escape the house.

"Why did you stay here?" I found the courage to ask Justin's parents during the first leg of our journey.

"Where else would we have been able to raise seven kids and afford to put them all through college?" his mom responded.

She had a good point. Justin's family knew how hard it was for a Black family to find stability in America. Both of Justin's grandfathers sought refuge in northern cities to escape the violence of the rural South, where they were raised. His dad's dad often recalled the evening when, as a little boy, he watched a Black man be lynched while neighbors stood by and did nothing, and his mom's dad told stories of "the Klan" marching through his neighborhood and how white kids and Black kids spent much of their time hurling racial slurs at one another across the main road that segregated his small town. Escape to the North, however, did not mean they left the racism and hate behind. As the car bumped down the highway, which ran through vast, flat lands covered in naked trees, Justin's mom told me about growing up in Queens, New York, and watching the funeral of Martin Luther King Jr. as a five-year-old. That same year, her mom and dad made the decision to leave their all-Black neighborhood, which had once been a safe haven for Black families. Drugs, violence, and poverty were becoming more rampant, and that once-safe neighborhood was in decline. The final straw came when a little Black girl attacked Justin's mom in kindergarten.

"I still have the scar right here, see?" she told me casually, pointing to her left cheek, which bore the permanent mark.

By the time we arrived in Jackson, I understood that Justin's and his family's scars were both visible and invisible. While Justin's mom eagerly pointed out the first "barnyard"-style house that the family rented from a white man when he was a toddler, Justin stared forlornly in the opposite direction out the car window.

"It was only when some friends and family came around that they told us the flag hanging over the house's garage door was the Nazi symbol," she said matter-of-factly.

I didn't know if I should feel confused by the revelation or embarrassed for Justin. I tried to gently inch my hand toward his in a show of support, but he moved his into his lap. His dad pulled the car into the house's gravel driveway, and they momentarily mused over how little had changed since they resided there decades earlier. Our tour continued into the heart of Gallipolis, where a short street was lined with brick-facade buildings that very much resembled those back in the Northeast. They pulled into a mini-mart, but I opted to stay in the car. There was absolutely nothing about that town that felt inviting for someone who looked like me.

"Are you okay?" I asked Justin, who had been silent much of the trip.

He shrugged and shifted his body from left to right, as if he was unable to get comfortable. I had been offered only a glimpse into the trauma that he had spent a lifetime enduring. But that little bit was enough for me to finally understand: there was nothing I alone could do to suck him out of the vortex of racist abuse that both he and his family had been stuck tumbling in, like clothes in a dryer, for so long.

"Just write with me and we could save money," I stubbornly tried once more. "We could leave here."

He lowered his eyes and never even offered a response.

Shortly afterward, I booked a flight back to Trinidad for myself alone. I felt guilty, like I was abandoning him, as I sat on the plane and prepared for departure.

"Please secure your mask before assisting others," said the voice giving emergency safety instructions over the intercom.

My chest was so tight with sadness and anxiety. I could barely even breathe.

CHAPTER 8

Lethal Abuse

Is this how I die?

Each time a victim returns to their abuser, the capacity for abuse escalates. Eventually, the abuse can become fatal. I first began to be haunted by thoughts of my own death in my early twenties. Such thoughts were fleeting then, appearing briefly and then vanishing like a spirit. They were conjured by images of lynched Black bodies or fears that I had some undiagnosed medical condition. Thoughts of my own death became more frequent as I began to better understand America's cycle of abuse with its Black populace: the way destruction and death always seemed to follow times of progress. I wondered, would my time come after high school? Or maybe college? Would I be gunned down for a traffic violation on my way home from my graduation? Or struck by a stray bullet while enjoying my favorite sitcom on television? Would violence find me in my most prideful moment, in the same way that the vicious wave of white terrorism from organized groups like the Ku Klux Klan, the White League, and Knights of the White Camelia followed the era of Reconstruction? Did the rise in white supremacist hate groups and white violence that immediately followed the election of Obama,

America's first Black president, threaten my life? Would I become another Black health statistic? Eventually, I came to recognize the whispering voice in my mind as the part of my Black consciousness that understood that my mere existence repulsed, defied, and threatened the tenets of white supremacy. Such threat and defiance could warrant death. The louder I began to express my disdain for the oppressive forces that wreaked havoc on my life, the more violent the voice in my head became.

Is this how you want to die? Taking a bullet to the head? Skull cracked into bits, your brain strewn about?

To be a Black woman is to live, either consciously or subconsciously, carrying the burden that your death or destruction is imminent. Death trails your car at night when you are driving home from work and spot a police car in your rearview mirror. It is by your side at every doctor's appointment. Its threat grows with your belly during every pregnancy. It lurks behind every promise of love from a Black man. You are constantly haunted by statistics, and the statistics never look favorable.

According to the 2010–12 National Intimate Partner and Sexual Violence Survey, nationally, 45 percent of Black women experienced contact sexual violence, physical violence, and/or stalking by an intimate partner in their lifetime.[1]

According to the CDC, Black women ages twenty-five to twenty-nine are eleven times more likely as White women in that age group to be murdered while pregnant or in the first year after childbirth.[2]

As the scroll upon which your hardship is written into reality endlessly unfurls, it moves beneath you like you are running on a treadmill that you cannot keep up with, high above a canyon.

According to the U.S. Department of Health and Human Services, in 2017, African American mothers were 2.3 times more likely than non-Hispanic white mothers to receive late or no prenatal care.[3]

According to the CDC, Black women are three to four times more likely to experience a pregnancy-related death than white women.[4]

Yet Black women hope and pray that they can beat the odds and not only survive but thrive in spite of the looming dangers of Black womanhood. We stiffen our spines and soften our tone during police encounters to attempt to ward off the threat of becoming the next Lajuana Phillips, Crystal Danielle Ragland, Latasha Nicole Walton, April Webster, or Sandra Bland. We act as shields for Black men while knowingly leaving ourselves vulnerable to attack by those we desire to love and those who have built systems to destroy us. We bring children into this world to love, uncertain of whether or not we can protect them.

It was 2016 and the summer was mild as I stepped out of Newark International Airport. Only moments earlier, it had felt like the world had flattened while I sat on an airplane gliding above the gray, industrial city as we approached for landing. I was entering a dark dimension where I could not bring the colorfulness, joy, and carelessness I had inhabited while living in Trinidad for the past year. I healed from my breakup with Justin in Trinidad, finding relief from heartache in solo weekend beach trips and long chats with Granny, who had finally returned home and was living with my aunt in Trincity.

"Come back soon," she said when I told her I would be taking a trip to the U.S. "Don't get stuck out there."

As the plane descended, I already yearned for the warm feeling of home and of being immersed in a sea of faces of color. My status as a "Black" "minority" weighed on me while I hiked through the vast, clean, quiet, fluorescent-lit airport. Where I was going—back to Jersey City on a quest to help my mom pack up and finally move back to Trinidad—wouldn't be so bright.

"I made your favorite," Mom coaxed while she sped down the highway after she picked me up.

"Thanks" was all I could muster.

Her neighborhood looked worse than I remembered it—dingier

and more depressed. But when I opened the door to Mom's house, the familiar smells of home greeted me.

"Come on, cheer up!" she cajoled. "It's not gonna be so bad."

As always, Mom had prepared my bribe: food. A single whiff of her special curried crab and dumplings made my mouth water. I rushed to the kitchen to fix a plate. When my taste buds exploded with the savory sweetness of the crabmeat and its sauces, I found myself more open to her America. Three months of my life was a small price to pay to keep Mom company and help her figure out how to sell her house and move back home with me. I planned to work, save up some money, jog every day, and return to Trinidad with a full bank account and the best body I ever had. I envisioned returning with luggage filled with chocolates and goodies for Granny and clothes and new bathing suits for myself.

But one man would change my plans.

It was a sunny, quiet summer afternoon when I stumbled upon him, bouncing a basketball in the local park by himself. I asked if I could join.

"If you want to," he responded casually.

He was tall and athletic with smooth mahogany skin and the perfect smile. His name was Gabriel. I took note of his attractiveness but played it off like I barely even noticed him. He chest-passed me the ball and I threw it up toward the hoop.

Swish!

"Oh, so you can shoot?" he asked patronizingly.

I rolled my eyes and dove toward the ball to get the rebound.

"Yeah, and I bet I could destroy you one on one too."

He was a twenty-eight-year-old mental health worker at the local hospital who was born in Jersey City, New Jersey, and raised there by his Haitian parents. While we shot around, he explained that he was working evening shifts at the hospital, as well as going to school and doing an internship in order to complete his master's degree in social work.

We connected instantly. I was impressed that, like me, he stood in defiance of systemic racism. He hadn't been gobbled up by Greenville, Jersey City's violence or beaten down or incarcerated by its prejudicial justice system. He was a part of a very small demographic: a Black man who not only survived but thrived, despite American oppression.

"When I went for the interview for my job at the hospital, the secretary thought I was there for a janitorial position," he recalled with a laugh.

He told me stories of being stopped and frisked daily while on his way to school and getting his head slammed against the pavement by police after refusing to lower all of his car's windows during a routine traffic stop in the middle of the winter.

"I'm ready to go back home," I sighed, exhausted and missing Trinidad. "I think my soul is dying."

"Don't worry, I'll keep it alive until you leave."

He offered to give me a ride home, and I accepted, not quite ready for our chance meeting to end. All of my dating experiences had taught me to be exceedingly protective of my feelings, but his charm was disarming.

"I don't know what you are doing later, but I was thinking about going to Six Flags," he said as we made our way down Garfield Avenue toward my house. "You wanna come?"

That evening, we sped down the turnpike toward exit 7a, blasting soca and hip-hop tracks. I peered out at the cloudy gray sky and then turned my gaze toward the factories bellowing dark smoke lining the highway. Typically, the sight of expansive industrialism would make me yearn for the mountain ranges and clear blue skies in Trinidad, but his company kept my mind from wandering back home. As we zoomed by, Jersey's industrial landscape eventually softened to reveal forests of oak trees and rolling green pastures, and I relaxed into the passenger seat with a smile.

When we got to the theme park, we jumped out of the car on a single mission: to ride "Nitro." Once the tallest in the park, the blue-and-yellow roller coaster was our agreed-upon favorite. We waited the extra twenty minutes on line just to ride in the front car so we could hang over the edge until the entire coaster crept over the first hump to take its plunge. As the coaster snaked out of the station, making a left before ascending the steep hill, I clamped my hand tightly onto the yellow lap bar in front of me.

"You can't hold on. You have to throw your hands up!" he screamed over the beating wind.

Oh, hell naw, I thought to myself.

Right before the drop, he grabbed my hand tightly and threw it into the air. I was shocked at first, prepared to hold my breath and close my eyes—the way I had learned to cope with the horror of dangling 184 feet in the air waiting to free-fall. But when I looked over at him, he had a wide grin, with both of his arms raised high above his head, excited as a child on Christmas. I gathered all the courage I could muster, let go of the lap bar, and raised my free hand into the sky, with the other still holding his. As the roller coaster took its plunge, it felt like my heart was lifting out of my chest cavity, struggling to keep up with the rest of my body. The roller coaster barreled down the track, cutting through the wind at eighty miles per hour.

"Woooooooooohhh!" everyone in the train screamed at different pitches.

I joined in soprano, as if the star of a roller-coaster-train-car choir.

By the end, I was teary-eyed and my heart was racing, but I felt exhilarated. He was panting, still trying to catch his breath and beaming.

"You wanna ride again?" he asked before the coaster parked in the station.

"Absolutely."

After that day, we spent all of our free time together. In the mornings, we exchanged texts full of jokes, smiley-face emojis, and hearts. During his breaks at the hospital, he would pick me up and we would share a box of lamb-and-rice halal food and exchange stories about our lives.

"My parents were almost never home," he explained one day. "They were always busy working at the church or trying to help my family from Haiti."

Despite stereotypes that branded Haitians as voodoo-inspired witch doctors, most became staunchly Christian as a result of colonialism.

Haiti's history is complex and unique.[5] Haitians were the first Black revolutionaries in the Western Hemisphere to win their freedom from slavery and French colonialism by revolting. In 1791, formerly enslaved Toussaint L'Ouverture led enslaved Blacks to capture the island, killing and exiling many of the land's white inhabitants. Inspired by the French Revolution's "Declaration of the Rights of Man," the insurrection lasted for over a decade, ending in 1804 when Haiti became a sovereign nation. The uprising sent shock waves across the world, all the way to Europe, where fears of losing control of European colonies in the Americas mounted, prompting a vengeful backlash. Although in the eighteenth century Haiti was France's wealthiest colony (then known as Saint-Domingue), it would be reduced to pain, hardship, and rubble in the centuries after its emancipation, beginning when the French arrived with warships in 1825, demanding the country pay millions in reparations.

Since that day, Haiti has paid its former colonizer over $21 billion in reparations,[6] plunging the country into economic duress that has created widespread social instability.[7] By the time a catastrophic earthquake rocked the tiny nation in 2010, it was already buried in poverty, poor housing conditions, and violence from years of being subjected to unfair trade sanctions that can be traced back hundreds of years to white anger over Black freedom.

Gabriel's family inherited that history—a complicated but proud one. One steeped in colorism, self-hate, and protectionism but simultaneously strengthened by pride and unity.

"My mom would make us kneel on vegetable graters," he disclosed with an uneasy laugh one day.

I cringed at the abuses of corporal punishment, but he never flinched a single time while telling stories—not even of the time his father hit him with the buckle of a belt, leaving a scar on his shoulder, or of the times he had to go outside and get a tree branch so his grandmother could make a switch out of it. But those dark moments of talking about our pasts were outshined by the bright times we spent together in those three months.

Summers in Jersey were short compared with those in Trinidad—only two to three months at most—so we made sure to spend as much time as possible outside enjoying the warm weather. Every evening, we went to the local basketball courts to team up and shoot against other players. We were an unstoppable team who often beat out our competition at two-ball—a shooting game where two teams show off against each other to sink the most three-pointers.

"What is this, some *Love & Basketball* shit?" one male opponent asked us. "I wish I could find a girl to do that with."

The question of love had certainly begun to creep up on me. But I fended it off like a madwoman.

"I'm not interested in anything serious," I declared one day, when it started to feel like things were moving too quickly.

I was hell-bent on escape and feared our time together would become a distraction from my goal of getting back to Trinidad as quickly as possible.

"God sent you for me," he said. "I don't think I want to share you."

A Black woman consumed by fears that I would never find a Black man "suitable" for my love, I had to admit that I also viewed him as being sent from above. Still, I was torn between my love of Trinidad and Tobago and my love for a man. Perhaps I could just have them both.

By that time, the reality that people of color and minorities were unwelcome in the United States was more clear than ever, and I could no longer repress my desire to leave the country. An unexpected presidential candidate had begun to gain traction that summer, as the election that would follow Obama's tenure began to loom. Donald Trump was white, wealthy, and slippery with bravado. Through unorthodox and stylized rallies, he'd made a name for himself "telling it like it is" and giving the almost-all-white working-class Americans who felt they'd suffered through the last eight years a candidate behind whom they could throw the fire of their anger and entitlement. Trump promised to return the country to its "family values." In Trump, conservative white America, which was struggling to find redemption, found a savior. Trump's presidential campaign hinged on the veiled racism and conspiracy that underpinned his simple slogan "Make America Great Again." That slogan pledged to return the country to a bygone era when white supremacy and paternalism equaled dominance and intelligence. He promised to build a border wall to protect the nation from dangerous outsiders like Mexicans, whom he disparaged as "drug dealers, criminals, and rapists." He branded Black Lives Matter protesters "thugs" as they fought to secure basic civil liberties. Yes, his campaign was marred by his history of blatant misogyny and allegations of sexual assault, but all it seemed to mean was that his win would exonerate any white men who wanted to openly degrade women.

"Grab 'em by the pussy" became a rallying cry for women all across the nation who were outraged after a leaked recording of the candidate was circulated by the media.

By then, Mom's neighborhood felt like it was under siege. Arguments, loud music, and police sirens blared all day. The dark nights brought sounds of gunshots and the screams of men high on PCP.

"HEEEEELP!" I heard a man hollering around midnight one night. "THE DEEEEEVIL IS AAAAFTER MEEE!"

His desperate shrieks continued for thirty minutes before the police arrived and subdued him, then put him in an ambulance.

Neighbors began to disappear one by one. First, a friendly young man in his twenties with locs who was frequently outside playing with his daughter and the neighborhood kids vanished. We had often exchanged greetings or made small talk as I prepared to take my usual afternoon jog. When days went by and I didn't see him, I asked another neighbor if he was all right.

"I'm sorry, baby, but he got shot," she said.

He had been up the block at the corner store when a man approached him, opened fire, and shot him in the head. His face haunted me in vivid nightmares. In them, he would always be smiling and waving at me, but there would be a gaping hole, oozing with blood, where I imagined the single gunshot pierced his forehead. Only weeks later, another young man who lived right across the street was murdered. They cordoned off the front of his house with yellow police tape that stretched all the way to our sidewalk and drew chalk lines in the crime scene. By then, I was more angry at the inconvenience than outraged over the murder. Living in a constant emergency state—where police vehicles or ambulances blaring sirens could come from any direction (even on a one-way street) at any moment, where drug busts occurred regularly, with SWAT teams breaking down your neighbors' doors, and where domestic violence and murder were commonplace—meant it was easy to become emotionally numb to Black pain.

After what had felt initially like a perfect union with Gabriel, there was now no shortage of drama that would regularly send my life spinning out of control. Relatively fresh out of an on-again-off-again relationship with his ex-girlfriend when he met me, he told me his family was still reeling from their breakup. As the president of the church, his father played an integral role in keeping "the community" (which was almost strictly Haitian) together, and Gabriel's ex's father was the church's vice president. Often discriminated against in America, Haitians had learned that their survival depended on their ability to stick together. Gabriel's union with his ex was supposed to unify the families and strengthen the institution. Unbeknownst to me, many in his community seemed to think I was the only thing that stood in the way.

When I first found out about "the ex," I urged him to be sure to follow his heart.

"She is crazy," he said, dismissing my empathy. "I would never want to be with her."

Then "crazy" literally came knocking. It began with an onslaught of emails.

You better leave my man alone, we have been building for ten years plus, one read.

You just a bum bitch, another declared.

Simultaneously, my "perfect" mate was spiraling out of control.

"I don't want you talking to him anymore!" he screamed in my face when a platonic male friend sent me a text message late one night.

"Who is over there with you?" he demanded another night.

But I was sleeping alone in my room at my mother's house. I pinned his blowups on the stress of having to deal with his family and everything unfolding with his ex.

"You know Donald Trump's wife Melania did soft-core porn?" I jokingly inquired over dinner, trying to cut the tension that had become commonplace in our relationship. "So much for conservative values, eh?"

He shrugged and pushed his food around his plate with a fork, avoiding eye contact.

Still, Trump managed to defeat Hillary Clinton to become the forty-fifth president of the United States of America. Headlines labeled Trump a dangerous narcissist. An abuser. A racist. They pointed to disturbing commentary he made about his daughters on national television and exposed his corruption, his failed businesses, and his tax evasion. The toxic potency of white dominance was impossible to ignore. Right-wing conservatives embraced Trump, their concerns about his temperament assuaged because, in a time of angst about white power and influence, he proved the white male viewpoint remained the omnipotent majority one. The liberal left papered over America's acceptance of white supremacy and sexism by declaring, "Not my president!" and treating Trump like a cavity-induced toothache that could be remedied with a drill and a filling, a tactic that didn't acknowledge the deeply rooted system that emboldened him and that couldn't be so easily fixed. Whether Americans admired or despised Trump, he was familiar. He was the embodiment of the country's pathology, a walking, ranting incarnation of its idealized self: white, male, self-absorbed, powerful, wealthy, arrogant, and entitled. Ultimately, the rise of Trump stirred discomfort in some but failed to rattle the shared faith in the great nation. Both sides of the political spectrum believed America could absorb the shock of the Trump presidency. That democracy would ultimately reign supreme. As I watched his mostly white supporters, many of whom toted Confederate flags and spewed racism like hissing, venomous snakes, become more vocal and visible, I feared for the safety of every Black person all across the nation.

Then came what I thought would be a far more welcome surprise.

"I'm pregnant," I told Gabriel one evening at the park while sitting in his car. I eagerly awaited his reply, sure that he'd see this as a positive development.

"You tryna trap me?" he fired back.

I was devastated and confused. Up until that moment, it had felt like he was the driving force behind our courtship: his frequent calls, his abundant text messages wishing me a good day or singing my praises, his repeated desire to "only be together" all served as proof. But that day, everything flipped. I went home stunned. He called moments later, apologizing for his outburst and begging for me to forgive him.

"There's just so much going on, Tiff," he pleaded. "I love you and I want to have this baby with you."

And there was a lot going on. As soon as we told his family about the pregnancy, they began to pressure us to get married—even though I wasn't the woman they'd pinned their hopes on. His parents needed to legitimize our relationship in the eyes of the church, and Gabriel wanted to prove to them that he wasn't a screwup. He had long been branded the family's "black sheep" for his resistance to the very narrow upbringing he was supposed to submit to. As an adolescent, he opted out of church on Sundays to participate in baseball leagues and hang out with friends his mother did not approve of. In college, he decided to pursue social work instead of a degree that could secure him a more lucrative career. Now he was threatening to spit in the face of tradition, once again, by having a baby out of wedlock.

"Let's do it," he coaxed daily.

Though I liked Gabriel, I never trusted him to make good financial decisions, ones that would ensure resources set aside for health care. He lived with his parents, yet he never made it to the end of the month with money in the bank, typically opting to splurge on food from restaurants, gas to aimlessly drive around, and other indulgences. I accepted his financial shortcomings as a matter of immaturity and imagined he would eventually evolve. But if I dared to marry him, I would leave myself vulnerable to not being able to afford health insurance, and our combined incomes could push me out of the income bracket to receive free health benefits. Instead, I urged practicality—for us to remain single so I could continue to receive Medicaid, free state health insurance that would guarantee affordable medical care for the duration of my pregnancy. For two young people buried in student loans, living with their parents and barely eking out a living, the additional burden of figuring out co-pays would be untenable.

"We can put all of the money we'll save towards a down payment for a house!" I argued.

He eventually acceded to my plan and I remained on Medicaid. I was conservative America's worst nightmare: a Black woman "taking advantage" of the system. A "welfare queen."

Upon registering for Medicaid, I was automatically assigned an HMO, which decided where I could access services—in my case, a health center not far from my Jersey City residence. I called and scheduled my first appointment, thrilled to find out details about the tiny new life growing inside of me. I excitedly imagined exchanging stories about impending motherhood or getting advice from other mothers in the waiting room.

"Nope, I don't care if it's a boy or a girl," I proudly rehearsed in my head, anticipating what other interested mommies-to-be would ask.

The doctor's office was in a two-story, brick-front building that looked just a little run down, right across the street from a park that was a frequent venue for huge fights that would end in police using pepper spray and Tasers to disperse groups of rowdy Black children. A nurse directed me to a seating area to fill out a packet of information attached to a clipboard, and I waited for my name to be called. Two other young Black women in their twenties were already seated. One was heavyset and had an enormous belly protruding from a shirt that uncomfortably clung to her body and barely covered her navel. She gave me a small, welcoming smile, revealing a gap where her front tooth should've been, as I took a seat across from her. The other, a petite woman with a tiny, perfectly round bump and wearing black-and-purple Jordans, skinny jeans, and a hoodie, sat nearby chatting loudly on her phone. The room reeked of poverty and hardship.

"They best not tell me I have to come back again today, cuz I have to work," she declared, both into the phone and to those of us in the waiting room.

"I hate when they be doing that," the other girl piped up.

"It happens a lot?" I asked.

"Mm-hmm-huh," she responded.

"The last time I missed the whole day and the boss was getting on me about it," the other girl continued her conversation on the phone.

I shrugged.

"You look like you about to pop," I said with a chuckle, trying to lighten the mood.

She gave me a weak smile.

"I'm eight months," she replied, exhausted. "They say I gained too much weight with this pregnancy, but most of the time I feel like all I have the energy to do is eat."

I lowered my eyes to hide the judgments brewing internally. Mom always warned me that I struggled immensely with concealing my opinions, even when I didn't utter a single word, so I evaded her gaze to avoid giving myself away. I took note of each of these women's struggles and tried to relieve my own circumstances of such burdens in my mind: (1) I worked from home and would never have to choose between making appointments and making a living; and (2) I was an avid exercise en-thusiast, so there was no way in hell I would get as fat and dejected as the woman sitting across from me. I was nothing like those women, I concluded.

"Drayton," a nurse called.

I waved goodbye to the women and sprang out of my seat toward the examination rooms.

"Room one after you fill this up in the bathroom," the nurse said, handing me a cup to pee in.

I relieved myself and handed the cup off to the nurse, dashed toward the room, and then plopped down on the examination table, my legs wagging as they dangled above the ground like a child's.

"The nurse will be with you shortly."

The walls in the room were bare, except for a poster showing a dia-gram of the female anatomy and a pregnant woman with a peachy com-plexion and a fetus turned upside down in her belly. I scanned it for any insights about what was going to happen to my body. Then another nurse, a short Black woman with green scrubs, came in and took my weight, height, and blood pressure.

"The doctor will be with you shortly," she said, gently closing the door as she left.

The doctor popped right in after her departure. He was a meticu-lously dressed white man with coiffed hair, wearing a suit with perfectly fitted pants and a tie. His nails were well manicured.

"So, how are you feeling, Ms. Drayton?" he questioned.

"I'm pretty all right."

He flipped through my chart perfunctorily and then sat in an office chair across from me.

"All right, well, I'm going to have the nurse schedule your next ap-pointment for three weeks from now to get more details on your medical history," he went on. "Drink some water and make sure you put your feet up and get rest."

And just like that, the appointment was finished. One nurse scheduled me to meet with the head nurse in four weeks; I would not be scheduled to see the doctor for another six weeks.

"There's no way this is right," I told my mom over dinner. "I'm not sure if he was there auditioning for *America's Next Top Model* or to be the host on *Queer Eye*. There's no way in hell he touches vaginas with those hands."

We exchanged jokes at the doctor's expense and laughed until we cried. But I knew my health was no laughing matter. The next day, I spent hours on the phone trying to change my HMO plan so I could beg my previous gynecologist to take me on as a pregnant patient. At first, she was hesitant to take on a patient who was well into pregnancy, one who already received care from another doctor. She had a full roster of patients and already spent seven days a week running between the delivery room at the hospital and her office across the street. But my begging and insistence proved successful.

She did an ultrasound the day of my first appointment and printed pictures for me of the tiny life growing in my belly. I peered at the black-and-white images, trying to decipher the baby's head, hands, and mouth, but could make out only a black shadow sprinkled with white specks.

"We're gonna run a couple of tests and do some blood work," she said with a smile. "I'm glad you came in now, because you almost missed the time frame for some of these tests."

One of those tests was called "nuchal translucency screening," an ultrasound test that helps to identify possible chromosomal problems like Down syndrome. It was supposed to be done between weeks eleven and thirteen of pregnancy. I was already thirteen weeks pregnant, and had I not changed health-care providers, I would've sat at home with my feet up drinking water while, unbeknownst to me, the narrow window for testing closed. A nurse came in at the end of my visit and filled vial after vial with my blood to send off to the lab to be tested for everything from vitamin deficiencies to genetic abnormalities to even the sex of the baby. They scheduled my next appointment for six weeks in the future, but I got a call in less than a week.

"Ms. Drayton," said the familiar voice of the doctor's receptionist when I answered, "you are going to have to come down and see the doctor."

My blood work had turned up an abnormality, but they refused to give me details by phone. Both Gabriel and my mother tried to reassure me that everything would be okay, but I could not sleep for the hours between the call and the time I was scheduled to see the doctor. My hands perspired and quivered as I sat in the examination room awaiting the news. I tried to suppress my worst fears, but scary thoughts swirled in me. *Is the baby okay? Is the baby alive? Do I have cancer? Which one of us is about to die?*

The door swung open and the doctor appeared with a clipboard in her hand. She flipped through the chart, peering at tiny numbers written in boxes labeled "leukocytes," "hemoglobin," "platelets," and other words then unintelligible to me.

"Have you been feeling all right lately?" Dr. Muhammad began.

The question caught me off guard. I had been feeling more tired than usual and noticed a patch of missing hair at the front of my hairline, but I chalked it up to the pregnancy and hormonal changes.

"Your tests show that your T4 levels are really low, which indicates hypothyroidism," she continued.

Hypothyroidism is serious. After a quick (and perhaps ill-advised) Google search I learned that, left untreated, it can cause high blood pressure, anemia, muscle pain, and weakness. Hypothyroidism also significantly increased my odds of having a miscarriage, premature birth, or even stillbirth. Babies whose mothers don't have enough thyroid hormone circulating in their blood during pregnancy are also more likely to have intellectual disabilities, because the hormone is needed for proper fetal and neonatal brain development. I clicked through link after link of web pages on the subject before I just sat in front of my computer with a blank stare. My eyes welled with water as I tried to choke back the shock and horror of only narrowly avoiding becoming just another Black maternity statistic.

The doctor prescribed me levothyroxine to help get my hormones to the proper levels and assured me that we had caught the problem in time. But I spent sleepless nights wondering how many Black women across the country were less fortunate than I was to happen upon a competent, caring health-care provider. How many Black women were told to drink water and put their feet up while the tiny lives fighting to develop inside them suffered?

The synthetic hormones gave me a bit more energy and the missing patch of hair began to grow in, but I struggled to find the motivation to do very much. I was stuck in the midst of the winter, bouncing between my mother's small two-bedroom house and Gabriel's family's basement, both in neighborhoods embroiled in constant tragedy. Police sirens, vigils for murdered young men, loud verbal altercations, and gunshots were the backdrop to my daily life. Soon I felt myself spiraling into the darkness of depression. I yearned for the warmth of my home country's embrace and spent every waking hour lost in thoughts of my return. I replayed images of myself jumping up and down in the mud at fetes, holding Niki's hand. And the many days "liming" by the beach with a cold drink in hand while friends and family exchanged jokes and laughter.

He pick and pick until he pick shit! I said to myself, giggling at the memory of my Trini girlfriend explaining why her former mate ended up with a woman who stole his money and left him for another man.

I had to dig within myself to find sustenance to help my soul survive through those times in Jersey, replaying as often as I could the animated, hysterical stories told by Trinidadians in their sweet, melodic accent, to afford me some relief from depression. But I broke under the weight of my cold, dark reality: in the basement of a house belonging to a family who did not like me or in the home of my mother, where I was often left alone while she went to work. By my sixth month of pregnancy, I barely ever got out of bed. I couldn't find any desire to write or even walk. I longed for home and spent days crying over my decision to leave. I needed an escape, but by then life felt like nothing more than a debilitating feedback loop that rendered me financially dependent on Gabriel and my mother and unable to find the will to work. After each decline of my debit card balance while shopping for maternity clothes or for other basic necessities, I struggled back to bed. I missed important writing deadlines and new opportunities for work. With every missed opportunity, I became more broke and less able to provide for myself, further reinforcing my desire to remain in a perpetual supine position. One morning, I awoke beside Gabriel in our cold, dark basement lair with an idea I imagined would brighten my spirits.

"I think I'm gonna go visit Karla in Florida for a few weeks," I said.

At that time, my old and dear friend Karla was living with her husband in a three-bedroom townhouse she'd purchased in Orlando. A trip would offer us ample opportunity to catch up and would give me a cheap getaway, where I could at least bask in the Sunshine State's healthy rays. Perhaps, I thought, I could even muster the courage to begin writing again.

"You just want to spend all of my money, don't you!?" Gabriel screamed, spittle erupting from his mouth and wetting me like a sprinkler.

It was true that weeks earlier, I had borrowed a hundred dollars from him to purchase bloomers to stuff my oversized belly into and a couple oversized T-shirts and pairs of pants. His response now both startled and enraged me. He screamed in my face, calling me a gold digger and complaining that I was just using him for his money. The disconnect between the reality of my living in our parents' houses while pregnant and his alleging I was after him for money dumbfounded me.

"I never said that!" he argued after the fight settled. "I love you and I know you aren't like that."

The only relief from the depressing environment was food. And oddly, that was one expense that Gabriel never spared. Together we frequented Colombian, Dominican, Thai, Chinese, and Indian restaurants, placing orders for pad kee mao, chicken tikka masala, green curry, General Tso's, and lamb biryani to go. The buttery flavor of the naan or the spicy sweetness of the chicken tikka masala touching my taste buds were my only moments of joy and pleasure.

"Your blood pressure is too high," my doctor advised during a routine checkup.

She warned of preeclampsia, a blood pressure–related disease that claims the lives of thousands of new mothers and their babies annually. I pledged to be more mindful of my eating habits. Then I went home and ordered Domino's and ate pizza and wings while watching movies with Gabriel. On the day I was unexpectedly admitted to give birth, I was 220 pounds. It was August 21, 2017, and a partial solar eclipse was forecast to take place. I went to the doctor for a routine checkup, and even though my due date wasn't for several weeks, I was instructed to go to the hospital right away.

"There isn't enough fluid around the baby," my doctor explained.

She wanted me to deliver right away to avoid any risks or complications. When we arrived at the hospital's entrance, staffers in colorful scrubs were crowded at the door wearing makeshift solar eclipse glasses fashioned from cardboard boxes. Gabriel and I watched in awe as the sky darkened in the middle of the day. We passed a pair of solar eclipse glasses between us to catch a glimpse of the moon moving in front of the sun, obstructing it from view. The magic of that moment could be eclipsed only by the sight of my daughter when she first emerged from my body. A nurse gently placed her on my chest, and my thoughts froze as I watched her wriggle around in the warmth of my bosom. I named her Lea after Gabriel's grandmother, who had only recently passed away. She was my gift from the universe, and her birth offered Gabriel and me a chance at a fresh start. Upon learning that New Jersey was one of the first states to afford men paid paternity leave, I urged that we go to Trinidad shortly after her birth. Paternity leave would cover the trip that I imagined would change our life. Free from the burdens of work, American racism, and life in the "hood," I knew we could figure out how to move forward with building our life and family.

When the plane landed at Piarco International Airport, we collected our things from baggage claim and vowed to leave all of that emotional baggage and trauma back in the States.

"I want you," he said. "I want my family."

We immediately acquired the status of a nuclear family. I was working on a small book project and he had money coming in from taking paternity leave. We were able to secure a roomy two-bedroom apartment in a gated community with a pool, not too far away from my aunt's neighborhood in Trincity. Our new abode boasted a huge walk-in closet that I carefully organized into sections for "Daddy," "Mommy," and

"Baby." The first morning we awoke comfortably in our own space, it felt like we had been able to secure the life we deserved as two young, college-educated adult professionals. We walked around the neighborhood every morning and evening, hand in hand, taking turns wearing the baby strapped onto our chests in her carrier. The birds chirped all about us, singing their sweet melodies, as passersby in cars gently beeped their horns in a show of their support for our little family. We eventually became acquainted with many of our neighbors, who would wave as we passed, greeting us, "Mawning!" and "Aftanoon!" Our life was sweeter than a Julie mango. Gabriel looked so peaceful and happy in our new environment. And I was grateful to be able to expose him to the existence that I discovered when I first traveled to the twin islands of my birth. One filled with natural beauty and brown and Black faces living in peace. One where the police rode by us, giving us nods of approval instead of pinning us with apprehensive stares. In those moments, the girl with no home and the man from the hood were finally afforded privilege. My "happily ever after" seemed within my grasp.

Early one morning, I awoke to the sound of Gabriel's voice. It was energetic and full of excitement.

"It's so great here!" I heard him reporting. "The place is great and we have a pool right in front."

I stepped out of the room to find him sitting at the dining table with his phone propped in front of him. In the six weeks that we had been there, he had never once received a phone call from friends or family, so I was delighted to see him share his happiness with someone he knew. I walked around the table to catch a glimpse of who was on the receiving end of his eagerness. It was his mother, and her face was contorted and angry, filled with displeasure and contempt.

"You need to come back and go to work!" she forcefully asserted.

He shot me a look full of anger and shame. I immediately backed away and mouthed "sorry" to him for intruding on his conversation.

"She is such a bitch," I reported to my mom when I spoke to her later that day.

I ridiculed and imitated her "disgusting" accent while retelling the details of her warning to her son.

"She gonna order him to come back to spoon-feed him heaps of her nasty cooking," I continued.

It is not that I didn't enjoy Haitian meals prepared by Gabriel's mother, but I knew pitting our cultures against each other would be an assured win for me. Haiti was a poor, disenfranchised country that was predominantly Black, so everything associated with it was less than, and I knew that fact would always give me the upper hand whenever I felt backed into a corner. I played that hand frequently, pointing out the many ways that association with my background conferred me power and privilege. And even though I often spoke of raising our children to be multilingual, in support of his belief that they should speak English, Creole, and French, I really saw no value in his native tongue.

"We should visit Haiti one day," Gabriel suggested while he pushed the stroller through our Caribbean neighborhood.

"I guess," I responded, unenthused by the prospect of being surrounded by poverty.

In the past, those feelings of superiority and deep-seated pity for Gabriel and his native land had fueled much of my desire to "save" him, in spite of the way he treated me. Though I had pure intentions when I invited Gabriel to partake in my life and enjoy the privileges I had discovered by venturing back to my homeland, I was also quietly asking him to disavow his own upbringing, country, and culture. When his paternity leave came to an end, his job had already begun to lure him back with promises of a promotion and pay upgrade. My commitment to saving him from America, and his family culture, would be put to the test.

I found out I was pregnant with our second child within weeks of our return to the U.S. Gabriel was already back working full-time shifts at the hospital and I was living at home with my mom, who tried her best to accommodate us, despite barely having enough space for herself in the small house.

"Let's go to dinner tonight," I texted him after my eighteen-week checkup.

I told him it was supposed to be a treat and my mom would watch our daughter. Right after work, he picked me up and we jumped on the highway toward Red Lobster. His eyes were puffy and he was sullen. He barely spoke the whole way there. When we were seated at our table, I crept away, saying I needed to use the bathroom. I returned with the server, who was carrying a cake with "It's a Boy!" written across it in blue. That morning, the doctor had called me to schedule my next appointment and also to share the news. It was the first moment in my life that I ever cried with joy—our little family was about to be complete with the birth of our baby boy. I wanted to have two children close in age so they could share the bond I shared with Stefan in childhood, and Gabriel wanted a son to throw baseballs with in the park and nurture into the athlete he was never allowed to be.

Gabriel watched as the server placed the cake in front of him, but his demeanor remained flat. It was impossible for me to imagine that he did not share my excitement, so I pushed on, eager to draw out a response.

"We are having a boy!" I gleefully reiterated.

A small smile spread across his face, signaling a lukewarm reception of the news. The server applauded and told us "Congratulations" before walking away.

"You aren't excited?" I asked when we were alone.

He shook his head as if awakening from a trance and reached for my hand.

"Of course I am, babe," he said. "I just had a bad day at work."

Then he began to divulge his long list of hopes and dreams for us and our unborn son: *I'm sure he is going to be big and strong. I can't wait to take him to the beach. We just have to save enough money and we can get our own place. I can't wait to get back to Trinidad.*

"I love you, Tiff," he said before we rose from the table.

If all went well, in a few months we would have a perfect family and enough money saved to run away to the Caribbean, where we would figure out our next move in a world of endless possibilities for a Black couple like us. As he held my hand during our ride home, I never imagined he would want to let the dream go. And then Father's Day arrived.

That morning, Gabriel confronted me in the kitchen as soon as he awoke, his face inches from mine, screeching at me. "Where were you and who were you with?"

He had spent the night with me and Lea at my mom's house, but I had crept out at 6:00 a.m. to sneak away to Walmart to purchase bacon, eggs, and pancakes for breakfast.

"The grocery?" I replied in confusion.

I lifted the plastic bags of groceries with "Walmart" printed across their sides. He lunged toward me and grabbed the bags from my left hand, rummaging through them like a DEA agent searching for drugs. When he did not find anything to confirm whatever suspicions were in his own head, he threw the bags on the counter and continued his rant.

"Who leaves the house at that hour for groceries?" he scolded. "You could've waited for me to get up and take you."

I watched him with equal parts confusion and disdain. He marched up and down the house's stairs, slamming doors in anger, waking our daughter and my mother, who rushed out from her bedroom in alarm. Then he stomped out of the house, shutting the front door behind him.

"What did you do?" my mom asked.

"I went to the grocery," I told her.

She didn't believe me and continued to question me, seeking a more sensible explanation. Gabriel's rage had landed full force in our family, interspersed between calm moments where we walked hand in hand while pushing our daughter through the park or giggled at each other's jokes while watching the sunset on the boardwalk of Atlantic City. The rest of the time was marked by eruptions of violence and sheer terror. My world was almost constant trauma, degradation, and uncertainty.

"I can't take this anymore," I said to him soon after the Father's Day outburst. "We each need to go to therapy."

"I'll do anything to make this work," he said.

I arrived at therapy with an arsenal of Gabriel's wrongdoings ready to unleash on my counselor. Her name was Elena, a curly-haired, petite Hispanic woman who wore black-rimmed glasses and spoke quietly and thoughtfully. She listened to me recount, session after session, the abuse I suffered. Gabriel's refusal to allow me access to the car he repeatedly called "ours." The way he withheld money, even from our daughter, forcing me to go to court to put him on child support. The way he screamed and threw tantrums whenever he didn't get his way or felt threatened.

"Well, why do you stay?" she finally asked one day.

I looked down at my protruding belly and took time to internally grapple with the question. The truth was that I was too invested in the dream I had for us. "Happily ever after" was the only end I could envision to my tale. I had found my Beast, and it was just a matter of time before the spell cast upon him would be lifted, freeing him of his anger and internal trepidation.

"A promise to change means nothing without action," she warned.

But it was hard to decipher the truth behind her words in a reality that swung between two extreme poles: hot flashes of anger and periods of potential-filled peace. On good days, our life was the perfect picture of sunny evenings and hand-in-hand walks through the park. Warm smiles and locked, transfixed gazes—blossoming flowers, manicured lawns, matching outfits, and confident poses. It sounded like a million "I love you"s, "I miss you"s, and "forever"s. Like giggles and playful banter and loud, joyful squeals. It tasted like first kisses, favorite meals, and sweet desserts.

Then, like turning off a light, the switch would flip. Storms were always brewing, and a bright, sunny day could give way to cloudy skies, pouring rain, and the bitter cold. Affectionate words would turn to screaming, yelling, lies, and false accusations.

Tell me who you were with!

Shirts tore, doors broke, windows shattered. Friends were lost. Police sirens and our baby wailed.

"If you press charges, we will have to open a CPS case—you could lose your child," an officer warned when they arrived at the behest of a neighbor's call.

Our relationship felt like quicksand: the more I tried to fight, the deeper I sank into it.

"He is such a good guy!" friends often declared.

"That is between the two of you!" his family said.

"But he will lose his job!"

"Think about the baby."

Strangers and passersby gave nods of approval whenever we walked down the street together, our daughter in tow. He did everything right: He proudly carried our baby strapped to his chest, his hand firmly clasping mine. He held down a job and finished his master's. He cooked, cleaned, and woke up in the middle of the night to feed and change the baby. He brought home dozens of red roses and pink tulips to surprise me on Friday evenings.

"You complete my life," he said.

And then he would do everything wrong, disappearing at night and refusing to disclose *his* whereabouts, leaving me to care for our toddler while pregnant. There was always a plausible reason for his disappearances. Car trouble. Working an extra shift. Cracking his phone screen. Doing a favor for his mother. I was always at fault for the outbursts— for asking why he came home late when I should allow him space and freedom. For expecting him to take care of our daughter after he came home from a long shift at work. The stormy weather was always followed by more flowers. More promises. More kisses. Then again by more screaming. More uncertainty. More violence. I could barely keep the facts straight in a world that shifted, flipped, and twisted so dramatically. I wondered how the same man who professed his love to me could degrade me in front of my family with taunts and acts of aggression. My *Beauty and the Beast* tale had turned to *Dr. Jekyll and Mr. Hyde*. I searched for meaning in every cold stare and prayed for continued calm in quiet moments. I traded respect for "love," the definition of which remained elusive.

I received an email early one morning from Gabriel's ex. I stared at the message, confused. The email contained a video of him checking into a hotel room. His ex was with him and they spent hours together in the room. It was the same hotel we had stayed in with my daughter for a little getaway on her birthday weekend. It was also the same day: August 22, 2018.

I felt sick. I was so tired of the relationship that I simply acquiesced.

"You can have him back," I responded plainly.

I was exhausted and just wanted peace.

When I confronted Gabriel, he leaned into his toxicity.

"She is just an evil, lying, manipulating bitch," he spit at me.

I told his ex about his response and she sent me a screenshot from her phone. It was a message from him, calling me those same exact degrading words. It took months to fully unravel the backstory: Gabriel had a long history of being abusive and aggressive. He had been trying to rope his ex back into a relationship for a while, promising that he loved her. He had been bad-mouthing me to anyone who would listen while purposely withholding access to finances for basic needs. I also learned that he'd promised to marry his ex and had been emotionally and financially abusing her when he met me (and then ghosted her).

"I'm sorry, I didn't know," I tried to explain to her.

I had been so caught up in the lies he had sold me that I had neglected to truly empathize with her. I had judged her not for the woman she was but based on her reaction to his abuse.

"You know he is doing all of these things on purpose," my therapist explained.

For so long, I had been branding him as "out of control." But finally the picture clicked into focus: He was completely in control the whole time. *I* was the one who had lost control. I needed to take my life back. And I took those first steps while bracing myself with his ex's support. Though we were very skeptical of each other at first, after being fed so many lies by Gabriel to keep the game going, we quickly recognized that we were the only two people willing to be honest with each other about our relationships. We also found we had a whole lot of mutual respect for and genuinely liked each other.

"We deserve better than this," we agreed after one of our hours-long sessions of trying to sort fact from fiction.

We were both victims working diligently to recover. We shared what we had discovered on our individual journeys. Both my relationship with my therapist and what I learned from Gabriel's ex helped me come to terms with what I was experiencing: *narcissistic abuse*. Having the words to explain what we had endured was affirming and freeing.

I spent many sleepless nights reading about and researching narcissistic abuse. I learned narcissism is a deeply disordered way of thinking that is the result of a lack of self-love and destroys relationships. Narcissists convince themselves that they are superior to others, but deep down they are driven by guilt and shame that plagues them because of early trauma. To avoid such feelings, narcissists rely on defense mechanisms that are destructive to themselves and others, especially those closest to them. Their abuse is cyclical and ever shifting—that is why victims often get caught in its trap. A relationship with a narcissist is dizzying and disorienting, swirling and whirling like a tornado, sweeping an unsuspecting person off of their feet and then violently tossing and twisting them about only to drop them back down—in either darkness or sunny light. Before the victim is able to process episodes of abuse, they are swept back into the relationship with love-bombing—the grand romantic gestures, compliments, and promises of love and affection that won us over in the first place. The potency of acceptance and love—especially after such a storm—makes the cycle incredibly hard to break.

You were sent to me from God.

You are perfect for me.

I love you.

Gabriel's words played in my mind like a broken record. It was so difficult for me not to believe them, though they stood in sharp contrast to the way he treated me. The lying. The financial abuse. The cheating. The numerous betrayals. The gaslighting and attempts to distort my reality. None of that felt like love. And yet when Gabriel's ex shared what he'd told her about me, his lies seemed alien and outlandish.

"You are just a gold digger," she reported he disclosed during one of their meetings.

"He doesn't love you," she warned.

How could the man with whom I shared a child and a life exhibit such maliciousness about me?

As I learned more about narcissism, I remembered the stories of the neglect Gabriel endured as a child whose parents did not have the time to care for him because they were too busy trying to make ends meet. The abuse he suffered as they tried to beat him into complying with their worldview, which they believed would save him from the traps of the hood. The whippings for having the "wrong" kinds of friends, coming home a few minutes late from school, or wearing a do-rag. The many tormenting police encounters where he was slammed on the sidewalk or against a wall while on his way to or from school as a teen. I worked hard to string together a narrative that would help me make sense of the years I spent in the fog of rationalizations and excuses, years that left me a victim.

"I've had enough," I quietly declared to Karla one day over the phone.

I wanted to call it off with him for good and finally gathered the strength to do it one mild winter night. We were sitting in the idling car, parked only a block away from my mom's house, when he again promised to "change" after getting home late and failing to relieve me from watching our daughter all day. I asked if he was out with another woman, my insecurities over his betrayal surfacing.

"You are always bringing up the past and don't let things go," he lectured.

He always demanded I let the past be the past, without ever truly making amends for his wrongdoing. But I knew there could never be reconciliation between us if he was incapable of fully taking responsibility for his errors and making me whole by changing his behavior. The desire to scream that I was done with the relationship was swelling inside me along with baby number two as I sat in the driver's seat. The thought was interrupted by the sight of a police car. My eyes followed the vehicle in my rearview mirror as it barreled down the street and made a U-turn to park right behind us. The swirl of the red and blue lights ricocheted against the night's shadows. My heart sank and we both froze. I placed my hands on the steering wheel.

"Do you have your permit?" Gabriel questioned, talking from the corner of his mouth, his body as stiff and unmoving as a corpse.

I prayed I did.

Four tall, white cops emerged from the police vehicle carrying flashlights. One approached my window and knocked on it with the butt of his flashlight.

"License, insurance, and registration, ma'am," he ordered when I rolled down the window.

I leaned over to the passenger side of the car, pulled open the glove compartment, and began to fumble with the stack of papers that fell out. Gabriel remained frozen as I shuffled through the papers, pulling out the registration and insurance. My hands were shaking, my heart racing as I tried to peer through the darkness to find my permit.

"I'm gonna need to see your ID, sir," the cop near the passenger-side door instructed.

"Ah, did I do something wrong?" Gabriel questioned.

"ID, sir."

Gabriel reached into his pocket carefully.

"It's in my wallet," he cautiously warned.

He slowly handed the officer his ID.

"I work at the courthouse," he offered.

It wasn't Gabriel's first interaction with neighborhood police, so he didn't press for acknowledgment when the officer ignored him. He knew an encounter with cops could turn violent or deadly in seconds. In a neighborhood rife with drugs, gangs, violence, and the boys and men who perpetrated such barbarity, the cops did not need to justify their behavior. Any violence that occurred would be justified by one fact: our Blackness.

"Sir, you are under arrest," the officer began. "Anything you say can be used against you in a court of law."

My eyes shot over to Gabriel.

"Wh-what is this about?" he stuttered as two police officers inched toward him, one with cuffs in his hands.

All of the rage and defiance he exercised on me was absent from this encounter with the police. Under the threat of these men, he shriveled and shrank like a decaying piece of fruit. As soon as he stepped out of the vehicle, one of the officers grabbed his arm and twisted his body, pressing it against the car's passenger door. His eyes met mine and I could see they were filled with horror and helplessness. Light pierced my eyes, forcing my attention back in the direction of the cop at my window.

"Your license, ma'am," he ordered, shining his flashlight right in my face.

My hands quivered as I returned to the stack of papers. I couldn't concentrate on the task, my mind flooding with thoughts of the Black people who had lost their lives under similar circumstances.

"Please, I have a paper permit," I started. "I know I put it in here but it's hard to find. Please just give me a minute."

"Ma'am, if you don't have a license to operate the vehicle, we are going to have to arrest you as well," the officer shot back.

I looked down at my hands, but they no longer looked like my own. They were frantically squirming and wriggling through the paperwork like worms uncovered from beneath a rock. They were not acting with a purpose or direction.

"Ma'am, get out of the vehicle."

The officer began to pull at the door's handle and I resigned myself completely. I couldn't fight anymore. The paperwork fell out of my hands onto my lap. I was frozen. I no longer even felt fear. I was completely numb.

"It's in the center console," Gabriel urged.

I looked at him and shook my head.

"It's in there, Tiff."

I mustered every last bit of energy in me and pulled open the center compartment to find a single sheet of paper: the permit.

The police allowed me to walk the block up the street to my mom's house and took Gabriel into custody. I sat on the sofa in my mom's living room as she called all of the nearby precincts to try to figure out where he had been taken. A couple hours into our search, the doorbell rang. They had released him upon finding out the warrant they had arrested him on was issued for an unpaid parking ticket.

"I can't do this anymore," I whispered as I held him in a tight embrace.

"We're gonna get out of here," he promised.

My anger over his past indiscretions faded in that moment. We were both safe and alive to hold each other for another day, and that was all that mattered while we were confined to a ghetto where living to see the next day was a daily feat. Our son was due in a few months, so we knew it was better to stay put, but my spirit had already floated back to the streets of Port of Spain seeking refuge. As I stared out my bedroom window onto the urban street below, I saw myself, slender and confident, parading through Port of Spain in a beaded bikini. The beauty of my homeland was transposed atop all of the ugliness of America, and imagining it there made the reality more bearable. But that year, it felt like America's abuse of Black people had become inescapable.

Every evening news report featured another Black death, plummeting me into an emptiness and despair that even my memories of home couldn't keep at bay.

March 18, 2018. Stephon Clark: shot in his grandparents' backyard after officers mistook his cell phone for a gun. "I can't handle this. I lay—I seen my grandson layin' out there," said Clark's grandmother on the night of the shooting. "He was just comin' home and y'all was comin' through the back. He don't have no gun. He don't carry no gun. Oh, my God. He got two children."

September 6, 2018. Botham Jean was shot and killed while eating ice cream and watching television in his own home by a white female officer, Amber Guyger. She claimed she thought he was an intruder in her apartment. Jean's younger brother Brandt forgave and hugged Guyger during her sentencing. A bailiff brushed the cop's blond hair in court. Jean's father, Bertrum, also stated that he forgave Guyger but had wanted a stiffer sentence.

October 11, 2018. The morning I awoke with contractions, my daughter was sound asleep on Gabriel's chest.

"I think the baby is coming," I whispered to him.

A wide grin spread across his face and he carefully slid out of bed to take Lea to my mom. We already had a bag packed and rushed to put on clothes. Within minutes, we were speeding down Garfield Avenue toward Jersey City Medical Center. I labored for hours before the doctor presented me with a cherubic newborn who weighed nine pounds and one ounce. When I held him in my arms, my mind and body eased and settled on a single thought: his freedom. In my mind's eye, I saw him playing and roaming freely through his neighborhood, as I had as a young child. I imagined him driving his first car to pick up his first date and the joy and laughter they would share. In all of my thoughts, he was living without fear and his brown skin was cherished. I nodded in and out of my dreams and the hospital room, where doctors, nurses, and their assistants were instructing me on breastfeeding or updating me about the health of the baby and necessary paperwork. When night came, I was moved to the recovery side of the maternity ward. It was already 10:00 p.m. and the maternity floor was quiet after a bustling day of births. Only the beeps of medical equipment and the shuffling feet of nurses, bobbing in and out of patients' rooms, could be heard.

Our newborn baby boy was lying so quietly in the hospital's bassinet beside me that I worried he wasn't breathing. I peeped over at him and watched in awe as his tiny brown body expanded and contracted with each inhale and exhale. He was a gorgeous sight nestled in a white-pink-and-blue-striped hospital blanket—his small hands cupping his perfectly round face.

BANG!

Gabriel slammed his fists into the wall, interrupting the moment. I tried to rise from bed to calm him and could feel the blood still oozing from inside me, my womb raw and throbbing from childbirth.

He stood near the door of the hospital room, angrily wagging my cell phone in my direction.

"You fucking him?" he asked.

Just a few moments earlier, he had been seated at the edge of my bed, cooing and whispering sweet promises to our baby boy. I had pretended to be asleep but looked on in appreciation.

"Daddy can't wait to take you to the park," he had whispered, his face only inches away from the baby, who grasped onto his index finger while sleeping. "Daddy's big boy."

The sound of a single *ping* had interrupted the picture-perfect bonding scene. It was a message from a male friend of mine who lived thousands of miles away, one I hadn't seen in years. He was congratulating us on the birth of our second child. The mere sight of the incoming text stirred a cyclone of rage within Gabriel. He tried to contain it, but his anger spilled out in a tirade.

"If you wanna fucking be with him, then go," he said.

I was too weak to argue, too vulnerable to fight to prove my love or to disprove his unfounded allegations. And by then I knew nothing I could say could quell the deep insecurity within him that constantly nagged and told him he wasn't good enough for or deserving of happiness. An insecurity that made him believe dominance and control were the only ways he could be sure about love.

Thoughts of our violent history created phantom sensations all over my body: My wrists throbbed where he'd grabbed them tight and pressed them against the wall because I told him I wanted to go out with friends months earlier. My back tingled where a long friction burn was left when he had ripped the shirt off my back a year before.

"Answer me!" he screamed. My hands were shaking and sweaty, my entire body frozen. I closed my eyes, submitting to a rapacious force that dragged me deeper and deeper into myself. His voice began to sound like a distant echo, the thumping of my heart overpowering his expletive-laden monologue. More thoughts cycled through my mind, creating their own powerful vortex.

How did I get here?

At only twenty-eight years old, I was the last thing I'd wanted to be: a statistic, a welfare queen, a Black woman dependent on WIC and Medicaid. I had given up my budding career as a writer to support his career. I had two babies with this man.

Despite all of my sacrifices, nothing I did extinguished his rage.

Still, I had returned to the relationship over and over again, falling prey to its patterns, distortions, and promises each and every time. Once buried in the depths of my subconscious, memories began to erupt like lava spilling out of a volcano into my conscious mind. Images of men, women, and children from my past and their angry words.

Nigger echoed through the air from an anonymous driver.

Negra puta exploded from the pursed lips of the mother of a crush.

Black bitch was repeated in chat boxes by white online gamers.

Black whore was uttered from the lips of a white lover.

Still shots from my childhood history books exploded one by one into full view: Black women and men dangling from trees. Whip marks across the backs of enslaved people. The shackles, chains, and contraptions forged from iron to enslave and torment them—my ancestors. White people spitting and jeering at a little Black girl as she clutched her schoolbooks. As those images settled, newer ones surfaced: my neighbor, a twentysomething Black man with locs, smiling and waving from across the street with a gaping, oozing bullet wound in his head. The sight of four white cops surrounding my car.

"Stop," I whispered under my breath, unsure where to direct my command.

"You gonna stop talking to and fucking all these men," Gabriel said.

I tried to speak again, but I began to shiver uncontrollably. The chaos, both inside my mind and outside in reality, began to mesh into a cacophony of sounds and blurred visions. I closed my eyes tightly, trying to block the light from the fluorescent bulbs that he had switched on and that now illuminated our previously tranquil room. The images flashed faster, like a seizure-inducing film: Gabriel and me happily holding hands as we plunged through the air on a roller-coaster ride during our first date. Him pulling me into an embrace when we exchanged stories about our pasts. Police slamming him onto our car after pulling him over for a warrant issued due to an unpaid parking ticket. The look of terror in his eyes when a childhood friend turned drug dealer showed up at our front door with a gun.

"Abusers seldom change," my therapist had warned when I shared such memories with her while trying to process my relationship with the father of my children.

I thought of America and the countless times I forgave the country for its poor treatment of me: After being forced out of my home time and time again by harmful policies. After being told I wasn't good enough or was unworthy of dignity and respect just because of my skin color. I forgave in spite of every theft of Black culture and in spite of every image of Black people being degraded and stigmatized by the media. After every violent police murder, including the many whose names have never been popularized by hashtags. I thought about the promises I made to work harder and do better to mend my relationship with the country in the midst of such clear degradation. And how I begged the country to love me back, despite clear evidence that it had no regard for me.

Then everything went silent.

When I opened my eyes, Gabriel was gone. I looked over at our baby, who had somehow managed to sleep through the entire episode. He was still lying on his back, but now it looked to me as if his hands were placed over his ears.

I felt guilty that I couldn't protect him and likely would not be able to in the future, if our circumstances remained the same. I so badly wanted to create a storybook moment worthy of his birth, but the fact was that we lived in a country where boys and men who looked like him were regularly gunned down by police while unarmed. Where millions were locked behind bars, slammed against brick walls or cold street pavement while being stopped and frisked. Where gang violence

claimed the lives of far too many. Where there was nothing Black
mothers like me could do to stop it. And where many of our men had
already been destroyed by the time they became fathers of Black boys
of their own. A lifetime of trauma and dysfunction rendered the father
of my children unable to truly connect with me. I was just another face
and body that he could not trust in a system where anyone, even those
closest to you, can become an enemy in the blink of an eye.

When he returned hours later, apologizing for his outburst, I nodded
up and down in full acceptance of his promises to do better. I was well
trained in my role as victim in the cycle of abuse and played it well, but
this time was different. For me, the moment of reckoning had arrived.
That night in the hospital, I knew I had to escape and end my cycle of
abuse—starting with America. I knew Gabriel and I would always have
a toxic relationship, and I had to find the strength to end it. I would
be able to do so only by finally refocusing my energy toward myself. I
vowed from that day forward to take back control of my life.

"You do whatever you want, hon," I responded plainly. "It's time I
start to take care of myself."

After the birth of my son, my stomach's skin stretched, sagged, and
dimpled from the fat that had accumulated beneath it as a result of
overeating to quell my anxieties and dull the pain and hurt. I was over
two hundred pounds and couldn't bear the sight of the woman I had
become. I began waking up early in the morning before the kids did
to brave the cold to walk or jog, swearing off unnecessary calories, and
affirming myself and my dreams. I ran past dilapidated homes and gray
industrial zones until I could see the Hudson River on the horizon, the
sound of soca beating its rhythmic drum in my ears with every step.
When I closed my eyes, I was in the streets of Port of Spain parading
with my sister, surrounded by a sea of people of every shade. I opened
them to the sight of the Statue of Liberty, America's beacon of freedom

and hope, and felt confident that I would soon be back at home in Trinidad, free of the hurt and pain I would leave behind.

"I will not live in constant abuse," I firmly declared to Gabriel one morning when I returned from my run. "I want to go back to Trinidad now."

He knew I was fed up with riding the roller-coaster relationship ride with him, and there was nothing left for him to say. His utterances were as meaningless as America's countless empty claims that it would finally make good on its promises of full citizenship and respect for Black people. *Abusers seldom change*, my therapist's voice echoed as my mind raced with fear, uncertainty, and disillusionment.

On February 19, 2019, Gabriel and I returned to Trinidad. We rented an apartment together and settled into giving our relationship one last shot.

"Our life is better here," he said. "I'm happy that we can afford things easier and get the kids away from all of that racism."

But the siren call of America's abuse had been whispering sweet promises, and he was secretly being hoovered back into its clutches. He was offered a new office job that would pay better and be less hectic, and his parents agreed to help him pay off his student loans if he stayed to help run the church and the family business. Even though I was grateful to have an escape from the relationship, I cringed as I watched him stumble back toward his old life.

"It makes more sense for me to save some money first before moving," he said during our last conversation about the move. "You stay with the kids. And I promise to go back to therapy."

I was relieved. I could handle being a single parent in the country that I loved, but I knew I wouldn't survive much longer in America, especially with him. Mom was reporting that back in Jersey City there was a threat that grew more violent with each passing year. Gunshots rang out closer to home. Police pulled my mom over with their guns drawn on her car, with my sister and nephew in it. Gabriel's abuse had also become more erratic and unpredictable.

"Go ahead and stab me!" he screamed at me one day while wagging a knife in my face. "You want to kill me, right?"

I had never made a single utterance of any desire to hurt him, but by then I knew of the narcissist's power of projection. Those were his own thoughts and intentions that slipped from his lips.

"I didn't mean it like that," he assured me afterward, but his words didn't matter.

The only remaining form of degradation and violence for the U.S. or Gabriel to exact upon me was death. The day he returned to America, I was freed from both threats, the Atlantic Ocean putting thousands of miles between me and my abusers.

The Lord is my light and my salvation; whom shall I fear?

CHAPTER 9

—————

The Breakup

"It is our duty to fight for our freedom. It is our duty to win. We must love each other and support each other. We have nothing to lose but our chains."

—ASSATA SHAKUR

The moment a narcissistic abuser recognizes that you see them for what they are and that you have the strength to leave the relationship is the most dangerous. The gaping void inside your abuser is filled only by narcissistic supply—the love, attention, praise, control, and even hate and derision—of you. Absent the fuel, a narcissist's inner emptiness engulfs them in feelings of shame and inadequacy, which they rabidly fight against rather than face their true nature. They must maintain belief in their righteousness and superiority, despite all of their evildoing and shortcomings, and will stop at nothing to protect their belief. Even if the real cost of their delusions of grandeur threatens to destroy everything, including themselves.

On January 6, 2021, I received a message from Karla containing a single question: "How did you know?"

Washington, DC, was under siege by violent insurrectionists, who were directed by then-president Donald Trump to storm the Capitol to stop the certification of the election that he'd lost to Joe Biden. My best friend was shocked and confused as the attack unfolded and couldn't understand how I had warned her of the likelihood of such violence months earlier.

"I dated a man like Trump," I said. "I know how far they will go to win."

I spent the entire year of my life prior to that day trying to wrestle freedom for myself and my family from the grip of my abusers. After I officially broke up with Gabriel, he enlisted America's court system to try to reclaim control of my life. The pair would attempt to rip apart my family and continue their reign over my physical and spiritual body. But I had already received a message from the universe, and it had different plans for me: During Carnival 2020 Niki came bearing an unexpected message. One that promised we would be *free*.

As the maxi snaked through the hills of Maraval, the cool breeze was both refreshing and invigorating. It was 4:00 a.m. on February 24, 2020, Carnival Monday morning, and I was sitting on the bus with my sister and our friend Katrina—a woman with Trini roots who lived in California but made the pilgrimage to Trinidad for the annual celebration every year. We were making our way to Port of Spain to partake in J'ouvert, all wearing matching orange shirts with the word "Clay" written on them for the band that we would be jumping with. I imagined Carnival 2020 would be the best of my life. No longer burdened by the thought of having to return to America after the festivities, I was finally completely at ease. The sound of music from the big trucks beckoned us as we neared the city's center, the traffic becoming denser as we approached. As soon as we came close to a band filled with big trucks blasting soca, we jumped out of the bus, excited to be lost in the sea of revelers. The bass rattled through my body, awakening my spirit. I sipped my drink as my body twisted and swayed in appreciation of the rhythm. People chipped, wined, and rolled their waists. The cloak of respectability had been cast aside.

I turned to Niki and her face was contorted with emotion.

"The ancestors, they are here," she said.

Tears were streaming down her face.

I watched her in silence, uncertain of how to respond. I had never seen my sister cry publicly before and felt woefully unable to comfort her. I participated in no religion and had no spiritual inclinations, so I turned to Katrina for help mustering a response. I was grateful when she immediately sprang into action and wrapped her arms around my sister.

"They said we are going to be free this year," Niki cried out, louder this time. *"We are going to be free."*

I didn't understand her use of the future tense. I was already free, falling into what felt like an endless abyss of excitement and ecstasy. I had her by my side, and Mom was back at home caring for our kids. We had made it safely to Trinidad and were renting a house together with a pool surrounded by a garden that had an expansive view of the ocean. Mom was making passive income from renting her house in New Jersey to a friend, and Niki and I were working online, making a steady income from home.

"We are already free," I said to Niki before breaking from our group to wine with a random man, my cup of rum and pineapple juice splashing from side to side as our hips rocked together.

We danced in the streets for hours under black lights affixed to our band's trucks that made our eyes, our teeth, and the white writing on our shirts glow neon. We dumped colorful paint all over one another and anyone else who looked too clean or untouched. When the sun rose in the sky, we retreated home to prepare for Monday Mas. I had made good on my promise to myself to lose weight and find the sexiest costume for the festivities, and I was excited to hit the road in full regalia. Back at home, I gently strapped on the wired bra top to my costume and pulled on the bikini bottom over a pair of nude-colored tights, then positioned the feathered wings and headpiece in place. When I gazed upon myself in the mirror, I was both enamored and inspired by what I saw: the woman staring back from my reflection looked strong, confident, and empowered. It was hard for me to believe that we were the same person. She had been through hell and back, but you could barely even tell because she looked so happy and at peace. The gems on her Yuma Carnival costume glittered and glistened as she turned from side to side, checking herself out. I was ready for the road again. To jump and wine. To revel and tumble in waves created by soca music—the rhythm and the pulse of the people.

When the festivities came to a close, Niki and I took the kids to Tobago, where we relaxed on its idyllic white sands as the children splashed in the clear blue-green water. We video-chatted with a happy Stefan, who had moved to Switzerland with his husband, a tall, cute European guy he met in New York City. I was in nirvana. I stretched out under a palm tree, watching it dance in the breeze as if participating in its own Carnival parade.

"Tiff, it was so beautiful," Niki said in a whisper. "The message I got from the ancestors:

"We are going to be free."

I couldn't help but trip over the way the statement undermined my current moment of bliss. Why was our freedom a matter for the future, when we had everything I could've dreamed of at that moment? I pushed aside her pronouncement, not allowing the unease it had spurred to take over me. But the seed had already been planted and thoughts had already begun to blossom in my mind of what Niki's prophecy of future freedom even meant.

Mom made it to our tiny island refuge right on time, mere months before the COVID-19 pandemic would shut everything down. For Mom, it took plenty of convincing from us that it was her time to break it off with America in November 2019. She felt like she had not accomplished what she set out to do when she left her homeland. She hadn't saved up enough money to retire or buy a house in Trinidad, and we kids were still struggling to find stability. She was ashamed that she would be judged for all she hadn't achieved. Ultimately, she made the leap of faith only after I used my secret weapon against her.

"The grandkids need you," I urged.

I was relieved when Mom finally booked her ticket to come home. A couple months later, Trinidad and Tobago closed its borders to stop the spread of a virus that would upend life as we knew it. The importance of that decision weighed on all of us as we watched COVID-19 ravage America. Had she remained in New Jersey, she would have been on the front lines of the war against the pandemic. From our haven in Trinidad and Tobago, she watched the hospice unit she worked on become a COVID-19 unit. While she lounged with my son, swinging in a hammock under a mango tree, she listened to the dire complaints of ex-coworkers, who never had enough personal protective equipment. She completely avoided conversations with some of her friends and co-workers at the time, feeling guilty that she got out while they were stuck in the trenches.

"I just can't call her," she told me, referring to her friend Diana, a fellow nurse from Barbados with whom she had for nearly ten years exchanged dreams of how their respective lives would be when they returned home.

When Mom found out Diana died during the time that they were on a speaking hiatus, she cried for days. She knew Diana had also lost her house to foreclosure and had left behind two daughters who had little support.

"I couldn't tell her I made it home," Mom kept repeating through tears.

I knew the situation was grim, but Mom took the brunt of the emotional shocks. Her phone kept ringing with calls from the friends she had left behind in the States who were struggling to find their way in one of the darkest times in modern history. But eventually, the depths of the horror of the moment also caught up to me.

Early one sunny morning, while scrolling through Facebook, I watched the video of George Floyd taking his last breaths under the knee of a Minneapolis police officer. The sound of waves meeting the shoreline and my children's giggles created the soundtrack for the devastating images. My mother came out onto our sunny front patio, a cup of coffee in one hand and her phone in the other.

"Mom, we are refugees," I said to her.

I scrolled through the day's news headlines and terror came crashing in on me like a rogue wave. Suddenly I was back in America, plunged into an abyss of systemic racism captured in heart-wrenching detail by the deaths of George Floyd, Breonna Taylor, Trayvon Martin, Tamir Rice, John Crawford, Michael Brown, and the endless list of names of Black children and adults who have lost their lives to police brutality. . . . As days passed and deaths from COVID-19 and from the protests began to mount, it became even more clear to us abroad how precarious remaining in the U.S. would've been.

"I can't breathe" were the words uttered by both George Floyd and Eric Garner before they died under the weight of a police officer. Thousands of health-care workers and women of color would also struggle to breathe as they fought to win their own battles against COVID-19. Many of their lives were claimed by the ravenous disease. Mom could've been a part of that statistic.

"Mommy, look—chocolate!" My daughter's sweet voice came tumbling in like a lifeline, lifting me out of the depths of America's darkness.

She extended her small brown hands toward me, covered in melted, sticky gooeyness. I reached out to pull her in close, burying my face in the nape of her neck. Her tiny body comforted me. The tides turned and I noticed the sun was still shining, the breeze was still blowing, and we were safe. Not a day went by that I didn't celebrate: we escaped.

Not too long after that, I stumbled upon a song a Trinidadian artist, Jiselle Singer, released called "Billion Dollar Dream." The sound of the artist's sweet voice posed questions that were the most pressing to me in that moment:

> *Will you stand up?*
> *Will you stand up?*
> *Will you stand up for your rights?*
> *Will you get up?*
> *Will you get up?*
> *Don't give up the fight*

It felt like the universe had sent me a message. I listened to the song while on the beach and was overcome with gratitude and sadness for the sacrifices of those who came before us and died in bondage with only the dream and hope that the next generation could experience true freedom. For those whose lives were claimed or tormented by the evils of racism and all other forms of abuse. Then I thought of my African ancestors and their allies of all hues who fought in the name of liberation and equality, many of whom remain faceless and nameless in the untold history of how the dreams enslaved Africans carried of freedom for themselves and their people materialized into a reality centuries later. The intrusive images of Black people's deaths and pain no longer overwhelmed my thoughts. Instead, I could feel those old Black souls pulsating through my blood and veins to the steady rhythm of my heartbeat. Through my DNA and that of every Black person in the Western Hemisphere, our African ancestors and their stories live on. It's a story of survival. Of surviving months crowded into the bellies of ships while shackled like beasts across the Atlantic Ocean. Of surviving centuries of enslavement, violence, and oppression. However, as I scanned the moonlit ocean and my eyes fell upon my mom, daughter, and son on its sandy shores, exchanging whispers and giggles while pointing at colorful Christmas lights strung upon a nearby tree, I realized that Black life is not defined simply by survival but by magic. All of the forces of good, both seen and unseen, had conspired to put us all together, safely, in that beautiful moment. In a moment when Black women in America were soaring to heights unfathomable only decades earlier, a global reckoning with white supremacy was underway, with Black women leading the charge, spurred by the refusal to allow the continued abuse and oppression of Black people and other minorities. That night, I recognized I was not alone in battle. And I would never give up the fight.

The Lord is my light and my salvation; whom shall I fear, I heard my mom whisper.

Her mantra floated away into the universe. Finally, I understood the power of living on a Black woman's prayer.

———

Reconciliation

Whenever people learn that I decided to leave America, they often ask if I would ever return. Others wonder if I could ever make amends with the father of my children, when they learn the reasons for our breakup. The truth is that I hope to heal and move on from the hurt and pain of the past and work toward a brighter future, but there is no certainty that the goal is a shared one—either by America or my children's father.

The paths to reconciliation, for both victim and abuser, converge at a place of growth, understanding, accountability, and making amends. It is the victim's obligation to self to heal the wounds that left them vulnerable to abuse and it is the abuser's obligation to the victim to offer both apology and restitution.

As I started my journey to healing, the hardest step was coming to terms with my own participation in the cycle of abuse in both my personal life and in American racial stratification. How had I allowed others to dictate my value or my worth? Or even outright degrade me? Why did I accept so many lies and distortions? Offer so many chances to the undeserving? Why did I devalue others based on their race or nationality?

Through the process of healing, I learned that for the victim to escape the cycle of abuse, they must accept their role in the dynamic and let go of the dreams and promises that kept them entrapped and beholden to their abusers. For me, that kind of letting go required higher education, therapy, resources, time, and support. Through my own healing, I recognize that for people of color to collectively heal from systemic abuse, the journey within our community begins with acceptance, self-love, and self-care. The good news is that we have more tools now than ever before. I have found support for my own healing on social media platforms where groups have been established to help survivors of narcissistic abuse and even combat systemic inequality by equalizing access to traditionally white and male-dominated industries. In fact, I owe much of my writing success to a private Facebook group where women writers and editors all coalesce to offer mentorship, guidance, and work opportunities to combat gender- and race-based inequality. In such acts of camaraderie and activism, glimmers of hope shine brightly.

However much healing these strategies can offer, though, true reconciliation cannot be achieved absent the work and dedication of abusers to not only confront their behaviors and be accountable for them but also commit to change and make amends to victims. Years after I finally escaped the trauma of an abusive relationship with my ex and the father of my two children, there remains no viable path for us to heal, move on, and establish a healthy co-parenting relationship. He has never apologized for his transgressions and refuses to financially support our children. Instead I see him using the family court system as a means of continued abuse, manipulation, and control. As I reflect on America and its failure to ever truly hold itself entirely accountable for the murder, enslavement, and oppression of millions of Africans and their descendants, and as I witness the racialized abuses Black people continue to endure, I am forced to grapple with a lesson I learned all those years ago in therapy that lit a fire under me to leave: abusers seldom change.

Yet my hopes and aspirations for my children, my family, and the United States of America are grounded in the possibility of realizing the most improbable outcome. For I am the unlikely realized dream of my ancestors—a free, educated, powerful Afro Caribbean American woman standing in her truth and awarded a platform from which to write and control my own narrative, only a few generations removed from enslavement, illiteracy, and extreme poverty. Though I have been told it is unlikely that the American government will ever publicly take responsibility for systemic racism or implement social and economic policies to ensure that racism is entirely eradicated, I will never lose hope.

My life, my journey, my heartbreaks, and my testimony stand testament to the power and magic of Black women to make the unfathomable a reality.

Further Reading on Reconciliatory Justice

Mary Frances Berry, "Taking the United States to Court: Callie House and the 1915 Cotton Tax Reparations Litigation," *Journal of African American History* 103, no. 1–2 (Winter/Spring 2018): 91–103, https://doi.org/10.1086/696360.

Ta-Nehisi Coates, "The Case for Reparations," *The Atlantic*, June 2014, https://www.theatlantic.com/magazine/archive/2014/06/the-case-for-reparations/361631/.

Thomas Craemer et al., "Wealth Implications of Slavery and Racial Discrimination for African American Descendants of the Enslaved," *Review of Black Political Economy* 47, no. 3 (September 2020): 218–54, https://doi.org10.1177/0034644620926516.

Darrick Hamilton, "Baby Bonds and Reparations," interview with Mark Miller, *Evanston RoundCast*, podcast audio, February 20, 2021, https://evanstonroundtable.com/2021/02/20/baby-bonds-and-reparations-a-conversation-with-dr-darrick-hamilton/.

Marcus Anthony Hunter, "Seven Billion Reasons for Reparations," *Souls: A Critical Journal of Black Politics, Culture, and Society* 20, no. 4 (2018): 420–32, https://doi.org/10.1080/10999949.2018.1607483.

Rashawn Ray and Andre M. Perry, "Why We Need Reparations for Black Americans," Brookings Institution, April 15, 2020, https://www.brookings.edu/policy2020/bigideas/why-we-need-reparations-for-black-americans/.

ACKNOWLEDGMENTS

I believe each individual human life is like a poui tree. Our spirituality and our connection to the ancestor is very much like the soil in which a tree finds nourishment and unconditional sustenance. Our history and culture ground us in our human experience and steady us through stormy weather, just as roots do. Our families and friends are like the bark—our visible, sturdy support system without which we could never grow to great heights. Our branches are the institutions, communities, and people within them who inspire us to reach out toward the universe and infinity, where dreams can become real. Each of our flowers represents our achievements and moments of growth that adorn us and make us beautiful.

I want to take a moment to acknowledge those who have played the most critical roles in my life—a most beautiful, blossoming poui.

First, I dedicate a moment of recognition to those who came before me who have passed on to the realm of the unseen. You all made this fantastical moment of my life a possibility through your indefatigable commitment to betterment and justice. I thank you for inspiring me, guiding me, and protecting me even when I may have been naive to your many interventions on my behalf.

Next, to my sweet island home, Trinidad and Tobago, and to Mama Africa: The rhythm of the steel pan, tassa, djembe, and the sound of the bass line will forever make my hips roll like the ocean's waves and allow me to float away into pure bliss and joy. Your flavorful, sweet, spicy, and succulent foods always comfort me. Your history bolsters my sense of pride and worthiness. My love for you is a flame that burns bright in times of prosperity and endures through times of hardship.

My dear family: Granny, Mom, Niki, Stefan, Aunty Pat, Glen Davidson, and my beautiful babies, Marcus, Lea, and Liam, I love you all dearly. And of course, my life would be incomplete without the amazing folks who I am fortunate to call friends: Karla Garcia, my best friend, my friend soul mate (and my personal financier in times of need), thank you for all the laughter and insights you have shared over the years. Jessi Munoz (and your wonderful mom and dad) and Liliana Chavez, who always made your home mine, and Robert Overton, who bailed me out in Hawaii when I was cash-strapped and always encouraged me to write a book before I even truly believed I was worthy. Josh McCarther, one of the smartest men I have ever known, who I will always love dearly. Kern Bruce, to whom I am connected through shared nationality and the purest love of art. And to Luca Castillo and Landis Wiedner, thanks for stepping in at crunch time and helping me to finish strong.

I am eternally grateful for Mrs. Boguslavsky, who made her classroom feel more like a home for us wayward, loud-mouthed kids. And to the New School and my mentors, Darrick Hamilton, Susan Shapiro, and Benjamin Jealous. Susan, thank you for your unwavering support and guidance over the years. You helped me find a path to success as a writer. I also want to thank my agent, Susan Golomb, for advocating on my behalf, Penguin Random House/Viking for this extraordinary opportunity, and Laura Tisdel for believing in my story and helping me to bring it to fruition in the way I envisioned. Lastly, Jenée Desmond-Harris: you are my fairy godmother who made one of my biggest dreams come true. This project may never have happened without you and *The New York Times*. Thank you.

I share this book with the world, one of the many vibrant accomplishments that now add color to my life, because of the many who believed in me, supported me, and never let me be defeated even in trying times.

Thank you to all who have published, read, and supported my work over the years. I hope I have made you proud.

NOTES

Chapter 2: Devalued

1. Olivia B. Waxman, "President Trump Played a Key Role in the Central Park Five Case. Here's the Real History Behind *When They See Us*," *Time*, May 31, 2019, https://time.com/5597843/central-park-five-trump-history/.
2. J. Stanley Lemons, "Black Stereotypes as Reflected in Popular Culture, 1880–1920," *American Quarterly* 29, no.1 (Spring 1977): 102–16, https://doi.org/10.2307/2712263.
3. Catherine Bowler, *Blessed: A History of the American Prosperity Gospel* (PhD diss., Duke University, 2010), https://hdl.handle.net/10161/2297.

Chapter 3: Discarded

1. Ian Bernard, "The Zong Massacre (1781)," *Black Past*, October 11, 2011, www.blackpast.org/global-african-history/zong-massacre-1781/.
2. Henry Louis Gates Jr., *100 Amazing Facts About the Negro* (New York: Pantheon, 2017), 9.
3. Peter Wagner and Bernadette Rabuy, "Following the Money of Mass Incarceration," Prison Policy Initiative, January 25, 2017, www.prisonpolicy.org/reports/money.html.
4. Michele Goodwin, "Invisible Women: Mass Incarceration's Forgotten Casualties," *Texas Law Review* 94, no. 2 (December 2015): 353–96, https://texaslawreview.org/invisible-women-mass-incarcerations-forgotten-casualties/.

Chapter 4: Calm

1. Bruce Lesh, "Post-war Suburbanization: Homogenization or the American Dream?" (lesson plan, Franklin High School, Baltimore County Public Schools, no date), www.umbc.edu/che/tahlessons/pdf/Post-War_Suburbanization_Homogenization(PrinterFriendly).pdf.
2. Shawn A. Ginwright and Antwi Akom, "African American Out-Migration Trends: Initial Scan of National and Local Trends in Migration and Research on African Americans" (report prepared for Mayor's Office of Community Development Task Force on African American Out-Migration, San Francisco State University College of Ethnic Studies, no date), https://sfmohcd.org/sites/default/files/FileCenter/Documents/2127-Product%20I%2007-18-07.pdf.
3. Michael A. Lindsey et al., "Trends of Suicidal Behaviors Among High School Students in the United States: 1991–2017," *Pediatrics* 144, no. 5 (November 2019): e20191187, https://doi.org/10.1542/peds.2019-1187; Zara Abrams, "Sounding the Alarm on Black Youth Suicide," American Psychological Association, January 28, 2020, www.apa.org/news/apa/2020/black-youth-suicide.
4. Leslie M. Harris, *In the Shadow of Slavery: African Americans in New York City, 1626–1863* (Chicago: University of Chicago Press, 2003), 279–88.
5. Barbara Ehrenreich, "Up Close at Trinidad's Carnival," *Smithsonian*, February 2009, www.smithsonianmag.com/arts-culture/up-close-at-trinidads-carnival-45542504/.

Chapter 5: Moving the Goalposts and Gaslighting

1. Gary B. Nash, *The Unknown American Revolution: The Unruly Birth of Democracy and the Struggle to Create America* (New York: Penguin, 2006), 254.

2. Marcelo Rochabrun and Cezary Podkul, "The Fateful Vote That Made New York City Rents So High," ProPublica, December 15, 2016, https://www.propublica.org/article/the-vote-that-made -new-york-city-rents-so-high.

3. Gretchen Livingston and Anna Brown, "Trends and Patterns in Intermarriage," Pew Research Center, May 18, 2017, www.pewresearch.org/social-trends/2017/05/18/1-trends-and-patterns-in -intermarriage/.

4. Schott Foundation for Public Education, *Black Lives Matter: The Schott 50 State Report on Public Education and Black Males* (2015), http://schottfoundation.org/resources/black-lives-matter-schott-50 -state-report-public-education-and-black-males.

5. Richard V. Reeves and Katherine Guyot, "Black Women Are Earning More College Degrees, but That Alone Won't Close Race Gaps," Brookings Social Mobility Memos, December 4, 2017, www .brookings.edu/blog/social-mobility-memos/2017/12/04/black-women-are-earning-more -college-degrees-but-that-alone-wont-close-race-gaps/.

6. Kay S. Hymowitz, "The Black Family: 40 Years of Lies," *City Journal*, Summer 2005, www.city -journal.org/html/black-family-40-years-lies-12872.html.

7. American Association of University Women, *Deeper in Debt: 2021 Update*, last updated May 2021, www.aauw.org/app/uploads/2021/05/Deeper_In_Debt_2021.pdf.

Chapter 6: Healing

1. Janelle Duke, "The Story of the Merikens in Trinidad," National Archives of Trinidad and To-bago, August 14, 2015, https://nationalarchivestt.wordpress.com/2015/08/14/the-story-of-the -merikens-in-trinidad/.

2. Deena Zaru and Lakeia Brown, "Hip-Hop Has Been Standing Up for Black Lives for Decades: 15 Songs and Why They Matter," *ABC News*, July 12, 2020, https://abcnews.go.com/Entertainment /hip-hop-standing-black-lives-decades-15-songs/story?id=71195591.

Chapter 7: Hoovered

1. Theodore R. Johnson III, "Recall That Ice Cream Truck Song? We Have Unpleasant News for You," *Code Switch* (blog), *NPR*, May 11, 2014, https://www.npr.org/blogs/codeswitch/2014/05 /11/310708342/recall-that-ice-cream-truck-song-we-have-unpleasant-news-for-you.

2. Sean Nicholson-Crotty, Zachary Birchmeier, and David Valentine, "Exploring the Impact of School Discipline on Racial Disproportion in the Juvenile Justice System," *Social Science Quarterly* 90, no. 4 (December 2009): 1003–18, https://www.jstor.org/stable/42940652; Michael Rocque, "Office Discipline and Student Behavior: Does Race Matter?," *American Journal of Education* 116, no. 4 (August 2010): 557–81, https://doi.org/10.1086/653629; Leah A. Hill, "Disturbing Disparities: Black Girls and the School-to-Prison Pipeline," *Fordham Law Review Online* 87 (2018), article 11, https://ir.lawnet.fordham.edu/flro/vol87/iss1/11.

Chapter 8: Lethal Abuse

1. *The National Intimate Partner and Sexual Violence Survey: 2010–2012 State Report* (Atlanta: Centers for Disease Control and Prevention, 2017), https://www.cdc.gov/violenceprevention/pdf/NISVS -StateReportBook.pdf.

2. Smith et al., *National Intimate Partner.*

3. Danielle M. Ely and Anne K. Driscoll, "Infant Mortality in the United States, 2018: Data from the Period Linked Birth/Infant Death File," *National Vital Statistics Reports* 69, no. 7 (July 2020): 1–18, https://www.cdc.gov/nchs/data/nvsr/nvsr69/NVSR-69-7-508.pdf.

4. "Why Are Black Women at Such High Risk of Dying from Pregnancy Complications?," *American Heart Association News*, February 20, 2019, www.heart.org/en/news/2019/02/20/why-are-black -women-at-such-high-risk-of-dying-from-pregnancy-complications.

5. Brown University, Library of Haitian History.

6. Dan Sperling, "In 1825, Haiti Paid France $21 Billion to Preserve Its Independence—Time for France to Pay It Back," *Forbes*, December 6, 2017, https://www.forbes.com/sites/realspin/2017 /12/06/in-1825-haiti-gained-independence-from-france-for-21-billion-its-time-for-france -to-pay-it-back/.

7. Jose de Cordoba, "Impoverished Haiti Pins Hopes for Future on a Very Old Debt," *Wall Street Journal*, January 2, 2004, www.wsj.com/articles/SB107300144534788700.